GW00707243

HANDBOOK OF
UK CORPORATE FINANCE

HANDBOOK OF
UK CORPORATE FINANCE

Edited by:

JANETTE RUTTERFORD, MSc, MBA, PhD
Alexanders Laing & Cruickshank

DAVID CARTER, MA, FCA
Head of Corporate Finance Services
Peat Marwick McLintock

Text editor:

MARTIN SMITH, MA
Bankers Trust International Ltd

London, Edinburgh
Butterworths
1988

United Kingdom	Butterworth & Co (Publishers) Ltd, 88 Kingsway, LONDON WC2B 6AB and 61A North Castle Street, EDINBURGH EH2 3LJ
Australia	Butterworths Pty Ltd, SYDNEY, MELBOURNE, BRISBANE, ADELAIDE, PERTH, CANBERRA and HOBART
Canada	Butterworths. A division of Reed Inc., TORONTO and VANCOUVER
New Zealand	Butterworths of New Zealand Ltd, WELLINGTON and AUCKLAND
Singapore	Butterworth & Co (Asia) Pte Ltd, SINGAPORE
USA	Butterworths Legal Publishers, ST PAUL, Minnesota, SEATTLE, Washington, BOSTON, Massachusetts, AUSTIN, Texas and D & S Publishers, CLEARWATER, Florida

© Alasdair J W Watson 1988 (chs 10, 11)
© D A Ross & S Taiyeb 1988 (chs 12 & 13)
© Butterworth & Co (Publishers) Ltd 1988 (chs 1–9, 14, 15)

All rights reserved. No part of this publication may be reproduced or transmitted in any form or by any means, including photocopying and recording, without the written permission of the copyright holder, application for which should be addressed to the publisher. Such written permission must also be obtained before any part of this publication is stored in a retrieval system of any nature.

This book is sold subject to the Standard Conditions of Sale of Net Books and may not be re-sold in the UK below the net price fixed by Butterworths for the book in our current catalogue.

British Library Cataloguing in Publication Data

Handbook of UK corporate finance.
  1. Corporations—Great Britain—Finance
  I. Rutterford, Janette   II. Carter, David
  III. Smith, Martin
  338.7′4   HG4135

ISBN 0 406 10300 3

Typeset by Colset Private Limited, Singapore
Printed and bound in Great Britain by Billing & Sons Ltd, Worcester

Preface

In the last ten years, there has been a revolution in corporate finance. Although the UK has long led many countries in the sophistication of its stock market and the international range of financing options available, UK companies today enjoy an unprecedented variety of financing options.

This change has given increased power to the finance directors and treasurers of companies. Gone are the days when, once financing had been arranged, it was left until maturity and then replaced. Gone also are the days when contact with the City consisted of a once-every-two-or-three-years equity rights issue, with the remainder of the finance coming from straightforward bank loans provided by the neighbouring clearing bank.

Nowadays, the structure of the liability side of the balance sheet can be altered at a moment's notice. Not doing anything to alter the portfolio of liabilities is as positive an action by the finance director as consciously altering it. The finance executives of companies are permanently bombarded with telephone calls from a bewildering variety of institutions offering new types of finance, securities, currencies, hedging and speculative instruments, and on- or off-balance sheet finance.

This handbook is designed to provide an up-to-date, practical guide through the maze of financing alternatives available in the field of corporate finance. It concentrates on the opportunities available to UK companies in particular and, where appropriate, details the UK legislative, accounting and tax implications of each financing decision.

The book is in four main parts:

Part A has an introductory chapter which considers the fundamental decisions to be taken in the corporate finance area before a particular type of finance is raised. It concentrates on three main issues: the objectives of the firm; the debt versus equity decision; and the management of risk. Chapter 1 concludes with a brief description of the major changes to corporate finance and to the structure of the finance markets which have taken place in recent years.

The remainder of Part A considers the sources of equity capital available to the firm, from a full listing on The UK Stock Exchange to the unlisted securities and third markets and, for start-up situations, venture capital. The important role of takeovers and mergers in the UK corporate sector as a means of expansion and rationalisation, a role with which the finance director of the company is intimately concerned, is also covered.

Part B describes the main sources of debt finance for UK companies, concentrating on sources of sterling debt. The variety of types of debt finance has increased widely. No longer do firms rely on overdrafts, with one or two debentures or loan stocks for longer-term funding. Companies have access to maturities of debt ranging from overnight to 30 years, to fixed- or floating-rate debt, to unsecured debt or to debt linked to asset puchase or to working capital, to straightforward loans or to debt securities.

Part C covers the international sources of finance which are now available. Since the abolition of UK exchange controls in 1979, UK companies have had access to cheap and flexible overseas finance. The Euromarkets, centred in London, offer an efficient alternative to the more regulated and expensive UK markets. More recently, the swap markets have made the choice of geographic area for the source of finance irrelevant. Swaps allow companies to raise finance anywhere in the world, wherever is cheapest, and then swap into their preferred type of debt.

Part C also covers the all-important areas of futures and options and shows how the combination of options and futures contracts with more conventional forms of equity or debt finance allows the company to control the levels of risk in the balance sheet; in particular interest rate risk and currency risk.

Part D completes the survey by covering the legal and taxation aspects of corporate finance: factors which must be taken into account in any corporate funding decision.

August 1987

JR
DC
MS

Contents

CHAPTER 1

The role of corporate finance

J. Rutterford
Alexanders Laing & Cruickshank

1.01 THE FINANCIAL OBJECTIVES OF THE FIRM

Finance theory states that the principal objective of the firm is to maximise shareholder wealth. This should be done by investing in positive net present value projects: in other words, projects which are expected to return more than the cost of funds needed to finance them. The higher the cost of funds, the more profitable the project must be to warrant investment. The cost of funds will depend on three factors: the level of interest rates; the inherent risk of the project (its business risk); and the level of gearing in the company (its financial risk).

For example, a high technology or biotechnology start-up company will have high business risk; although it may be *expected* to make profits, the uncertainty attached to future cash flow estimates make it a risky project. Investors may require 30% or more expected annual return before being willing to invest their funds. In contrast, a well-established company making, say, knitwear, and contemplating the expansion of a production line by 20%, would have a much better idea of future cash flows and therefore require a lower expected return before being prepared to make the necessary financial investment.

The level of financial risk will depend on the relative proportions of debt and equity in the balance sheet in the company. The cost to the company of debt is cheaper than that of equity. Since creditors are promised a particular rate of interest and come before shareholders in the queue in the event of a default, they require a lower rate of return. However, the more debt in the balance sheet, the higher the interest obligations of the company, and the more likely that it will default if profits take a down turn. So, with a riskier investment and a higher porportion of debt, the shareholders will require a higher rate of return on their share of the funding. Table 1.1 below gives an example to illustrate the gearing effect of debt on the shareholders of the firm.

The cost of debt is straightforward: it is the interest cost, assuming that the principal amount of the debt will be repaid. So, on a 10% ten-year loan, the cost of debt is 10%. The cost of equity is less obvious. Many observers of capital markets consider the cost of equity to be the dividend yield on the shares. In the UK stock market, this is currently around 3%. But this concentration on cash flow cost ignores the fact that dividends are expected to increase over time, thereby increasing the cost to the company. The cost of equity is thus the dividend yield plus the expected annual growth rate on the dividends, giving a total cost to the firm higher than that of debt.

Table 1.1   Effect of gearing on equity shareholders

	Profits before interest £	Interest £	Profits after interest £	Profits per £ share £
(A) *All equity*				
100 £1 shares	50	—	50	0.50
	40	—	40	0.40
	30	—	30	0.30
	20	—	20	0.20
	10	—	10	0.10
	0	—	0	0
				Range: £0 to £0.50
(B) *50 £1 shares*				
£50 debt @ 10%	50	5	45	0.90
	40	5	35	0.70
	30	5	25	0.50
	20	5	15	0.30
	10	5	5	0.10
	0	5	− 5	− 0.10
				Range: − £0.10 to £0.90

The overall cost of capital to the firm is the average cost of all the types of finance employed, weighted according to the amounts used. This is known as the weighted average cost of capital. Table 1.2 below gives an example of its calculation.

Table 1.2   Calculating the weighted average cost of capital

Cost of equity

Suppose DIV = expected dividend next year
PRICE = current share price
GROWTH = expected dividend growth rate per annum

$$\text{Cost of equity} = \frac{\text{DIV}}{\text{PRICE}} + \text{GROWTH}$$

If DIV = 4p, PRICE = 100p, GROWTH = 15% pa

$$\text{Cost of equity} = K_E = \frac{4}{100} + .15 = 19\%$$

Cost of debt

Suppose INT = pre-tax interest rate
TAX = corporate tax rate

Cost of debt = INT(1 − TAX)

If INT = 12% and TAX = 35%

Cost of debt = K_D = .12(1 − .35) = *7.8%*

Weighted average cost of capital

This is simply the average of the costs of debt and equity, weighted by the *market* values of the debt and equity liabilities of the company.

Weighted average cost of capital $= K_O = \%D\ K_D + \%E\ K_E$

If $\%D = 30\%$ and $\%E = 70\%$

$K_O = .30 \times 7.8\% + .70 \times 19\%$

$K_O = 15.6\%$

In summary, the role of the finance director is twofold. First, to ensure that profitable projects are entered into and, second, to minimise the cost of capital. This book concentrates on how the latter objective can be achieved through the optimal choice of finance for the company.

1.02 THE DEBT v EQUITY DECISION

One of the major unresolved problems in corporate finance is how a firm should decide on its level of gearing, in other words, how it should choose its debt-equity ratio. In practice, many firms conform to an industry norm, either because they feel comfortable with this or because the norm reflects limits imposed by banks and other creditors. For example, the covenant on a bank loan or trust deed of a debenture stock might allow no more than twice the shareholders' funds to be raised in debt, or an interest coverage ratio (earnings to interest due) might be imposed.

In theory, the choice of capital structure may be crucial to the long-run survival of the firm. It may be that there is an optimal level of debt in the balance sheet which would minimise the overall cost of capital. If this is the case, any firm which does not keep to this gearing ratio runs the risk of going out of business. Projects which are not attractive to the firm because it has too high a cost of capital could be attractive to firms who had attained this optimal ratio.

The main argument is as follows: the more debt (which is cheaper than equity) the company raises, the more expensive will be the equity cost because of the gearing risk to shareholders (see Table 1.1 above). So, on balance, the amount of debt should not make much difference to the weighted *average* cost of capital. However, other factors come into play: taxation; and bankruptcy risk. The interest payments on debt are deductible against profits for tax purposes. This is not generally true for dividend payments on equities. This lowers the cost of debt relative to the cost of equity and seems to encourage high gearing. On the other hand, the more debt there is, the more likely that the company will default and have to go into liquidation. If there are costs to this default, too much debt in the balance sheet could be expensive.

The conclusion to these arguments is that some compromise amount of debt is optimal. However, this is not very helpful to corporate finance managers, especially when an international comparison is made. Table 1.3 below shows typical debt-equity ratios for companies in the main industrialised countries. On a superficial analysis of column 1, using OECD data, companies in countries with higher post-war growth rates, in particular France, Germany and Japan, appear to use higher debt-equity ratios. However, there are problems of measurement of debt-equity ratios across national boundaries, with different accounting standards in each country. The ratios in column 2, derived from more recent and complete data, and adjusted where possible for accounting differences, show smaller variations between countries. Also, the tax and bankruptcy systems in these countries differ, so that the attractions of debt relative to equity may be very different.

Table 1.3   Corporate debt-equity ratios in the US, UK, France, Germany and Japan

	Total debt to total assets (OECD, 1982) %	Total debt to total assets (Rutterford, 1984) %
US	37	24
UK	50	21
France	73	30*
Germany	63	19
Japan	83	35

*1983 data

The attractions of debt relative to equity have also varied in the UK over time. Under the classical taxation system, in operation between 1965 and 1973, equity was less attractive than now, because dividends were taxed twice, once at the level of the firm and once in the hands of shareholders. Since 1973, the UK has operated an imputation tax system, which gives relief from double taxation at the basic rate of income tax, reducing the tax burden on dividends and hence the cost of equity to the firm. Indeed, the lower the corporate tax rate relative to the basic rate of income tax, the less attractive debt is for tax reasons. See Table 1.4 below for an example of this.

Historically, the tax advantages of debt relative to equity for UK companies have not been as low as current levels since before the Second World War. However, one very important point is that the tax advantage of debt will depend on whether or not the company does actually pay corporation tax. Although the apparent tax advantage of debt is currently low, UK companies do now have substantial corporation tax liabilities. They have lost the generous first-year capital allowances available in the 1970s which meant that many companies did not pay corporation tax and so were unable then to benefit in practice from the theoretical tax advantage of debt.

Average debt-equity ratios in the UK gradually increased after the Second World War, reached a peak around 1974 and have fallen somewhat since. A typical debt-equity ratio would now be around 20% to 30%, measured as debt to total capital (depending on whether balance sheet or market values are used), compared with 14% to 17% in 1950 and 25% to 40% in 1974. Bankers' limits tend to be expressed in book terms.

However, the problem of off-balance sheet finance has never loomed so large as now. Whatever gearing ratio appears on the balance sheet, actual gearing may be much higher. Although leases now have to be capitalised on the balance sheet (see ch 9 below), there are many property and asset financing schemes, for example, financing through subsidiaries which do not have to be consolidated and so do not appear on the group balance sheet of the company. Corporate finance has become more sophisticated in recent years but UK accounting standards have not kept up with the rate of change.

Table 1.4   *Tax advantage of corporate debt*

	Geared company £	Ungeared company £
(A) 52% corporate tax rate, 30% basic personal tax rate		
Corporate profit	100	100
Interest	(20)	—
Pre-tax profit	80	100
Tax @ 52%	(41.60)	(52)
After-tax profit	38.40	48.00
Total investor payout		
Dividend*	38.40	48.00
Interest (after tax)	14.00	—
Total income	52.40	48.00
(B) 35% corporate tax rate, 30% basic personal tax rate		
Corporate profit	100	100
Interest	(20)	—
Pre-tax profit	80	100
Tax @ 35%	(28)	(35)
After-tax profit	52	65
Total investor payout		
Dividend*	52	65
Interest (after tax)	14	—
Total income	66	65

*Basic rate assumed already paid on dividends (ACT)

One final point on the debt versus equity decision. The choice of debt and equity may be affected by ownership considerations. The majority of equity finance for British companies is still provided by retained earnings with no ownership implications for shareholders. The raising of *new* equity, however, raises the spectre of dilution of ownership (which is why the Stock Exchange, until very recently, upheld the pre-emptive rights of existing shareholders to new issues of shares. (See ch 2 below.)

A small firm might therefore prefer to raise as much debt as possible to retain majority control of the shares or to issue non-voting shares, as was done in the past with companies such as Marks & Spencer and Rank Organisation. Eventually, though, these companies grew to such an extent that they reached the debt limits imposed by creditors and were forced to issue equity — with voting rights. The dilution of ownership control of course increases the risk of takeover.

It used to be thought that size would be protection against predators, but recent experience in the US and UK markets, for example the battle for Distillers in 1986, has shown this not to be the case. Firms can use high gearing ratios to finance the acquisition of other firms as large, or larger, than they are: this is known as leveraged buyouts. Again, we see how important the gearing ratio can be.

1.03 THE MANAGEMENT OF RISK

The objective of the corporate finance director is, as we have seen, to minimise the cost of capital to the firm. Once he has decided on debt or equity, the next question is which *type* of debt or equity. For equity, there is usually only one type — voting ordinary shares — although the use of debt convertible into equity and the use of preference shares are reasonably common: see ch 2 below. For debt, the decision is more complex, given the range of choices available in terms of maturity, type of interest payment, market-place, currency, etc.

When deciding on the type of debt, the objective again will naturally be to minimise the cost of the debt. But the risk to the company of the different kinds of debt must be borne in mind.

1 Interest rate risk

Suppose the finance director wishes to arrange the funding of a five-year project. Which maturity and interest type of debt should he choose? This will depend on three factors: how much the company wishes to relate the financing to the project; the relative costs of the different types of debt; and the company's view on what is going to happen to interest rates.

If the debt is to be closely linked to the project, then a five-year loan would appear appropriate or, rather, one whose cash flows are closely correlated with the cash flows of the project would be appropriate. The closer the correlation, the less the risk that the firm will at any point in time be unable to meet its interest payment commitments. So, for example, an investment in property, with low cash flows initially but a high expected capital gain, lends itself to the use of deep-discount or zero coupon fixed interest debt (see ch 7 below). A cash-generating project, on the other hand, could be financed with normal fixed or floating rate debt. Some firms prefer fixed interest rate debt because the cost of the financing is known in advance, facilitating forward cash planning. Others prefer floating rate debt, believing that their cash flows are correlated with interest rates.

Recently, combinations of fixed and floating rate debt have been made available through the use of options attached to debt. For example, a company can choose floating rate debt where the maximum and/or minimum interest rate is fixed. For example, if the current floating rate is 10%, the firm can lock in a rate of between 8% and 10%, using what is known as a 'collar'. Alternatively, it can choose to benefit from falling interest rates whilst protecting itself from higher rates by using only one side of the collar, known as a 'cap'.

As well as using the combinations of fixed and floating rate debt now available, the finance director can also choose to switch between fixed and floating rate debt at any time, through the mechanism of a swap (see ch 10 below). For example, the debt raised might be a five-year fixed rate eurobond issue, but this could be swapped immediately after the issue, or at any point during the life of the bond, into floating rate debt.

The swap mechanism allows firms to satisfy their second objective: to minimise the cost of debt. This is because swaps enable anomalies in the relative valuation of companies in the world's capital markets to be exploited. It may be that the extra interest coupon required of company B relative to company A in the eurobond market for fixed rate debt is different to the relative interest payments required of them in the floating rate bank loan market. By each raising debt in the cheapest market, and then agreeing to swap interest rate flows, they can minimise their cost of capital.

However, the choice of fixed versus floating rate debt, and short versus long maturity debt also hinges on the interest rate expectations of the finance director.

In efficient markets, interest rates should reflect expectations. In other words, if interest rates are expected to rise, the interest rate on long-term debt will be higher than for short-term debt, and vice versa. In a risk-neutral environment, long-term interest rates should just be the average of the constituent short-term rates. Thus, a company finance director should expect the same average cost of debt for his five-year project whether he raises five-year money, one-year money rolled over each year, or ten-year money repaid early.

In practice, this relationship between short- and long-term rates may not hold exactly, because of the maturity preferences of investors and companies seeking debt finance. It may be that companies wish to fund relatively long, to match long-term projects, whereas investors prefer lending short, because of uncertainty about the future. In these cases, long-term rates would be at a premium to the average of short-term rates. A finance director who funded his five-year project with one-year money rolled over could therefore expect a lower average cost of debt, but at the expense of uncertainty over his funding costs.

In the sterling debt markets, the evidence seems to point to a more complex picture. At the short end of the maturity spectrum, say up to five years, there is little or no premium on long rates relative to short rates. Also, at the long end, 15 years or over, the premium appears unimportant because of demand for long-term debt investments from the life assurance companies and pension funds. The premium is probably most important around 10-year debt, where there is no natural UK investment population.

Excluding the possible uncertainty premium, which is small in any case, the conclusion as far as funding is concerned is that the finance director cannot expect ex ante to reduce interest rate costs by selecting a particular maturity of debt or by choosing floating rate rather than fixed debt, unless he believes that he has a clearer view of future interest rates than the market as a whole. By constantly switching between maturities and fixed/floating rate debt, the finance director is attempting to 'beat the market'. There is no evidence that this can be done on a regular rather than random basis. Of course, if there are anomalies between markets, due to cross-border inefficiencies, as are exploited by interest rate swaps, interest rate costs can be reduced.

2 Currency risk

The same arguments apply to currency risk. If a finance director wishes to finance a US-dollar project, the best way to do this is with dollar debt. This gives the closest correlation between the project's cash flows and the debt's cash flows. The currency mix of the debt portfolio should therefore reflect the currency mix of the assets of the firm. Any mismatch means that the finance director is incurring currency risk, again because he believes that he has a better view of future interest rates and exchange rates than the market as a whole. Exchange rate theories suggest that, ex ante, the expected cost of debt in any currency should be the same. Higher interest rates are related to the weaker currencies. The problem with exchange rates, as with interest rates, is that there are leads and lags with these adjustments, so that it is tempting to calculate how one could have reduced debt costs by being financed in sterling between 1985 and 1987 and in US dollars between 1982 and 1984.

As far as individual cash flows are concerned, the finance director has the choice of hedging or not, using the forward or futures markets. (This also applies to interest rate risk.) For example, if a dollar cash flow is expected in three months' time, the finance director can do nothing (thereby effectively selling at the future spot exchange rate) or he can sell forward, locking in the forward rate. Naturally, the forward rate reflects expectations of future spot rates. The finance director again has to trade off the desire to hedge risk against any beliefs that the forward rate under- or over-states the likely future spot rate.

1.04 THE STRUCTURE OF CORPORATE FINANCE MARKETS

The major changes in the market for corporate finance have been securitisation, internationalisation, and changes in the structure of the intermediaries bringing together the companies seeking finance and the investors providing the finance.

1 Securitisation

The traditional mechanism for the provision of equity finance was via the stock market for publicly quoted firms and through finance agencies, such as **3i**, for smaller firms. The debt market was dominated by the banking sector, with the UK corporate bond market almost completely dormant since 1973. Some use was made of the euromarkets, either through floating rate bank loans or eurobonds.

The most recent trend has been the emergence of debt securities as a more common form of debt finance than traditional bank loans. This mechanism essentially bypasses the banks as providers of funds, using depositors' money, and goes direct to the investors via issues in the capital markets.

The attraction to corporate borrowers is that it is usually cheaper and is more flexible. For example, it is common for the AAA credit-rated firms to be able to raise debt in the eurobond markets at interest rates below LIBOR (the base bank lending rate) and close to LIBID (the cost of funds to banks themselves). It could be argued that eurobond investors are myopic (or the banks were making excess profits) although there are tax and secrecy advantages for investors in the eurobond markets which may explain most of the reduction in the interest rates they require, relative to normal bank lending rates. The liquidity of the debt instruments should also reduce their cost.

The flexibility for corporate borrowers is due to early redemption provisions often built into the securities, the variety of maturities, currencies and coupons available, and the ability to swap into alternative forms of debt at any time.

2 Internationalisation

Following the removal of exchange controls in the UK in 1979, many other countries have reduced or removed the barriers to international investment so representative of the 1970s capital markets. UK firms can now raise debt in many capital markets, influenced only by the relative expected cost, since the currency and interest swap markets enable the firm to switch into its preferred coupon, maturity and currency debt. There are still some costs, for example the SEC disclosure requirements in the US, which make some markets inaccessible for all but the largest UK companies.

3 Intermediaries

There are two main changes in the intermediaries which companies use to reach their ultimate investors: the switch from clearing banks to investment banks; and the impact of deregulation on the split between agents (brokers) and principals (market makers).

As mentioned above, the securitisation of the debt finance markets has led to the need for banks with access to a retail investor clientele. Their role is to issue debt securities on behalf of companies and to sell them to investors on a world-wide basis, in return for a fee, rather than lending at an interest rate premium over their cost of funds. The need is for a distribution network, serviced by a sales-force, and an ability to buy and sell the securities at any time, to preserve liquidity, serviced by a market-making capability. Thus, the typical intermediary is international in outlook, has a broad investor clientele, has sufficient capital to make markets in securities, and is rewarded by fee income (and market-making profits). Many of the more traditional commercial banks are rapidly attempting to convert themselves into these investment banks.

The second major change has been in the UK market where 'Big Bang' has meant the deregulation of the UK stock market, with the abolition of fixed commissions, of the separation between acting as agent and acting as principal, and of the membership cartel. The implication for the company wishing to raise finance on the UK markets is that it is now more likely to deal with a 'securities house' able to offer the merchant bank skills on security issues, the placement power of the stockbrokers, the market-making power of the jobbers, and the investor clientele in the form of the funds that they manage for insurance companies, pension funds, etc.

The potential conflicts of interest inherent in housing all these company services under one roof are obvious and have been highlighted by various scandals. The government has attempted to impose greater control on the City in the form of the Securities and Investments Board, which has statutory powers, but is concerned that too much regulation will drive many financial services companies and banks to other, more flexible, market centres. The major advantage that UK companies have in terms of corporate finance is that one of the most sophisticated financial centres in the world is on their doorstep.

Equity

CHAPTER 2

Raising equity capital

P. R. Mitchell
Clifford Chance

NB Except for the Appendix, this chapter is prepared on the basis that the Financial Services Act 1986, is fully in force which, however, will not be the case before March/April 1988. Readers should consult their own legal advisers on the position prior to this.

2.01 INTRODUCTION

This chapter is in two parts. The first describes what shares are and what rights and liabilities arise when they are issued, both for the shareholder and the issuer. It also describes how the law restricts the circumstances in which a company can issue new shares. The second part describes the requirements which exist where the issue of new shares is to involve obtaining a listing or quotation on a recognised stock exchange.

PART I

2.02 CLASSES OF SHARES

1 General

A share is an intangible bundle of rights in a company, which both indicates proprietorship and defines the contract between the shareholders. The terms of the contract, i e the particular rights attaching to a class of share, are contained in the articles of association of the company. Class rights principally affect dividend, voting entitlement and return of capital upon liquidation. The most common classes of shares are ordinary, preference and deferred. Where no class rights are specified the holder will be deemed to have unrestricted 'equity rights'. The term 'equity capital' includes all types of issued share capital except shares limited to a specified amount as regards dividend and capital. Evidence of ownership of a share is by entry on the company's register of members, and only secondarily by possession of a share certificate.

Capital may be nominal (or unissued), issued, or paid-up; the difference between the second and third categories is the amount not yet called up and the shares, which are therefore partly paid and may have abridged participation rights.

The Companies Act 1985 postulates that in the case of a company having a share capital the memorandum of association, in its capital clause, must state, apart from the authorised capital 'the division thereof into shares of a fixed amount' (s 2(5)(a)). It is thus not possible to issue shares in the UK of no-par value.

2 Ordinary shares

In the absence of any contrary provisions in the articles, ordinary or 'equity' shareholders will be entitled to dividends (if declared and subject to any share-holders ranked higher in priority), the exercise of one vote per share held, and the right to a pro rata proportion of the company's assets upon a winding-up of the company. It is the right to participate in a due porportion of the assets which distinguishes ordinary shares from other classes of shares and, therefore, provides the holder with the greatest potential return on the capital invested. Every company limited by shares and registered under the Companies Act 1985 has ordinary shares, although they may be divided into sub-classes ('A' Ordinary and 'B' Ordinary, etc) to confer special rights inter se.

By virtue of becoming a member of a company through the purchase of shares, a person also becomes liable to contribute to its assets in accordance with statute and the memorandum and articles. The degree of liability will depend upon the type of company concerned (ie unlimited company, company limited by guarantee or company limited by shares). An ordinary shareholder is liable, and liable only, to contribute the amount unpaid on a share which he has agreed to take up, or, in the case of partly-paid shares already issued to him, the balance. The mechanism for payment on partly-paid shares is a call, and the continuing liability of a shareholder to complete payment of the nominal amount (plus any applicable premium) is a debt obligation between the company and the shareholder. Unless otherwise provided in the articles or by separate agreement, a call may be made by the directors at any time on such notice as the articles provide. However, a call, on rare occasions, may not be made where the company has passed a special resolution under the Companies Act 1985, s 120, to establish reserve capital which is precluded from being called up until, and unless, the company commences liquidation.

Although a call will normally be implemented rateably on all members, or members of the same class, provisions may be supplied in the articles for a difference in amounts and time of payment between the shareholders on calls. In the event payment of a call is not made by the shareholder, the subject shares may be forfeited.

Ordinary shares may be issued as redeemable at either the holder's, or the company's option. This is increasingly popular with shares issued to institutions, eg on a management buyout, to close-end their participation and allow for an unrestricted stock market flotation in due course.

3 Preference shares

A preference share can, broadly, be described as a share possessing priority rights over ordinary shares. More specifically, a preference share may entitle the holder to a preferential right over lower-ranked ordinary shareholders to either dividends, return of capital in the event of liquidation, or both.

Although, typically, preference shares entitle the holder to the right to a fixed annual dividend, the right to receive repayment of any amount paid up on the preference shares on a winding-up and restricted voting rights (usually limited to cases where dividends are in arrears or upon liquidation of the company), many variations of such rights exist. For example, if holders of preference shares are given the additional right to participate pari passu with the ordinary shareholders in any of the company's profits or assets beyond the fixed preferential amount, the shares will be designated as 'participating preference shares'. Such shares are common with overseas 'open ended' investment companies which may have a UK listing.

An issue arises as to whether or not a preference shareholder is entitled to receive arrears of fixed dividends for any years the company earns no profit. Where dividends in arrear for any given year are expressed to become payable from profits earned in subsequent years *before* ordinary dividends are declared, the preference shares are classified as 'cumulative preference shares', as opposed to 'non-cumulative preference shares'. In addition, any cumulative preference dividends in arrear do not result in a debt owed by the company for the amount of such dividend. Rather, in the subsequent year in which a dividend is declared to compensate adequately the arrears, the dividend is treated as relating to the year in which it was actually declared. Consequently, a preference shareholder, even a cumulative one, does not have an absolute right to a dividend, but instead a right to receipt of any dividend which is declared and, thus, the company incurs no debt (or liability) to the shareholder until such declaration.

Nevertheless, there is a financial implication inherent in a preference share issue that the company's earnings are and will remain sufficient to meet the coupon rate, since declining to declare the requisite amount of dividend on the shares is often viewed as a sign of financial weakness in the company, and may, indeed, amount to an event of default which accelerates other loan repayments.

As with ordinary shares, preference shares are subject to the same liability to contribute amounts unpaid in compliance with the particular articles of association.

Preference shares which do not carry participating rights are not regarded as 'equity', in view of the decreased risk. Although having the usual characteristics of a share, they are closer to debt capital and may be issued virtually interchangeably with debentures. Debenture holders have creditor rights against the company, however, whose liabilities must be discharged in advance of any shareholder (including the holders of preference shares) in a winding-up. They are not, therefore, inherently an attractive form of security to an investor, unless accepted in conjunction with some other right in the company. Institutional investors can usually be persuaded to take a mix of debt and equity, which will include preference shares.

It is common for preference shares, by their terms, to be issued as redeemable. The redemption may be financed out of profits, or the proceeds of a fresh issue. If out of profits, a capital redemption reserve fund must be established, to prevent the distribution of a book profit which would otherwise be available as the direct result of the redemption. This is because the sum required for the redemption would be cancelled twice on the liabilities side of the balance sheet, i e under profit and loss and redeemable preference shares, but once only on the assets side. The fund is quite separate from any reserve fund to accumulate profits for the redemption.

4 Founders or deferred shares

Founders or management shares, which in essence are deferred shares, do not entitle the holders to receipt of a dividend or repayment in a winding-up until after preference and ordinary shares have been paid, and are usually associated with the promotion of a company. Deferred shares allow the promoter to enjoy a stake in the company without utilising equity capital which could be made available to other investors. Yet their issuance has the effect of diminishing the value of ordinary shares in instances where a considerable proportion of profits are allocated to the holders of them.

Any attempt to exchange founders or deferred shares for a larger nominal amount of ordinary shares (unless reserves are capitalised to meet the difference in nominal value) will constitute an unlawful issuance of ordinary shares at a discount even if such issuance is made through the reduction of a company's capital pursuant to the Companies Act 1985, s 135.

5 Convertibles

Convertible shares, because they are normally issued as unsecured loan stock but are convertible into ordinary shares at the holder's option, are often recognised as a hybrid class of both debt and equity. Theoretically, convertible shares can be perceived as a deferred issue of equity since during its pre-conversion status the holder will earn a fixed coupon, and then upon conversion the holder will begin to acquire the rights maintained by the ordinary shareholder.

In the case where the convertible shares are being issued by a new company and the success of its operation may be viewed as speculative, the investor would find this class of share desirable because of the ability to convert shares held into equity of the company should the company continue to grow successfully, or seek a listing.

The term 'convertible' also applies to preference shares which are convertible into ordinary shares in specified circumstances.

2.03 PRECONDITIONS TO THE ISSUE OF SHARES

1 Authority to allot

Before a company may proceed to issue shares, it is imperative to ensure that the directors are empowered with proper authority to issue shares in compliance with the Companies Act 1985, s 80.

Under s 80, the directors of a company may be granted authority to allot 'relevant securities' either by (i) the company in general meeting, or by (ii) the company's articles. As defined in s 80(2), 'relevant securities' refer to the shares of the company other than those indicated in the memorandum which are to be taken by subscribers, or shares allotted in pursuance of an employee's share scheme; and includes any right to subscribe for, or to convert any security into shares of the company other than those shares so allotted. Additionally, any authority granted, whether by general meeting or articles, may be in respect of a general or particular exercise of that power as provided in s 80(3) and may be either unconditional or subject to certain conditions. The maximum amount of relevant securities which are capable of being allotted and the date when such authority expires must be specified as well.

In specifying the expiration date of the authority to allot relevant securities, such period of authority must not exceed five years under s 80. Consequently, where the authority originates from the company's articles at the time of original incorporation, the five-year limitation will be calculated from the date of incorporation. Conversely, where the authority is granted by the company in general meeting by means of a resolution, the calculation begins from the date the relevant resolution is passed. However, authority (even if granted by the company's articles), may also be revoked or varied by the company in general meeting by ordinary resolution, regardless of whether it alters the articles (which would normally require special resolution).

Where authority is granted by resolution, many companies consider it a wise precaution to renew automatically the original authority at each annual general meeting, so as to ensure that capital is available for whatever adventure arises in the succeeding 12 months. It is also good practice to increase the nominal capital under the Companies Act 1985, s 121(2)(a) in line with the directors' authority.

Criminal penalties may be imposed, under s 80(10) upon any director who knowingly and wilfully contravenes or permits or authorises the contravention of s 80. However, the validity of any allotment is not affected.

2 Pre-emptive rights

Under the Companies Act 1985, s 89(1)(a) a company is not permitted to allot shares to any person prior to first making an offer to existing holders of 'relevant shares' or 'relevant employee shares' on the same or more favourable terms, of a proportion of those securities which is as nearly as practical equal to the proportion in nominal value held by him of the aggregate of relevant shares and relevant employee shares. A 21-day period, during which pre-emptive rights may be exercised or refused, must elapse before shares may be allotted or the offer withdrawn. Moreover, the 21-day period in which the pre-emptive offer must be made and the manner in which it must be made and served are governed by the Companies Act 1985, s 90 and not the applicable provisions of the company's memorandum or articles.

Equity securities included within the statutory pre-emption rights include securities which consist of or comprise a right to subscribe for, or convert any security into, equity shares. This includes convertible preference shares or loan stock (see above). Although it is necessary to make a proportionate offer to existing equity shareholders when debentures convertible into ordinary shares are issued, no further offer falls to be made to equity shareholders when the debenture holders do, in fact, exercise their conversion rights.

If the company proposing to allot shares is a public company, conferment of pre-emptive rights to existing equity shareholders is required. If, on the other hand, the company is private, the pre-emptive rights under s 89 may be excluded under a provision contained in the company's memorandum or articles. Under the latter circumstances, if a requirement or authority provided in the memorandum or articles is inconsistent with the requirements under s 89(1) and 90(1)–(5) (regarding method of service) and s 90(6) (regarding period of offer) it has the effect, under s 91(2), of a provision excluding the pre-emptive rights under s 89(1).

In an attempt to reconcile the provisions pertaining to authority to allot securities and pre-emptive rights, the Companies Act 1985 permits specific disapplication of s 89 in certain instances. Section 95(1) states that where the directors have general authorisation for the purposes of s 80, power may be given by the articles or by special resolution to allot equity securities under s 80 authority, effectively as if s 89(1) did not apply to the allotment. However s 95(1)(b) specifies that s 89(1) may apply to the allotment with such modification as the directors may determine. A public company can waive or modify statutory subscription rights only in respect of a specific number of shares already comprised in the company's nominal capital or in respect of equity securities if the issue of those shares or securities has already been authorised, and the waiver is effective only while the authorisation to issue those shares or securities can be exercised.

Exemption from s 89 is conferred where the allotment is of equity securities which are to be paid up wholly or partly otherwise in cash. By way of example, these provisions would not apply to shares issued on a share for share basis. Exempt status also applies to any allotment of those securities which would, aside from a renunciation or assignment of the right to allotment, be for an employee's share scheme. These exemptions are equally applicable to public and private companies.

3 The Stock Exchange and pre-emption

These basic statutory requirements are supplemented by Stock Exchange and institutional requirements. Until 27 October 1986, as a basic condition for applications for listing for public companies, issues for cash of securities having an equity element had, in the absence of exceptional circumstances, first to be offered to existing equity shareholders in proportion to their holdings, unless agreed otherwise by shareholders in general meeting.

The principles underlying The Stock Exchange's past insistence on the system of rights issues were:

(a) the shareholders collectively are the proprietors of the company, each having a stake proportionate to the size of his or her shareholding;
(b) only the individual shareholders, therefore, can consent to any arrangement whereby their proportionate stakes can be modified or reduced;
(c) where the company seeks to increase its assets by issuing new shares for cash the existing shareholders must be given the opportunity to maintain their proportionate stakes by subscribing new cash; and
(d) in the event that individual shareholders are unable or unwilling to subscribe new cash, they must at least be given the opportunity to obtain value by selling their rights in the market.

In future, the rule is modified to allow shareholders to agree to waive the statutory pre-emption rule for the ensuing 12 months at the annual general meeting, and, if this is done, the company will be absolved from the need to seek specific sanction on each occasion.

Neither at the time shareholder approval is sought, nor on the occasion of any consequent issue, will The Stock Exchange seek to impose any monetary or percentage limit to the amount of such issues. They will, however, require that shareholders be informed of any such issues by way of a note to the accounts presented to the next AGM.

Provided that the blanket approval has been secured at the AGM the only cases in which specific approval for an individual issue must be sought is when the intended subscribers are directors of the company or their associates, or are already substantial shareholders or associates. In these cases specific prior approval must be sought and the proposed counter-parties must abstain from voting at the relevant meeting.

The new arrangements, by requiring at least annually a waiver of their rights on the part of shareholders, barely maintains the earlier principles. Because, however, no limit in terms of total monetary value or percentage need be specified when seeking this clearance, it will be difficult for shareholders to make an informed decision. They could be voting themselves into a position whereby they give blanket approval to a large issue at a deep discount to third parties, which would have the effect, not only of reducing their proportional stake, but also of depressing the price of the shares they still hold.

There is also the consequence that, if shareholders waive their right to pro rata participation, it will be open to the directors to negotiate with one or more investment banks for the sale to them of the new shares as a block for them to distribute as they see fit (but subject to certain restrictions under the Financial Services Act 1986). This would naturally tend to favour the clients of those major investment banks, brokers, or Stock Exchange conglomerates who have the capital resources and the distribution capacity to finance and retail large blocks of shares. Clients of other brokers, will not get an opportunity to participate, whether or not they are existing shareholders, unless the Stock Exchange were to require a spread of allotments similar to that which it appears willing to impose on initial issues above £2m value.

The investor protection committees of the major institutional investing groups impose their own requirements for the amount of 'free' shares to be available to directors to allot otherwise than on a pre-emptive basis. Normally this must not exceed 5% of the shares which are the subject of a s 89 authority. The Committees are strongly in opposition to the recent Stock Exchange relaxation.

2.04 PAYMENT FOR SHARES

1 Allotment of shares for cash

Consideration supplied in any of the following forms of payment will meet the qualification of payments in cash (including foreign currency) under the Companies Act 1985 s 738:

(a) cash received by the company;
(b) cheque received by the company in good faith, which the directors have no reason for suspecting will not be paid;
(c) the release of a liability of the company for a liquidated sum; or
(d) an undertaking to pay cash to the company at a future date.

Section 738 becomes relevant to public companies, as under the Companies Act 1985, s 106, any subscribers' shares in the company, together with any premium, must be paid up in cash. However, under s 106 and aside from these subscribers shares, s 99(1) permits shares allotted by any company (including any premium) to be paid up in money or money's worth, which includes goodwill and know-how. Additionally, unlike a private company, a public company is prohibited by s 99(2) from allotting shares in return for an undertaking given by any person that he or any other should do work or perform services for the company or any other person. If a company, nevertheless, engages in such undertakings, the holder of the shares is liable to the company for the nominal value of the shares, including any premium, for such proportion treated as being paid up, plus any appropriate interest.

2 Allotment of shares for non-cash consideration

A public company is prohibited by the Companies Act 1985, s 102(1) from accepting non-cash consideration payment for allotment of shares if the consideration is, or includes, an undertaking which is to be, or may be, performed more than five years after the date of the allotment. The language of s 102(1) indicates that the undertaking need not necessarily be certain to be performed more than five years after the allotment but rather, if there is even a remote chance it 'may' occur after such period, then the shares may not be allotted. If for some reason, though, shares are allotted in contravention of s 102 the allottee becomes liable to pay the company the nominal value and premium element of the shares treated as paid up by the undertaking, plus any appropriate interest.

3 Valuation of consideration

With the exception of a takeover or merger by way of share for share exchange, a public company is restricted by s 103 of the 1985 Act from allotting shares as paid up as to their nominal value or any premium 'otherwise than in cash' unless the consideration is independently valued in a report to the company, submitted by a person appointed by the company, during the six months prior to the allotment of shares, and a copy of the report is sent to the company and the proposed allottee of the shares. The evaluative report is generally required to be made by an 'independent person'. An 'independent person' is defined in s 108 as one who is qualified at the time of the report to be appointed or continue to be the auditor of the company. The specific contents which must be included in the report are as follows:

(a) the nominal value of the shares to be wholly or partly paid for by the consideration in question;
(b) the amount of any premium payable on the shares;
(c) the description of the consideration and, as respects so much of the consideration as he himself has valued, a description of that part of the consideration, the method used to value it and the date of the valuation; and
(d) the extent to which the nominal value of the shares and any premium are to be treated as paid up:
    (i) by the consideration;
    (ii) in cash.

Section 103, however, does not apply in the case where any outstanding credits of a company's reserve accounts, or its profit and loss account, is applied in paying up (to any extent) any shares allotted or any premiums on shares allotted, because the amount applied will not constitute consideration for the allotment. Nor will it apply to the allotment of shares by a company in connection with a takeover or merger with another company by way of exchange of shares.

Minimum payment of shares on allotment is commonly required. For example, public companies are prohibited by s 101 (except in relation to an employees' share scheme) from allotting shares unless paid up at least one-quarter of their nominal value, together with the whole of any premium. Any contravention of s 101 will result in the share being treated as if one-quarter of its nominal value, together with any premium, had been received. In turn the allottee is liable to pay the company the minimum amount which should have been received under s 101 (minus any value of consideration actually applied in payments up to any extent of the share and any premium on it), plus any applicable interest.

Although allotting shares at a discount is not permitted, a company is not prohibited from allotting shares at a premium but in accounting terms such premium, whether cash 'or otherwise' is to be transferred to a share premium account. Similarly, where payment received is non-cash consideration and the value of the assets exceeds the nominal value of the shares issued, this excess must be transferred to a share premium account. The payment of dividends out of money received by a company in respect of share premiums is prohibited by the

Companies Act 1985, s 130. There are concessions in respect of share premiums arising on future issues of new shares in consideration of the acquisition of shares of another company (s 131).

PART II

2.05 METHODS OF RAISING CAPITAL

1 General considerations

The methods employed by companies to raise money are less the result of the preferences of directors and their advisers than the dictates of the market. A small private company, unless identified for growth and subsequent stock market flotation by a venture capital institution, is unlikely to attract support for investment outside the small circle of its existing shareholders, and will rely heavily on bank borrowing or leasing arrangements. In any event it could not sustain the expenses of a public issue. Most of what follows therefore relates to larger-scale financings of: 1 substantial private companies prepared to re-register as public or restrict their offerings to private placings or subscriptions; and 2 public companies without an existing listing or quotation. Such companies should be advised to float new or existing capital on to one of the four UK markets for public offerings: The Stock Exchange; the Unlisted Securities Market; the Third Market; or the 'over-the-counter market' provided by individual securities dealers. The requirements for each are set out below. Major companies already possessed of a listing or quotation have, especially in the current climate, a ready public market for new equity, whether or not issued by way of rights.

The methods of raising equity usually employed are private placing or subscription, public issues by placing or subscription offer for sale, and introduction where that involves making available additional equity.

2 Private placing or subscription

The Financial Services Act 1986, s 170 provides that no private company may issue or cause to be issued in the UK any advertisement offering new securities in that company. That restriction will not apply to:

(a) advertisements having a private character, whether by reason of a connection between the person issuing them and those to whom they are addressed or otherwise;
(b) advertisement dealing with investments (ie shares or debentures) only incidentally; or
(c) advertisements issued to persons who are sufficiently expert to understand any risks involved.

A private company is any company which is not formed, or does not re-register, as a public company under the Companies Act 1985, Part II, and which in so doing satisfies the minimum capital requirements of s 45 of that Act, ie an issued share capital of £50,000 of which at least one-quarter must be paid up.

Thus new equity for a private company, even one whose issued capital already exceeds the minimum needed for re-registration can only be raised by offers to existing members or employees who satisfy the 'private character' test or outsiders who have been approached on an individual basis and who are either 'professionals' or sophisticated businessmen. This will cover the great majority of private placings to investors such as Investors in Industry plc and other institutions. Under the Financial Services Act orders may be issued defining the circumstances in which even these exemptions apply, e g so that if written offers are made to sizeable groups of shareholders or workers either a formal prospectus may be required or the offer must be made through an authorised person whose 'investment advertisements' comply with new Conduct of Business Rules. This confirms the difficulty for a small private company in raising new cash unless the existing proprietors agree to subscribe or institutions can be persuaded to participate. Increased equity can also be created by capitalisation of profits or reserves but this is essentially only a balance sheet operation and does not create new money.

Both private and public companies make substantial use of 'private placings' to one or more institutional investors, whereby an offer document containing particulars of the proposed issue and relevant financial and other information about the company is prepared and circulated through a broker or merchant bank to a selected 'private' list of the potential subscribers.

Although the issue could equally be done by direct subscription, a placing has the advantages that:

(a) the intervention of an intermediary, who as an 'arranger' of deals under the Financial Services Act 1986, Sch 2 will be required to be authorised or exempted from being so, gives institutional investors comfort that any offering material will be properly prepared and presented, and that the intermediary will have carried out a due diligence exercise on the company;

(b) the broker or bank can introduce its own clients to the company;

(c) it may be possible to arrange for the issue to be underwritten, thus providing a guarantee of the necessary cash; and

(d) the company's bankers will often be prepared to extend their credit lines 'on the back' of an equity issue which has been carefully researched and supported by the institutions. This is particularly true for venture capital or management buy-out situations.

Placings of a private company's shares are not suitable where large amounts are to be raised unless the company intends, either immediately or within a stated time, to seek a Stock Exchange listing or Unlisted Securities Market quotation. Except where the shares placed are to be retained by the institutional holders for long-term investment (and even here they will want an eventual opportunity for sale or redemption), the issuing house will be offering securities to clients who may wish to resell but cannot find a ready buyer and an easily ascertainable market price because of the private company's restrictive transfer provisions. The Rules of The Stock Exchange preclude brokers from placing securities for which a listing is not being sought and an issuing house will not in practice undertake 'public' placing of unlisted securities. If a private company wishes to raise capital among a wider clientele it must re-register as public and seek a listing or quotation.

A private placing document, not being a public investment advertisement, will not be a 'prospectus' for the purposes of the Companies Act 1985 and will not need to contain the matters formerly set out in Sch III to that Act (now the Financial Services Act 1986, s 162). However, in practice issuing houses require the issuer to comply as nearly as possible with the regulatory requirements so that the institutional or other subscribers will find information about the company in a recognisable form and secure an appropriate degree of investor protection. This compliance, and the accompanying verification process, is often lengthy, and involves the use of specialist corporate advisers, including lawyers. (The issuing house may, to reduce costs, consent to the same firm acting both for the company and for the house.)

For details of public placings on The Stock Exchange see below.

3 Public issues by direct subscription

Issues of shares directly to the public may only be made by public companies. Unless a full listing for the shares is obtained, the issue ranks as an 'offer of unlisted securities' and is governed by the Financial Services Act 1986, Part V. The shares are treated as 'unlisted' for those purposes even if they are quoted on some other exchange, e g the Paris Bourse or New York Stock Exchange. Section 160 of the Act provides (subject to exceptions) that a company may not issue an advertisement offering securities which amounts to a 'primary or secondary' offering unless:

(a) it has delivered for a registration to the UK Registrar of Companies a prospectus relating to the securities, i e one that complies with the requirements of the regulations made under the Financial Services Act, s 162; or

(b) the advertisement is such that no agreement can be entered into in pursuance of it until such a prospectus has been delivered.

A 'primary' offer is an advertisement issued otherwise than in connection with securities admitted to dealing on an approved exchange, inviting persons to subscribe for, or underwrite, shares or which contains information calculated to lead directly or indirectly to their doing so. A 'secondary offer' is an advertisement issued, e g by a person who has acquired the securities from the issuer with a view to issuing such or advertising in respect of them.

The prospectus registration requirement does not apply to a non-listed offering where other securities of the issuer (whether or not of the same class) are already dealt with on an approved exchange and the exchange certifies that persons likely to consider acquiring the securities to which the offer relates will have sufficient information to enable them to decide whether to do so. An 'approved exchange' means, principally, the Unlisted Securities Market of The Stock Exchange but could, in time, include various over-the-counter markets. There are also rules which modify the requirements for securities already dealt on an overseas exchange (Financial Services Act 1986, s 162(3)).

On the occasion of a *new* issue other than on The Stock Exchange, therefore, a statutory prospectus will always be needed for direct public subscription in addition to compliance with the rules of the participating exchange.

Where a full London Stock Exchange listing is sought for the shares, no prospectus has to be filed, but instead the company issues and registers listing particulars the contents of which are prescribed by section 3 of The Stock Exchange's *Admission of Securities to Listing*, ('*the Yellow Book*'). This in turn is based upon certain requirements of EEC Directives and was adopted as recently as 1984. The actual mechanism for listing is covered by the Financial Services Act 1986, Part IV, which deals with such matters as matters as the general duty of the issuer to disclose the material facts in the listing particulars (s 146), compensation for false or misleading particulars (s 150) and the persons who are legally responsible for the contents of the particulars (s 152).

An application for listing will not normally be considered unless the company's listed securities are expected to have an initial aggregate market value of at least £700,000 in the case of equity issues and at least £200,000 in the case of debt securities, although in practice a company is unlikely to apply for a full listing unless it will result in a market capitalisation of at least £5m. There is a further requirement that at least 25% of any class of issued equity share capital (or securities covertible into equity capital) must be in the hands of the public, that is persons who are not associated with the directors or majority shareholders.

A company must usually have a trading record of at least five years before an application for the listing of the shares will be considered. In view of this a company whose assets consist wholly or substantially of cash or short-dated securities will not normally be regarded as acceptable for listing.

Non-underwritten offers to the public on first listing are now unusual in that the company has no protection against the risk of the issue being under-subscribed. One of the methods indicated below, each of which involves an intermediary, will be proposed, although of course this increases the costs as a proportion of the total proceeds (the other main elements being advertising, the preparation of the prospectus with an accountant's report, and capital duty on the shares allotted at the rate of 1%).

4 Public placing

In this case there is no general offer to the public and the shares to be sold are offered to private and institutional clients of the issuing house (which is usually the company's sponsor) through The Stock Exchange or Unlisted Securities Market. Listing particulars or a statutory prospectus are required.

To ensure that an adequate market in the shares will develop, The Stock Exchange requires at least 25% of all shares being placed to be offered to market-makers so that the general public has the opportunity to subscribe. The Stock Exchange has imposed a maximum sum of £3m on the monetary value of shares being sold by placing, and if the expected capitalisation of the company is now to exceed £15m an offer for sale is necessary.

The issuer will enter into a placing agreement, or placing letter, with the sponsor whose principal terms, including the amount of the placing fee and any of other charges, must be mentioned in the 'General Information' section of the statutory prospectus. If the sponsor uses his 'best endeavours' to place the shares, this leaves the possibility of under-subscription, although the reputation of the sponsor may be damaged in the market if this happens. If the placing agreement actually specifies that subscriptions for all the shares will be paid, this amounts to an underwriting of the issue and the fee payable by the issuer is accordingly higher.

5 Offer for sale

When this method is adopted the company usually agrees to allot the securities, which are intended to be offered to the public, to an issuing house or broker. The issuing house then makes an offer to the public, to sell the securities at a some-what higher price, thereby earning its commission.

When a company is floated it frequently happens that the existing shareholders wish to sell some of their shares at the same time as further capital is raised for the company by the issue of new shares. In the event the issuing house will also agree to purchase some of the shares already in issue and the new and existing shares will then be offered to the public at the same price, pursuant to the offer for sale. The issuing house will often find others to sub-underwrite part of the issue.

An offer for sale by tender is in most respects similar to an offer for sale at a fixed price, but the important difference is of the price at which the shares are subsequently purchased by the public. The purpose of a tender is to ensure that any excess over the minimum tender price is available to the company (or existing shareholders). This is in contrast to a fixed price issue where, if the issue price is pitched too low, the purchaser of the shares may stand to make a substantial short-term profit.

In any offer for sale by tender the issuing house fixes a minimum tender price for the securities and then invites offers from the public at this or any higher prices. Subject to two qualifications, the securities will be allotted to applicants who apply for them at or above the striking price, which is the highest price at which sufficient applications (including applications at a higher price) are received to cover the total number of shares offered. The first qualification is that the issuing house will usually reserve the right to give preferential treatment to the company's employees, directors and pensioners by alloting shares to them at the minimum price rather than the striking price. The second qualification relates to the need to establish a proper market in the shares, for which a reasonable number of shareholders is required.

The relative complexity of the offer by the tender procedure has not prevented it becoming an increasingly popular method of raising equity capital in the market, e g with the recent flotation of Virgin plc.

It will be noticed that an offer for sale of whatever type involves the sub-sale by the sponsor to the public. Since the public are not actually subscribing for shares (which have already been allotted, albeit probably on renounceable letters) to the sponsor, but purchasing them, it could be argued that the prospectus or listing particulars requirements do not apply to them and that they are not relying on it.

However, the Financial Services Act 1986, s 150 provides that the persons responsible for listing particulars shall be accountable for their accuracy to any acquirer (ie whether subscriber or purchaser) who suffers loss. Such accountability ceases if it can be shown that the responsible person believed, having made such enquiries (if any) as were reasonable, that the statements in the listing particulars were true and not misleading, or that the matter whose omission caused the loss was properly omitted and:

(a) that he continued in that belief until the time when the securities were acquired; or
(b) that they were acquired before it was reasonably practicable for steps to be taken to bring a correction to the attention of persons likely to acquire the securities in question; or
(c) that he continued in this belief until after the commencement of dealings in the securities following their admission to the Official List of The Stock Exchange and that the securities were acquired after such a lapse of time that he ought in the circumstances to be reasonably excused (s 151).

The Stock Exchange is the competent authority to judge whether any of these circumstances apply.

There are thus three duties cast on the persons responsible (as to the definition of such persons, see section 2.07 below). First, that the listing particulars, which substitute for a filed prospectus, are accurate. Second, that if the shares are reoffered by the sponsor or issuing house all the relevant information is repeated to their clients (except to professional investors who can assess the risks on the basis of lesser information). Third, that if the accuracy of the information is compromised by later events, efforts must be made to issue supplemental statements which continue to offer a full and balanced picture. The requirements for supplemental listing particulars are set out in the Financial Services Act 1986, s 147.

Where shares are offered on an unlisted market, so that there are no listing particulars, then an equivalent obligation arises as regards the prospectus which is filed with the Registrar of Companies. Thus, s 164 of the Act provides that where a prospectus has been registered 'and at any time while an agreement in respect of those securities can be entered into in pursuance of that offer:

(a) there is a significant change affecting any matter contained in the prospectus whose inclusion was required by rules applying to it; or

(b) a significant new matter arises the inclusion of information in respect of which would have been so required if it had arisen when the prospectus was prepared;'

the person who delivered the prospectus for registration shall deliver a supplementary prospectus containing particulars of the changed circumstances. It should be noted that this obligation can become 'time expired' in the same way as in the case of a full listing.

Effectively, then, there is no difference in the level or duration of responsibility of the issuers of offers on The London Stock Exchange or on the approved exchange or elsewhere.

6 Introductions

A company may also obtain a listing instead of, or after, USM quotation by way of an 'introduction', if no new issue of securities is contemplated but the securities to be listed are already of such an amount and so widely held for their adequate marketability when listed can be assessed. Applications for introductions to a full listing would be favourably considered, for example, when the securities are already listed on another stock exchange or where the company's securities are sufficiently widely held to fulfil the requirements as to marketability.

2.06 PUBLIC ISSUES — THE CHOICE OF MARKET

1 The London Stock Exchange

Since late 1987 The Stock Exchange has been technically divided, following its merger with the International Securities Regulatory Organisation ('ISRO'), into the International Stock Exchange and the Securities Association. The Exchange became a recognised investment exchange for the purposes of the Financial Services Act 1986. The Association became the regulatory arm for brokers and dealers who seek authorisation to carry on investment business within the meaning of the Act. It is as an exchange that we refer to it here.

The main factors for a board of directors of a public company in deciding whether to go for a full Stock Exchange listing, an Unlisted Securities Market quotation or the Third Market may be summarised as follows:

(a) Trading record

For Unlisted Securities Market (USM) entry, The Stock Exchange will accept companies with a three-year record, as against a five-year record generally required for full listing. A shorter record may be allowed in certain exceptional cases, such as a new but thoroughly researched project, and the Third Market, requirement is only one year.

(b) Size of company

Typically, the size of company entering the USM is smaller than that seeking a listing. The majority of USM companies have a market capitalisation of between £1m and £10m, whereas it is uncommon for companies with a capitalisation of less than £10m to seek a listing.

(c) Shares bought to market

It is only necessary to put 10% of shares in public hands on the USM as against 25% for listing. Thus a company on the USM is less prone to interference, scrutiny and takeover. This ability to part with a lower percentage of the share capital, yet still achieve a quotation, is particularly attractive to the growing company, whose proprietors may be reluctant to part with a significant portion of the equity at an early stage.

(d) Expenses

Entry to the USM will usually cost less than entry to the listed market, regardless of the method of entry which is chosen. The principal savings lie in advertising costs, Stock Exchange fees and, often, professional fees.

(e) Reporting requirements

Reporting requirements are similar for both markets. However, requirements of circulars to shareholders on material acquisition or disposals are relaxed. Broadly, whereas a listed company has to report transactions exceeding a level of 15% on relative size, for a USM company the level is 25%. The requirement for audited figures referred to in a prospectus to be not more than six months old in the case of listing is relaxed to nine months for a USM company. All applications for an initial listing by way of placing, introduction or open offer must be submitted to the Secretary of the Quotations Department of The Stock Exchange in writing. The application, together with all supporting documentation (including the listing particulars), must be lodged by a broker member firm of The Stock Exchange which will act as the intermediary between the Quotations Department of The Stock Exchange and the company or its advisers in relation to any matters arising in connection with the application. Where listing is being sought for shares of a particular class in a company, the listing must be sought for all the issued shares of that class and not just for the specific shares included in any public offering.

The Stock Exchange maintains a complete discretion to accept or reject applications for listing subject only to judicial review if it is adjudged to have exercised its discretion unreasonably. Compliance with all of the requirements of the *Yellow Book* may not of itself ensure an applicant's suitability for listing.

The flotation of a company on The Stock Exchange is customarily sponsored by an 'issuing house', usually one of the merchant banks, or by a firm of stockbrokers. The issuing house (or the brokers) will advise the company on the appropriate type of issue, the offer price in respect of the shares to be issued, the size of the issue and so on, and will also co-ordinate the timing and documentation.

It is the directors who are responsible for the accuracy of the information contained in the prospectus, and indeed they are required to make a statement to that effect in the offering document, but The Stock Exchange attaches particular importance to the role of the sponsors which involves satisfying themselves on the basis of all available information that the company is suitable for listing. The choice of sponsor is important as the sponsor's name and reputation can contribute to the success of an issue. Before agreeing to act as sponsor a merchant bank or firm of stockbrokers will make careful enquiries about the company as their reputation depends in part on the quality of the companies they bring to the market.

The sponsors should on the applicant's behalf submit proof listing particulars and the proof memorandum and articles of association. The formal application for listing together with listing particulars in final form must be lodged with The Stock Exchange at least two days before the application for admission of the securities to the Official List. Admission is likely to be granted a few days after the listing particulars are advertised. Where equity securities in which no market already exists are introduced to the market, an interval before the commencement of dealings is normally necessary to enable a realistic price to be established. Accordingly dealings normally begin in the week after that in which the listing particulars are advertised and the subscription money is received.

2 The Unlisted Securities Market of The London Stock Exchange

For the purposes of the Financial Services Act 1986, all securities which are not entered on the Official List are 'Unlisted' and a separate set of provisions apply (see below). The USM is classified as an 'approved exchange' along with many other exchanges overseas whether or not they themselves are primary or secondary markets.

The relative advantages of the USM as against full listing have been considered in 1 above, and it is here only necessary to refer to the possibility of transfer from one to the other. The Stock Exchange in its original proposals issued in December 1979 envisaged that companies entering the USM would be expected, after reaching the appropriate status, to move to a listing. At present, less than 10% have done so.

Currently, where the company has entered the USM on the basis of a full Companies Act prospectus, including a report on a full five years' results, a further formal accountant's report will not be required in connection with a transition to listing provided the fundamental business of the company, including its size, has not changed significantly and it has complied with the provisions of the USM's General Undertaking. In these circumstances the company is considered to have complied with the normal admission requirements included in the *Yellow Book*, and adequate information will be publicly available through Extel cards, although listing particulars will still be required.

3 The Third Market

The new Third Market which began trading the shares of eight companies in January 1987, requires only one set of statutory accounts to have been produced or the ability to demonstrate that the intended project has been properly researched and can reasonably he expected to produce significant income within 12 months. There is no specific requirement to announce half-year figures or any minimum proportion of the share capital which must be in public hands. The Companies Act prospectus requirements apply where there is an issue of shares.

4 The over-the-counter market

Any person authorised to carry on investment business by the appropriate self-regulatory organisation recognised under the Financial Services Act is entitled to make a market outside The Stock Exchange, unless he is a member of The Stock Exchange itself. There is thus no single 'over-the-counter (OTC) market', but a number of different brokers, dealers and 'share shops' who are prepared to quote a price in the securities of a company which is not admitted to The Stock Exchange. The number of companies involved is, however, at present relatively small.

Share offers on the OTC are subject to the Companies Act prospectus requirements and the Part V requirements of the Financial Services Act 1986.

2.07 DOCUMENTS FOR A FULL LISTING

1 Accountant's report

Having decided to prepare say, for an offer for sale and appointed professional advisers, the first step will be to ask the reporting accountants to prepare a full long-form report on the company and its subsidiaries. This report will contain much of the information which is required to be disclosed in the listing particulars and provides the starting point for the assembly of the full information. As a general principle, The Stock Exchange will not grant a listing for securities when the latest audited accounts reported on are in respect of a period which ended more than six months before the date of the listing particulars (*Yellow Book*, section 4, para 6). For this reason it is not unusual for audited interim accounts for the first half of the current year to be prepared so that the offer for sale may be made eight to eleven months after the previous year-end.

2 List of documents

A pro forma list of documents is set out below to give an indication of the relative complexity of a full issue and the time scale that it is likely to take. The more important of the documents are discussed in the sections that follow:

List of documents

ABBREVIATIONS USED

The company	:	Coy
Sponsors	:	SP
Stockbrokers	:	BR
Reporting Accountants	:	RA
Auditors	:	A
Solicitors to the company	:	SOLS
Solicitors to the issue	:	S to I
Registrars	:	R
Printers	:	P
Valuers	:	V
Receiving bankers	:	RB

LIST OF DOCUMENTS

| (a) | Listing particulars stamped by Stock Exchange | All parties |
| (b) | Verification notes and replies | S to I/Coy |

(c)	Offer for sale agreement	SOLS/S to I
(d)	Sub-underwriting letters	BR
(e)	Acknowledgments of responsibility	Directors
(f)	Form of application	SP/R
(g)	Employee's form of application	SP/Coy
(h)	Fully paid renounceable letter of acceptance	SP/R
(i)	Letter of regret	SP/R
(j)	Model code for securities transactions	SP
(k)	Press release	SP
(l)	Notes for City editors	SP
(m)	Full advertisement	SP
(n)	Abridged particulars	SP
(o)	Extel card	SP
(p)	Estimate of expenses	SP
(q)	Appointment of registrars	Coy/S to I
(r)	Appointment of receiving bankers	SP
(s)	Display documents	SOLS
(t)	Consent of government broker	SP/BR
(u)	Application for listing	BR
(v)	Directors' declarations	Directors
(w)	Certified copy of certificate of incorporation and all other certificates on change of name	S to I
(x)	Certified copy completion board minutes	S to I
(y)	Specimen definitive share certificate	Coy/S to I/R
(z)	Declaration as to filing of listing particulars	SOLS/SP
(aa)	Stock Exchange fee	Coy
(bb)	Listing particulars	SOLS

3 The listing particulars

The requirements of The Stock Exchange as to the contents of listing particulars are set out in the *Yellow Book* section 3. These Rules are an amalgam of statutory requirements under Part IV of the Financial Services Act 1986 together with additional matters required by The Stock Exchange itself.

In addition to the detailed requirements there is a general requirement that additional information, according to the particular nature of the issuer and of the securities for which listing is sought, must be included to the extent necessary to enable investors and their investment advisers to make an informed assessment of the assets and liabilities, financial position, profits and losses and prospects of the issuer and of the rights attaching to such securities. Furthermore, The Stock Exchange may require disclosure of such additional information as they may consider appropriate in any particular case.

The Stock Exchange may only authorise the omission from listing particulars of information which represents a requirement of the Listing Regulations if they consider that:

(a) such information is of minor importance only and is not such as will influence assessment of the assets and liabilities, financial position, profits and losses and prospects of the issuer; or

(b) disclosure of such information would be contrary to the public interest or seriously detrimental to the issuer.

Although the power of The Stock Exchange to authorise the omission of other information not representing a requirement of the Listing Regulations is not limited to the above circumstances, the *Yellow Book* makes it clear that The Stock Exchange will normally have regard to those circumstances in authorising any such omissions.

The *Yellow Book*, (March 1987 revision) ch 2, section 3 specifies the requirements of companies and is itself divided into seven Parts which deal with the following matters:

Part 1: the issuer, the persons responsible for listing particulars, the auditors and other advisers

The issuer must indicate its name, registered office, date of incorporation, place of registration and registered number, auditors, bankers, brokers and solicitors. In addition the listing particulars must contain a formal declaration of responsibility by those responsible for its content in a form prescribed.

Part 2: the securities for which the application is being made

Full details must be given of the shares being issued including a summary of their rights. Information must be given as to the terms and conditions of the issue and marketing of the relevant securities where such issue or marketing is being effected at the same time as or within 12 months prior to admission. The offer price and method of payment must be specified as well as the period within which the offer is open. The underwriting arrangements must also be specified. The directors must state that the company has sufficient working capital.

Part 3: general information about the issuer and its capital

The company's principal objects must be stated and a full description given of its authorised and issued share capital. If shares representing more than 10% of the voting capital of the issue will remain unissued, it must be stated that no material issue of shares will be made without shareholders' consent. Information must be given as to any person who could exercise control over the issuer or who holds more than 5% of the issuer's capital. Particulars must be given of any options over any capital of the issue or any of its subsidiaries. Any material litigation and any material contracts (not being contracts entered into in the ordinary course of business) must be summarised. Certain documents must also be put on display and be available for public inspection.

Part 4: the group's activities

The principal activities of the group must be described, stating the main categories of products sold and/or services performed and any significant new activities. The relative importance of different categories of activity must be given together with details of the location, size and tenure of the principal establishments. Any fundamentally important patents, licences or other contractual arrangements or new manufacturing processes should be summarised. The average number of people employed and material changes over the previous three years must be disclosed and information given regarding the group's principal current and future investments.

Part 5: financial information concerning the issuer or group

Information must be given with respect to the profits and losses, assets and liabilities, financial record and position of the group in the form of an accountant's report for each of the last five completed financial years (or such lesser period as may be acceptable to The Stock Exchange). The information for the last five financial years should also be set out as a comparative table. The issuer's profit or loss per share after tax and its dividend per share in each case for the last three years must be shown. If more than nine months have elapsed, or six for a new issue, since the end of the financial year to which the last audited accounts relate then there must be a financial statement (which need not be audited) covering at least the first six months of the current year. Any significant change in the financial or trading position of the group since the date of the latest financial statements should be stated. Full particulars must also be given of the group's borrowings.

Part 6: the management

The names and other relevant business interests of the directors of the issuer must be stated together with details of the aggregate remuneration paid to them. Disclosure must be made of all interests of the directors in the share capital of the issuer, any loans given by a member of the group to a director and any share schemes for employees. Details must be given of all existing and proposed long-term service contracts with directors.

Part 7: the recent development and prospects of the group

General information is to be given regarding the trend of the group's business since the end of the last financial year and information on the group's financial and trading prospects for at least the current financial year. Where a profit forecast appears (which is not obligatory but is frequently included for marketing reasons) the principal assumptions must be stated and the accounting policies and calculations for the forecast must be examined and reported on by the reporting accountants. In addition, the issuing house must report whether or not they have satisfied themselves that the forecast has been made by the directors after due and careful enquiry.

It must be stressed that the above represents only a brief summary of the very detailed requirements of the *Yellow Book*, ch 2. A certain amount of the information to be given with regard to issues of equity securities need not be given on an issue of debt securities, and ch 1 indicates the differing requirements of The Stock Exchange in respect of various types of issue.

4 Renounceable letter of acceptance

The allotment of shares on renounceable letter of acceptance enables successful applicants to renounce shares in favour of subsequent purchasers rather than transfer shares only by using stock transfer forms. Furthermore, dealings are enabled to take place free of stamp duty for up to six months after allotment. In practice, unless the shares are initially only partly paid for, the period during which dealings take place in renounceable form is often limited to six weeks. The Stock Exchange *Yellow Book* section 9, ch 3 sets out Stock Exchange requirements in relation to all temporary documents of title.

5 Subscription and purchase agreement

The issuing house will enter into a binding contract with the company, the vendor shareholders, and the directors, to give effect to the offer for sale arrangements. The agreement will be conditional upon the grant of listing by The Stock Exchange, and will provide for:

(a) the purchase of shares from the vendor shareholders and for the subscription of shares in the company by the issuing house; and

(b) the subsequent offer for sale of such shares by the issuing house.

Directors' warranties as to the accuracy of the statements contained in the listing particulars will be included in the agreement, including confirmation that no facts have been omitted which would make any statement contained therein misleading. The directors will also be required to give warranties, inter alia, in respect of:

(a) returns filed with or delivered to the Registrar of Companies;

(b) the balance sheet and profit and loss account for the immediately preceding financial year;

(c) disclosure of unusual long-term or abnormal contracts;

(d) disclosure of litigation to which the company is or may become a party; and

(e) taxation liabilities of the company.

The agreement will include a provision for the company to bear all the costs of the offer for sale including a fee to the issuing house.

2.08 DOCUMENTS FOR USM

1 An accountant's report

As above.

2 List of documents

The abbreviations above still apply.

DOCUMENTS

(a)	Prospectus	All Parties
(b)	Verification notes and replies	S to I/Coy
(c)	Placing agreement	SOLS/S to I
(d)	Acknowledgments of responsibility	Directors
(e)	Pre-placing letter	S to I/BR
(f)	Placing letter and form of application	BR/S to I
(g)	Fully paid renounceable letter of acceptance	SP/R
(h)	General undertaking	SP/Coy
(i)	Model code for securities transactions	SP
(j)	Press release	SP/Coy
(k)	Box advertisement	SP
(l)	Estimate of expenses	SP
(m)	Appointment of registrars	Coy/S to I
(n)	Display documents	S to I/SOLS
(o)	Extel card	SP/S to I
(p)	Preliminary application for permission to deal in USM	BR
(q)	Formal applications by Stockbrokers (USM 1) and (USM 2)	BR/Coy
(r)	Certified copy of certificate of incorporation and all other certificates on change of name	Coy/SOLS

(s) Certified copy completion board minutes S to I
(t) Specimen definitive share certificate Coy/S to I/R
(u) Declaration as to filing of documents SOLS/SP
(v) Directors' declarations Directors of Coy/BR
(w) Stock Exchange fee (£1,500) Coy
(x) Sponsors power of attorney for signing prospectus SP

DOCUMENTS FOR FILING IN DUPLICATE AT COMPANIES HOUSE ON USM

(a) Prospectus SOLS
(b) Placing letter and form of application
(c) Consents
(d) Statement of adjustments
(e) Material contracts

3 Prospectus

The Financial Services Act 1986, Part V will apply to all offers of securities which are not the subject of a full listing under Part IV. It therefore covers the USM, other approved exchanges (including overseas exchanges) and all remaining public offers of shares or debentures. No investment advertisement relating to such shares or debentures is permitted to be issued in the UK unless:

(a) in the case of an offer on the USM or other approved exchange, a prospectus has been approved in advance by the exchange *and* delivered for registration; or,

(b) in the case of any other offer, has been delivered for registration;

and in either case the advertisement is such that no agreement can be entered into in pursuance of it until the prospectus has been approved and/or registered, as the case may be (ss 159–160).

These requirements are considered further under section 2.05, Public Issues by Direct Subscription', above.

By s 162, a prospectus must contain such information and comply with such other requirements as may be prescribed by rules made by the Secretary of State. Rules under the section may make provision whereby compliance with any requirements imposed by or under the law of a country or territory outside the UK is treated as compliance with any requirements of the rules. Further, if it appears to the Secretary of State that an approved exchange has rules in respect of prospectuses relating to securities dealt in on the exchange, and practices in exercising any powers conferred by the rules, which provide investors with protection at least equivalent to that provided by rules under the section he may direct that any such prospectus shall be subject to the rules of the exchange instead of the rules made under this section.

At the time of writing no rules have been brought into force under s 162.

In addition to the information required to be included in a prospectus by virtue of rules applying to it by virtue of s 162 a prospectus shall contain all such information as investors and their professional advisers would reasonably require, and reasonably expect to find there, for the purpose of making an informal assessment of:

(a) the assets and liabilities, financial position, profits and losses, and prospects of the issuer of the securities; and

(b) the rights attaching to those securities (s 163).

The information to be included by virtue of this requirement shall be such information which is to the knowledge of any person responsible for the prospectus or which it would be reasonable for him to obtain by making enquiries.

In determining what information is required to be included in a prospectus by virtue of s 163 regard shall be had:

(a)   to the nature of the securities and of the issue of the securities;
(b)   to the nature of the persons likely to consider their acquisition;
(c)   to the fact that certain matters may reasonably be expected to be within the knowledge of professional advisers of any kind which those persons may reasonably be expected to consult; and
(d)   to any information available to investors or their professional advisers by virtue of any enactment or by virtue of requirements imposed by a recognised investment exchange.

Where any significant change takes place which renders anything in an original prospectus out of date, a supplementary prospectus is required to be prepared and registered (s 164).

If in the case of any approved exchange the Secretary of State so directs, the exchange shall have power to authorise the omission from prospectus or supplementary prospectus of any information the inclusion of which would otherwise be required by s 163:

(a)   on the ground that its disclosure would be contrary to the public interest;
(b)   on the ground that its disclosure would be seriously detrimental to the issuer of the securities (subject as below); or
(c)   in the case of debentures, on the ground that its disclosure is unnecessary for persons of the kind who may be expected normally to buy or deal in the securities.

No authority is to be granted under (b) above in respect of information the non-disclosure of which would be likely to mislead a person considering the acquisition of the securities as to any facts the knowledge of which it is essential to have to make an informed assessment.

Subject to the various defences set out in s 167 of the Act, s 166 provides that the persons who are responsible for a prospectus or a supplementary prospectus shall be liable to pay compensation to any person who has acquired the securities to which the prospectus relates and suffered loss in respect of them as a result of any untrue or misleading statement or the omission from it of any material matter.

4 The contents of a prospectus

At the time of writing, no rules under s 162 have been produced. It is unlikely, however, that they will differ materially from the requirement of the Companies Act 1985, Sch III which they are intended to replace, which is accordingly reproduced as an appendix to this chapter.

5 Other documents

As for full listing: except that no listing particulars are required.

Mandatory contents of prospectus PART 1: MATTERS TO BE STATED

The company's proprietorship, management and its capital requirement

1(1) The prospectus must state:
(a) the number of founders or management or deferred shares (if any) and the nature and extent of the interest of the holders in the property and profits of the company;
(b) the number of shares (if any) fixed by the company's articles as the qualification of a director, and any provision in the articles as to the remuneration of directors, and
(c) the names, descriptions and addresses of the directors or proposed directors.

(2) As this paragraph applies for the purposes of section 72(3), sub-paragraph (1)(b) is to be read with the substitution for the reference to the company's articles of a reference to its constitution.

(3) Sub-paragraphs (1)(b) and (1)(c) do not apply in the case of a prospectus issued more than 2 years after the date at which the company is entitled to commence business.

2 Where shares are offered to the public for subscription, the prospectus must give particulars as to:
(a) the minimum amount which, in the opinion of the directors, must be raised by the issue of those shares in order to provide the sums (or, if any part of them is to be defrayed in any other manner, the balance of the sums) required to be provided in respect of each of the following:
  (i) the purchase price of any property purchased or to be purchased which is to be defrayed in whole or in part out of the proceeds of the issue,
  (ii) any preliminary expenses payable by the company, and any commission so payable to any person in consideration of his agreeing to subscribe for, or of his procuring or agreeing to procure subscriptions for, any shares in the company,
  (iii) the repayment of any money borrowed by the company in respect of any of the foregoing matters,
  (iv) working capital, and
(b) the amounts to be provided in respect of the matters above mentioned otherwise than out of the proceeds of the issue and the sources out of which those amounts are to be provided.

Details relating to the offer

3(1) The prospectus must state:
(a) the time of the opening of the subscription lists, and
(b) the amount payable on application and allotment on each share (including the amount, if any, payable by way of premium).

(2) In the case of a second or subsequent offer of shares, there must also be stated the amount offered for subscription on each previous allotment made within the 2 preceding years, the amount actually allotted and the amount (if any) paid on the shares so allotted, including the amount (if any, paid by way of premium).

4(1) There must be stated the number, description and amount of any shares in or debentures of the company which any person has, or is entitled to be given, an option to subscribe for.

(2) The following particulars of the option must be given:

(a)   the period during which it is exercisable,

(b)   the price to be paid for shares or debentures subscribed for under it,

(c)   the consideration (if any) given or to be given for it or the right to it,

(d)   the names and addresses of the persons to whom it or the right to it was given or, if given to existing shareholders or debenture holders as such, the relevant shares or debentures.

(3) References in this paragraph to subscribing for shares or debentures include acquiring them from a person to whom they have been allotted or agreed to be allotted with a view to his offering them for sale.

5 The prospectus must state the number and amount of shares and debentures which within the 2 preceding years have been issued, or agreed to be issued, as fully or partly paid up otherwise than in cash; and:

(a)   in the latter case the extent to which they are so paid up, and

(b)   in either case the consideration for which those shares or debentures have been issued or are proposed or intended to be issued.

Property acquired or to be acquired by the company

6(1) For purposes of the following two paragraphs, 'relevant property' is property purchased or acquired by the company, or proposed so to be purchased or acquired,

(a)   which is to be paid for wholly or partly out of the proceeds of the issue offered for subscription by the prospectus, or

(b)   the purchase or acquisition of which has not been completed at the date of issue of the prospectus.

(2) But those two paragraphs do not apply to property:

(a)   the contract for whose purchase or acquisition was entered into in the ordinary course of the company's business, the contract not being made in contemplation of the issue nor the issue in consequence of the contract, or

(b)   as respects which the amount of the purchase money is not material.

7 As respects any relevant property, the prospectus must state:

(a)   the names and addresses of the vendors,

(b)   the amount payable in cash, shares or debentures to the vendor and, where there is more than one separate vendor, or the company is a sub-purchaser, the amount so payable to each vendor,

(c)   short particulars of any transaction relating to the property completed within the 2 preceding years in which any vendor of the property to the company or any person who is, or was at the time of the transaction, a promoter or a director or proposed director of the company had any interest direct or indirect.

8 There must be stated the amount (if any) paid or payable as purchase money in cash, shares or debentures for any relevant property, specifying the amount (if any) payable for goodwill.

9(1) The following applies for the interpretation of paragraphs 6, 7 and 8.

(2) Every person is deemed a vendor who has entered into any contract (absolute or conditional) for the sale or purchase, or for any option of purchase, of any property to be acquired by the company, in any case where:-

(a) the purchase money is not fully paid at the date of the issue of the prospectus,
(b) the purchase money is to be paid or satisfied wholly or in part out of the proceeds of the issue offered for subscription by the prospectus,
(c) the contract depends for its validity or fulfilment on the result of that issue.

(3) Where any property to be acquired by the company is to be taken on lease, paragraph 6, 7 and 8 apply as if 'vendor' included the lessor, 'purchase money' included the consideration for the lease, and 'sub-purchaser' included a sub-lessee.

(4) For purposes of paragraph 7, where the vendors or any of them are a firm, the members of the firm are not to be treated as separate vendors.

Commissions, preliminary expenses, etc.

10(1) The prospectus must state:
(a) the amount (if any) paid within the 2 preceding years, or payable, as commission (but not including commission to sub-underwriters) for subscribing or agreeing to subscribe, or procuring or agreeing to procure subscriptions, for any shares in or debentures of the company, or the rate of any such commission,
(b) the amount or estimated amount of any preliminary expenses and the persons by whom any of those expenses have been paid or are payable, and the amount or estimated amount of the expenses of the issue and the persons by whom any of those expenses have been paid or are payable,
(c) any amount of benefit paid or given within the 2 preceding years or intended to be paid or given to any promoter, and the consideration for the payment or the giving of the benefit.

(2) Sub-paragraph (1)(b) above, so far as it relates to preliminary expenses, does not apply in the case of a prospectus issued more than 2 years after the date at which the company is entitled to commence business.

Contracts

11(1) The prospectus must give the dates of, parties to and general nature of every material contract.

(2) This does not apply to a contract entered into in the ordinary course of the business carried on or intended to be carried on by the company, or a contract entered into more than 2 years before the date of issue of the prospectus.

Auditors

12 The prospectus must state the names and addresses of the company's auditors (if any).

Interests of directors

13(1) The prospectus must give full particulars of:
(a) the nature and extent of the interest (if any) of every director in the promotion of, or in the property proposed to be acquired by, the company, or
(b) where the interest of such a director consists in being a partner in a firm, the nature and extent of the interest of the firm.

(2) With the particulars under sub-paragraph (1)(b) must be provided a statement of all sums paid or agreed to be paid to the director or the firm in cash or shares or otherwise by any person either to induce him to become, or to qualify

him as, a director, or otherwise for services rendered by him or the firm in connection with the promotion or formation of the company.

(3) This paragraph does not apply in the case of a prospectus issued more than 2 years after the date at which the company is entitled to commence business.

Other matters

14 If the prospectus invites the public to subscribe for shares in the company and the company's share capital is divided into different classes of shares, the prospectus must state the right of voting at meetings of the company conferred by, and the rights in respect of capital and dividends attached to, the several classes of shares respectively.

15 In the case of a company which has been carrying on business, or of a business which has been carried on for less then 3 years, the prospectus must state the length of time during which the business of the company (or the business to be acquired, as the case may be) has been carried on.

(Extract reproduced by kind permission of HMSO. Crown copyright reserved.)

CHAPTER 3

Venture capital

J. Hustler
Peat Marwick McLintock

3.01 INTRODUCTION

The expansion of the small business sector in the UK is seen by many people, not least the Thatcher Government, as one of the main factors in the revitalisation of the UK economy, since any significant increase in employment levels must come from the small and medium firms sector. Since 1979 the renaissance of the unquoted equity market, and in particular the venture capital 'industry', has played a significant role in changing attitudes and the achievement of the objectives mentioned above depends largely on a continuation of this initiative by all sections of the investment community. In particular, if significant investment is not allocated to the earlier-stage investment proposals over the next few years there is likely to be a slowdown in the rate of growth of investment activity into more mature venture capital proposals by fund managers, since the pool of available proposals will diminish.

This chapter will consider the history of venture capital in the UK and the providers and types of finance they offer. It will also look at the expectations and needs of both the venture capitalist and the entrepreneur. Consideration will also be given to some of the issues facing the venture capital industry in the coming years.

1 The nature of venture capital

Venture capital can be defined as the provision of equity finance to growing companies which are not yet mature. In reality, however, the package offered by venture capitalists often includes a variety of types of capital sometimes accompanied by loans.

There is a common misconception that the provision of venture capital is a somewhat altruistic occupation requiring investment in high-risk propositions, which will provide equally high returns at some unspecified date in the future. This view of course presupposes that the venture capitalist has unlimited finance and no immediate requirement to make a return on that investment.

In reality, the venture capital industry, as it is constituted in the UK, is primarily funded by the private sector and in that respect has the same duty as any other business: to maximise the returns to its investors.

It is important to realise that those providing the resources to the venture capitalist will look to making a return on the investment in a relatively short timespan. This return is normally achieved by selling the investment via an exit route (discussed in more detail below).

Venture capitalists are therefore looking for investments in high-growth/high-margin businesses where there is a reasonable expectation of a return within a foreseeable time frame. They are not, in the main, in the business of providing 'hope' capital to new businesses or long-term funds to mature companies with little prospect of the necessary growth within the foreseeable future.

Venture capital can be broadly subdivided into the following:

> seed or start up capital;
> 'second' round finance for young companies; and
> development capital for established companies.

A further role of the venture capitalist is the financing of management buy-outs (which are dealt with in ch 4 below) and expansion of investee companies through acquisitions.

2 Types of companies which should seek venture capital

Private companies, and unincorporated businesses, fall into two distinct categories — *proprietorial* and *entrepreneurial* — distinguished by the objectives of their owners.

A proprietorial company is a business, closely owned, which will provide its owners with a sufficient return to finance their lifestyle. The owners and managers of such businesses do not have the desire, or opportunity, to expand such companies beyond their present capabilities except, perhaps, on a gradual basis. Growth in such companies will be financed by the use of internally generated funds, normally retained earnings on the basis of which additional bank borrowings can be obtained.

An entrepreneurial company is typically in the early days of its development and the entrepreneur's own objective is to realise a significant fortune. The owner's driving force is to expand the company by, for example, the development of new markets or the introduction of new products. Such growth cannot be financed from within the company and falls outside the parameters set by the clearing banks. The company's main opportunity to raise finance is to take outside equity finance. Obviously a private company can not in reality issue shares or loan stock to the public in its early days and existing shareholders almost inevitably lack the financial resources to invest further funds. The entrepreneurial company must therefore turn to other sources. In the UK this could well be a venture capitalist.

At the outset, therefore, a proprietor will be reluctant to relinquish any of the equity, but an entrepreneur will realise that his long-term objective is only attainable by relinquishing equity at some stage, and he will therefore consider, at the initial stages of his project, a minority equity partner.

3.02 HISTORY

One has only to think of Queen Isabella financing Columbus, the East India Trading Company and the great European trading houses of medieval times to realise that the provision of risk capital is not a new phenomenon (in the case of Columbus it proves that the raising of venture capital has always been a difficult process!). However, the venture capital industry, as it is presently constituted in the UK, is a product of the twentieth century. During the nineteenth century the provision of finance to entrepreneurs gradually became more organised but it was not until the 1930s that the first professionally-managed venture capital fund, Charterhouse, was formed.

Progress during the next few decades was slow and by the mid 1970s there were only some ten funds in operation in the UK, the industry being dominated by ICFC (Industrial and Commercial Finance Corporation), now known as 3i.

Since the election in 1979, and encouraged by the success of the venture capital industry in America, the Government's attitude towards entrepreneurial activity has changed. Figure 3.1 below shows the growth in the amounts invested by specialist UK-based venture capital organisations in recent years.

Fig 3.1 Venture capital: growth in amounts invested

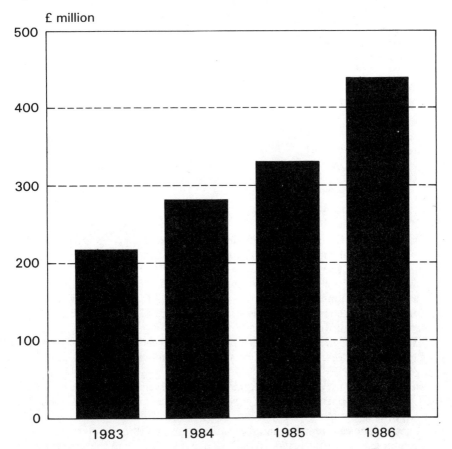

3.03 INVESTMENT BY INDUSTRY SECTOR

Figure 3.2 below shows an analysis of investments made by members of the British Venture Capital Association in 198(6) by industry sector. Buy-outs and acquisitions have been excluded from the analysis.

Fig 3.2 Venture capital: investment by industry sector – 1986

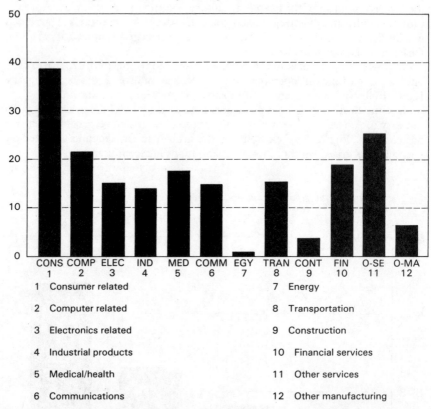

1	Consumer related	7 Energy
2	Computer related	8 Transportation
3	Electronics related	9 Construction
4	Industrial products	10 Financial services
5	Medical/health	11 Other services
6	Communications	12 Other manufacturing

3.04 THE VENTURE CAPITAL MARKET

The source of venture capital includes institutions and private investors. The opportunity to raise money from groups of individuals is still difficult to organise, although recent years have seen a rush of direct Business Expansion Scheme prospectuses. These are normally sponsored by one of the professionals in the venture capital industry. If you have a good proposal, therefore, and wish to raise venture capital, the normal route is to approach some of the 150 or so recognised managers of venture capital funds.

The success of the Business Expansion Scheme and the Unlisted Securities Market have increased the funds available from both the institutional and private investors.

An illustrative list of the major funds which make venture capital investment is set out in the Appendix to this chapter. These may be broadly categorised as captive funds and independent funds.

Captive funds are venture capital organisations established by investment institutions or major clearing banks to channel their own funds into venture capital.

Independent funds can take many forms but usually consist of a group of experienced venture capitalists who seek financial backing from a number of sources. These funds normally have a set life, typically ten years, at the end of which the fund is realised and distributed to its investors.

Whilst it is true to say that there is a surplus of funds available for venture capital proposals, most fund managers are unwilling to invest in young businesses which do not have the attributes of an integral proposal. Hence their claims that they receive an insufficient number of good quality proposals.

Most businesses will require a number of separate rounds of finance, typically as follows:

	Uses
Seed or start-up capital	To bring a research idea to the development stage.
	To set up manufacturing/ distribution/marketing.
Second round financing for young companies	To expand the range of products.
Development capital for established companies	To develop an alternative product or expand through acquisition.

The term venture capital can be used to describe all of these but more truly the first two should be described as 'adventure capital' and the rest 'development capital'.

The British Venture Capital Association survey of funds invested in 1985 showed that less than 40% of funds invested could be described as 'adventure capital', and this excludes the sums invested in management buy-outs which amounted to over £1b in that year.

In order to persuade the professional investor to commit funds to a business, the business plan must prove that there is a proven product to be sold to a well-researched market by, most importantly, an experienced management team. 'Adventure capital' proposals normally lack a part of this formula.

Two particular reasons are responsible for the lower than expected levels of institutional investment in the earlier stage proposals:

(a) a lack of experienced venture capital managers to manage the explosion of funds available and more particularly to nurse the younger companies which takes a disproportionate amount of time; and
(b) the need to prove to institutional investors that the returns are at least as good as from an investment in property or listed securities. In the mid-eighties we are seeing the lemons ripening before the plums. Thus many investors are reluctant to commit more funds until they see the successes (the plums) realising the expected profits.

3.05 SOURCES OF FINANCE

As we have seen it is more difficult to raise venture capital for younger businesses. In addition to this, there is the problem that to raise amounts of less than £250,000, is, perhaps surprisingly, more difficult than raising more substantial funds. Whilst seed or start-up capital often comes in smaller amounts there are recent examples of very large start-ups.

New businesses requiring less than £50,000 are usually funded by a bank loan adding to the equity capital provided by the entrepreneur. Assets are often purchased on leases and factoring of debt gives added working capital.

However, there exists an often quoted 'equity gap' for proposals requiring between £50,000 and £250,000. The banker will normally view this proposal as beyond his normal lending criteria, in view of the lack of security, and the venture capitalist sees it as proportionally too time consuming given the funds he has to invest and the limited time available to him.

Where then does one seek funds in this range?

1 Loan Guarantee Scheme (LGS)

The LGS was introduced in 1981 as a scheme to assist banks to supply medium-term loan finance to small independent businesses in situations where the risks were considered too great to justify conventional lending, and especially where inadequate security existed.

The loans are granted in amounts of up to £75,000 repayable over periods of two to seven years and the facility may be used as either a single loan or as a top-up to an ordinary bank loan. The loan guarantee facility can also form part of a total financing package which can comprise, amongst other things, equity investment from other sources. The Department of Employment guarantees 70% of each approved loan by the lender in return for a 2½% premium on the sum guaranteed. Whilst this may increase the cost of borrowing, the security offered by the guarantee may persuade the banks to reduce their interest rate so that the real cost may be reasonably competitive. However the entrepreneur will not be able to take advantage of this if normal bank lending would be available (e g loans secured by personal guarantees).

The LGS, whilst making additional finance available over and above that which the entrepreneur's own resources will support, does not meet the need of many small embryonic companies for straight equity finance if the money is required to purchase intangible assets or develop products or markets.

It has the effect, on what are usually under-capitalised businesses, of greatly increasing the gearing, with the problems that this poses both for the future liquidity of the business and the need to service a high interest cost.

2 The Business Expansion Scheme (BES)

The BES was established in 1983 as a successor to the 1981 Business Start-up Scheme. It offers individuals income tax relief for investment in qualifying unquoted UK trading companies with which they are not connected. Tax relief is at the investors' highest rate (or rates) of income tax on amounts invested of up to £40,000 per year. The investment must be in new, full-risk ordinary share capital and must be held for at least five years. Individuals may invest directly or through an investment fund ('the BES funds'), but the investor owns the shares in both cases. Certain types of businesses are excluded from the Scheme, including those dealing in land, shares and commodities, those leasing and letting assets and those providing financial services. There are also restrictions on the value of property assets the company can own.

Inland Revenue statistics show that approximately £105m was invested in over 700 companies during 1983/84, and in the following year £147m was invested in 787 companies.

This generous tax treatment for the investor therefore means that investment sums are often available for the higher risk proposals either from funds or groups of individuals. At present it is still difficult to find groups of individuals to invest in a project, which was certainly one of the objects of the scheme when it was set up.

3 Funds

Certain funds profess to cover this area, examples of which are 3i, of whose investments about half are for sums of less than £100,000, National Westminster Growth Options, who make quasi loans (with options) of up to £200,000, and new earlier stage funds like MTI Managers and JMI Seed Capital Fund.

The company seeking amounts of over £250,000 should experience no difficulty in raising venture capital from a venture capital fund so long as the proposition meets the overall criteria set down by venture capitalists for a successful investment.

However, in addition to seeking venture capital from a fund an entrepreneur should also consider whether an alternative might not be found in an industrial partner (UK or overseas) who may be able to provide technical or marketing expertise as well as just finance. An advertisement in the *Financial Times* will prove how many potential industrial partners exist as an alternative to a straightforward provider of equity finance. Such industrial partners would normally require at least 50% and often 75% of the equity so that, at 75%, the risks are reduced since losses can be group relieved for tax purposes.

3.06 THE VENTURE CAPITALIST

The venture capitalist is primarily looking for proposals which will provide his institution with a good return for his investment funds. Since funds available for venture capital are provided in the main by the large institutions, the risks associated with venture capital investments mean that they have to offer a better rate of return than the safer investments (with gilts yielding in excess of 10% per annum to redemption and blue chip equities returning nearer 20% per annum after including the rise in capital value). The venture capital funds need to be capable of returning in excess of 25% per annum compound. It is still early days to count the returns but initial indications imply that this rate will be achieved and the older US market is certainly showing these sorts of return.

Given that the venture capital funds will inevitably make investments which do not achieve their projected expectations, or which result in total losses, the managers will at the outset be seeking a return of approximately 50% per annum compound, possibly reduced if the risks are perceived to be lower than normal as in the case of management buyouts.

In assessing the return the investor will assume that the investment may be realised by means of a quotation on the Unlisted Securities Market after five years. Having reviewed the company's projections he will prepare a schedule of post tax profits which he considers achievable. To this he will allocate an approximate price/earnings ratio for the final year's profits to give the company a market capitalisation on the quotation. From the value attributed to his share he will deduct expenses and make allowances for any income received in the period and then be able to calculate the potential compound growth rate.

1 The financial package

Each investment house will have its own rules on how the 'deal' should be structured and most aspects are open to negotiation. It is therefore wise for the entrepreneur to consider his objectives with regard to the investment but not to be inflexible over most of them. The only way that an entrepreneur can be happy that he has achieved a fair deal is to look to more than one potential investor. It is for this reason that an investment cannot and should not be concluded between an investor and entrepreneur in under three months. Both parties need this time to ensure that the chemistry between them will last the length and master the hurdles of the proposed investment timespan. In addition it will not be possible to seek out and negotiate separate deals in under this timespan. These entrepreneurs who insist on concluding their investment deals within a faster timetable must realise that they may have sacrificed some extra equity for speed.

In designing the financial package an investor will want to ensure that he has an adequate share of the capital to reward him for his risks. However, he will probably not require or want a majority share (since the structure of his vehicle would not easily manage subsidiaries) and he will want to motivate the entrepreneur by future rewards from his substantial equity stake.

Often a potential problem arises in deciding on the size of the investor's equity stake when the investor calculates his return from a more conservative (ie lower) view of the company's future results than the entrepreneur's. This problem is overcome by allocating equity shares on a ratchet basis whereby the entrepreneur receives a greater number of shares the nearer he comes to achieving his original forecast results. An alternative method is to issue the investor a lower number of ordinary shares together with preference shares, which carry a fixed rate of return but would therefore not increase in value as the fortunes of the company improve.

The final aspect which the investor will want to ensure is some commitment on behalf of the entrepreneur. No investor wants to feel that an entrepreneur is overburdened by the worry of losing the amount committed but both investors and bankers will seek to ensure that the loss of the personal investment by the entrepreneur would 'hurt'.

A sensibly structured equity base will allow a reasonable amount of borrowings but not detrimentally affect a young business's opportunity to expand through a penal interest burden.

2 What the venture capitalist looks for

It is impossible either to define or measure accurately the inherent risk of an investment. An investor's judgment of the risk will depend upon his assessment of the possible gain or loss.

The venture capitalist ideally wants a proposal which already includes a sound and experienced management team with a proven product to be sold in a well-researched market. Specifically he will consider the following:

— Is the business a new venture?
— How good is the management team — how skilled are they in management, production, finance and administration?
— How will the investment be realised?
— Does the company possess the capability of achieving significant sales of the product within its market?
— Is the management determined to achieve high growth and returns?
— Will the management be motivated long-term?
— What is the customer base?
— How dependent is the business on its suppliers?
— Is the company entering a new market?
— What is the state of the market — declining, stagnant or expanding?

— How will the external factors, such as recession and currency fluctuations, affect the market?
— Is the product subject to rapid technological change?
— How will the company's competition affect the business?

3 Management

The above all help the venture capitalist form an opinion as to the desirability of an investment. However, more weight is given to some factors and notably the management team's ability to overcome problems of both success and failure.

The management team that the entrepreneur assembles is crucial to the success or otherwise of a venture and most venture capitalists inevitably require a proven management track record. A company grows by the skills of its management and the number of managers who are able to make the transition from running a small company to running a large one is, unfortunately, small.

A compound annual return of 40% over five years requires a company to increase in value by five times in the period. This can only be achieved by skilful management. Venture capitalists recognise that an innovative idea or product may be developed by an entrepreneur who lacks the management skills to exploit fully the commercial potential. In these circumstances the venture capitalist may suggest that suitable management is recruited to provide the necessary expertise. This is unfortunately difficult to achieve in many cases as British managers are reluctant to give up the security of their present employment for what is undoubtedly a potentially high risk business albeit with potentially high returns. It is important in these circumstances that the entrepreneur is prepared to give the incoming management sufficient of the equity to enable them to participate in these potentially high returns.

The other option open to the venture capitalist faced with this situation is to provide intensive management himself. This route is more commonly taken by venture capitalists specialising in seed or start-up capital. It will be appreciated that such a situation cannot exist forever and normally is utilised to allow the company to develop into the position where outside management can be recruited.

4 Product

Many venture capitalists operate in specific product areas or, more usually, will not consider certain product types, particularly in high technology industries where venture capitalists often have stated preferences. Irrespective of the type of product, the venture capitalist is looking for some unique selling point and development potential. It is also necessary to consider technological developments on a product especially in the field of high technology where the rate of development can be extremely rapid, with today's state of the art product being rapidly overtaken.

5 Marketing

When preparing business proposals marketing is often overlooked or only given cursory consideration. It is essential that management have a well thought out marketing plan supported, if necessary, by market research.

The venture capitalist will be looking for evidence that sales can be achieved by seeing that a market exists for the product and that the market share envisaged can be reasonably attained. They will also be looking to see that the market is capable of development and what action competitors can take to defend their market share.

6 Management commitment

A venture capitalist will almost certainly require the management to make a financial commitment to the business. The amount that management are required to commit to the project is an often intangible element of the financing package.

However, as a rule of thumb, management are normally required to commit enough of their personal wealth to be financially hurt if the venture fails, although not necessarily bankrupted.

The thinking behind this is that if a management team is financially committed to a project they will not walk away if the project begins to show signs of failure, and will work to bring the business round to financial stability.

There is a school of thought that asking management to devote a substantial part of their financial resources to a project is counter-productive. This is because management will be concerned to limit their own financial loss and will be less inclined to take the risks necessary to develop the business.

3.07 EXIT ROUTES

All that has been said so far presupposes that the venture capitalist will at some stage be able to liquidate his investment in an acceptable manner and reconvert to cash, often referred to as the 'exit route'. An investment which is not capable of being liquidated in some form is of no interest to the venture capitalists. Any member of management with an equity stake will have a similar objective in realising his investment, although probably with a longer time scale.

Set out below are those exit routes that are available to the venture capitalist with an investment in a successful company. In practice, the necessary steps will depend on the capital structure, but typically the institution will wish to liquidate its loan finance, exercise the conversion rights attributable to its preference capital or options and realise its equity. The principal convenient exit routes for the venture capitalist are going public, the company purchasing its own shares, or a takeover.

1 Going public

The company may not be suitable for a full Stock Exchange listing: in many cases the requirement for a five-year profit record will be a significant obstacle; in other cases it may not be of a sufficient size in terms of capitalisation to fulfil The Stock Exchange's requirement for an adequate market to be established. Two alternative methods of quotation are:

(a)   the Unlisted Securities Market; and
(b)   the Third Market.

(a) Unlisted Securities Market (USM)

The USM was instituted in 1980 to provide a market for the smaller or emerging company not eligible for a full listing. The principal requirements for entry to the USM are as follows:

(a) 10% of the total equity to be available to the public, compared with the 25% for a full listing;

(b) only a three-year trading record is required, compared with the five years for a full listing;

(c) audited figures included in the prospectus or particulars card not to be more than nine months old; and

(d) a box advertisement to be inserted (in abridged form) in one newspaper, compared with the normal costly advertisement of the prospectus in two national newspapers;

Flotations on the USM are effected mainly by an offer for sale (either at a fixed price or by tender) or by a private placing. For some companies, flotation on the USM is a prelude to a full listing at a later date.

The USM gives the venture capitalist the opportunity to dispose of part of his holding as early as possible and leaves him the flexibility of disposing of a greater proportion of the holding at a later date.

(b) The Third Market

Certain stockbrokers and dealers in securities make a market in the shares of companies which are neither dealt in on the USM, nor on the Official List of The Stock Exchange. The Third Market came into existence in early 1987 under the auspices of The Stock Exchange.

Flotation on the USM or the Third Market provides shareholders with a method of realising their investment. In both cases a document will be considered necessary at the time of entry to the market, to which the prospectus requirements of the Companies Act 1985 will apply.

2 Purchase of own shares

The Companies Act 1981 introduced legislation which, for the first time, allowed a company to purchase its own shares from shareholders, subject to various statutory requirements. This legislation was followed by provisions in the Finance Act 1982 for more favourable tax treatment of such purchases of own shares by trading companies, broadly allowing the gain to be treated as capital rather than a distribution (dividend). The tax consequences are complex and specific advice will always be required.

3 Acquisition by a larger company

A further opportunity for the venture capitalist and entrepreneur to realise their investment is the takeover of the company by a larger concern. Whilst this is rarely an option envisaged at the outset because the entrepreneur will wish to retain control and the investor is likely to realise a greater price by means of a listing, the aspirations of the business plan are often not achieved, making a listing impossible. Additionally, many companies can gain in their formative stages by a link to a stronger company particularly if it is time to exploit their product in overseas markets.

3.08 BUSINESS PLAN

An entrepreneur who has the attributes sought after by a venture capitalist should be able to raise the finance he requires. However, the entrepreneur needs to communicate his ideas and plans to the venture capitalist. This is normally done via a business plan which is normally the first contact between the entrepreneur and the venture capitalist. It must be remembered at all times that the business plan is primarily a selling document. Its purpose, initially, is to interest the venture capitalist in the project and it is therefore essential that the business plan should succinctly address the various aspects of the project after taking account of the requirements of the venture capitalist outlined above.

Whilst there is no ideal length for a business plan it is recommended that initially it is kept relatively brief: some suggest ten pages of narrative with a similar number of pages of financial information, but increasingly an even shorter document to interest the senior venture capitalist and incline him to set up a meeting at which you can sell the idea personally is welcomed. The full business plan will still be required and will also form the basis of the running of the business post investment.

The following headings cover the topics which are normally included in a business plan:

> summary;
> background;
> products and services;
> management and organisation;
> markets and marketing;
> methods of operation; and
> financial information.

1 Summary

The summary is arguably the most important section of the whole document, since it presents the venture capitalist with an overview of the proposal. If this section cannot stimulate sufficient enthusiasm in the venture capitalist in the time it takes to travel from Woking to Basingstoke on his journey home, he will probably read no further.

The summary particularly must carry the individuality of authorship of the team and must aim to sell fully the exciting investment opportunity of the idea. This cannot be done by excessive detail and must contain no facts which can be easily disproved. Whilst some potential investors will be put off because of their personal impressions or experience of a market or technology sector, if there is no such adversity, he must be generally enthused at the end of reading the summary.

It is always wise to ask a friend or colleague to read the plan and ask questions so that answers to the obvious questions can be addressed. Your accountant or business advisor will be happy to give advice and is an ideal 'sounding board'.

2 Background

For many proposals there will be little or no trading record and in these cases it is only necessary to outline the origins of the business. For established businesses this section will contain details of operations to date. The venture capitalist will always be interested in past performance as an indicator of future potential. If necessary the proposal should explain how a past poor performance will be overcome, resulting in the projection of attractive returns.

3 Products and services

The venture capitalist needs a precise description of the product or service concerned. Of particular interest will be the features which distinguish it from its competition, together with details of any market niche that is being filled.

The venture capitalist may well have no detailed knowledge of the industry and therefore the information provided in this section should be written in a form suitable for the layman to understand. Once interest in the plan has been shown, further assessment is likely to require more precise technical data.

If an understanding of the product or service can be enhanced by the inclusion of supporting material such as brochures, photographs or sketches, these can be submitted with the plan by way of appendices. Even an amateur video could help on occasions.

Any limitation which the product or service may have should be pointed out. If they are not, the venture capitalist may lose confidence in the entrepreneur's assessment of the estimated potential.

4 Management and organisation

Venture capitalists rank the capabilities of the management team ahead of all other factors in assessing a business.

The management team must be committed to the business and will ideally have a balance of diverse but complementary skills. It should be able to demonstrate an ability to perform the three essential roles required:

(a)   marketing and sales;
(b)   production and technical; and
(c)   finance and administration.

Where the team lacks any of these essential skills (which is likely for a new venture) the business plan should recognise these facts and indicate how this deficiency will be overcome. This may take the form of part-time staff or outside advisers to be substituted with a permanent post at a later stage when the business can afford it.

5 Markets and marketing

Under this heading sufficient facts should be presented to convince the venture capitalist that:

(a)   a good up-to-date knowledge of the market exists;
(b)   a market need has been identified; and
(c)   the planned approach to marketing will result in the projected sales.

It is important that the information is supported with facts and figures, where possible. Where surveys have been carried out or statistics are available, it may be possible to append these to support the conclusions reached.

An understanding of the market and an effective marketing strategy are vital for a company's success. This section must be prepared after careful consideration and research.

For those entering a market for the first time it is often difficult to substantiate any prediction of sales, since actual experience cannot be used for comparison. In such circumstances it is even more important to have carried out relevant research to be able to provide the venture capitalist with convincing evidence to support the prediction of sales. There are government-aided schemes which may help with market surveys.

6 Methods of operation

The processes involved in the manufacture of the product or the supply of goods or services should be explained. Those factors of the operation which give an advantage over competitors should be highlighted.

7 Financial information

If the venture capitalist likes what he has read so far he will then need to know all the financial details relevant to the business. The five topics generally covered are:

(a) financial projections for the business and the detailed assumptions on which they are based;
(b) risks and sensitivities;
(c) previous financial record;
(d) amounts of finance required; and
(e) financial controls.

(a) Financial projections and assumptions

The financial projections should demonstrate the potential of the business and determine the amount of finance required. These projections will also be useful as a yardstick against which the future performance of the business can be measured. The projections will normally consist of:

(a) projected profit and loss accounts;
(b) cash flow projections;
(c) projected balance sheets; and
(d) the principal assumptions.

The period over which projections should be prepared will vary according to the business. The well established business is usually able to prepare projections more accurately than a new venture, with the result that a five-year projection may be meaningful for the former but often a mere extrapolation for the latter. In the first year it would be wise to prepare the cash flow projections on a monthly basis and quarterly thereafter.

The plan should include the main assumptions on which the statements are based. It is not necessary to provide all the assumptions used providing those which have a significant effect on the projected results are shown. The projections must be keyed to what can be sold, therefore the projections should begin with sales forecast. (Many first-time entrepreneurs make the mistake of starting at the manufacturing cost level and assuming that the marketing department can sell everything they make for a profit.) Starting with a sales forecast will also define how much cash will be received, and when, after allowing for VAT.

(b) Risks and sensitivities

The venture capitalist will normally make up his own mind on the risk factors, but will take note of the company's own assessment and the business plan should give the assumptions most critical to the success of the business. Having determined these factors a sensitivity analysis of the projected results should be given.

These assumptions should be sensitised for a greater and lower than expected result. Surprising though it may seem, if a company does better than expected it often needs more cash. Notwithstanding this, experience has told venture capitalists that over 90% of all proposals will need more cash than originally anticipated and they will often raise the amount of investment to ensure that the management do not have to come back for more too soon. It is a common misconception that you are more likely to find an investor if you ask for as little as possible. In reality if the proposal is good, the larger the project, within reason, the more likely it is to find funding (viz European Silicon Structures, a start up which raised £60m).

(c) Previous financial record

The most recent management and audited accounts (where applicable) should be included by way of an appendix, with highlights extracted and included in the plan.

(d) Amounts of finance required

The amount of finance which a business requires will be determined from the projected cash flow. This will show when the greatest cash requirement arises and the estimated amount required after allowing an appropriate safety margin derived from the sensitivity analyses. From this the best forms of funding for the business can be determined. For example, a term loan might be appropriate for financing the purchase of capital items but inappropriate for the provision of working capital, where an overdraft could be more suitable. The amount of equity required will be determined on the sum needed for:

(a)   the amount needed to provide the capital base for bank borrowing; and
(b)   the amount required for purchase of intangible assets or finance of initial losses.

(e) Financial controls

The venture capitalist will want to see that management have up-to-date financial information to control the business effectively and efficiently. Brief details of the accounting systems and controls and the form of management and information should be provided.

3.09 THE ENTREPRENEUR'S REQUIREMENTS

Having prepared the business plan the next stage is to circulate it to venture capitalists. At first sight the selection of potential recipients of the business plan would appear to be a somewhat daunting task in view of the number of venture capital funds in existence.

However, many of the funds have some form of restriction, be it industry, geographical or size of investment, which make it inappropriate to send the business plan to them. It should be remembered that venture capitalists invest in about 1 in 30 plans they see. It is not normally a good idea to circulate a business plan to all potential venture capitalists at one time but to select a small number for the initial approach so that the project is not widely 'advertised' and so that any adverse feedback can be taken into account before sending it to any more. In any event the venture capitalists will be less enthusiastic to study it commitedly if they feel they are one of many. It is also wise to tell each one to whom the plan has been sent — in case they wish to syndicate the deal.

Hopefully from these approaches some venture capitalists will express initial interest in the project.

The next problem is to gauge which are serious contenders and reduce the list of potential investors to about three. The next stages in the negotiation are time consuming for the team and it is not wise to keep too many options open. When negotiating the financial package the problem is to select the venture capitalist most suited to the company. For those companies who are in a position to assess their potential investors, the following factors should be considered:

(a) the cost in terms of equity stake required, interest and share options;
(b) whether they are looking for a long- or short-term investment;
(c) the experience they have of the company's business and of providing capital;
(d) their time scale for making investments;
(e) whether they are in a position to offer further finance at a later date (eg for acquisition) and how quickly they could respond;
(f) whether they have contacts which might be of use to the company;
(g) what other services they can provide. For example, whether they give assistance with mergers, acquisitions, or flotations, and whether they offer consultancy services; and
(h) whether they allow the company buy-back or redemption options on their share of the equity.

However, the two intangible factors which often weigh heavier than any of the above are:

1 whether the chemistry is right between investor and investee. The initial years after investment are the toughest and the entrepreneur will want to feel that the investor is on his side;
2 what else they contribute besides finance. For example an investor may have a technical knowledge which can help bring a product to marketability.

Following these initial considerations, but at an early stage of discussion with the potential investors, the company should consider the following:

(a) the level of negotiation fees which will be charged by the fund (normally a percentage of the required finance);
(b) the estimated legal and investigation fees, and who will pay them;
(c) whether non-executive directors are to be appointed to the company's board, and at what cost;
(d) whether the directors will be asked to give warranties or indemnities in respect of the past activities of the company;
(e) what restrictions the investor will place on the company, for example on:
    (i)   directors' emoluments;
    (ii) the company's borrowing powers;
    (iii) alterations to share capital;
    (iv) the directors' opportunities to diversify or devote time to other activities; and
    (v)   the sale or transfer of control of the company; and
(f) what management accounting and other information the investor will want.

3.10 THE PROBLEMS

Many problems are encountered before, during and after investment by a third party. It is often said that it is only possible to raise money when it is not needed. As already stated it will take many months and much management time away from selling and running the business. It is therefore wise always to consider the company's long-term objective and be alive to the need for outside finance so that an attractive offer can be accepted whenever it comes. An initial introduction does not have to lead to an immediate marriage, but rather a long engagement, when both sides can get to know each other and formalise the marriage at some later date.

Statistics show that it is relatively more difficult to raise money in the North than in the South and sums of less than £250,000 pose an additional problem. Money is available for investment in the North but more time and effort is needed to find it. If it is not possible to raise the early stage finance through normal bank loans then the LGS or BES may offer the best options until the business is 'mature' enough to seek sums in excess of £250,000 from traditional sources. The main preferred exception to this rule is 3i where around half of their investments are for sums under £100,000.

The terms of the investment should be carefully studied to look for the 'hidden' benefits which accrue to investors if the plan results are or are not achieved (ie options if the company is successful or extra equity if it is not).

Many entrepreneurs do not realise the cultural change which will occur when a third party investor has been taken on board. From then on the family cannot have unfettered rights over their feifdom and the company's objectives become much more pecuniary, whereby the maximisation of profit is primary. The achievement of results normally relies on the staff as a whole and an entrepreneur needs to understand the investor's philosophy towards motivation of the staff (eg share option schemes).

The venture capital industry has seen explosive growth. An important side effect has been the shortage of experienced managers. The entrepreneur must be sure that the investor he chooses has a depth of relevant experience to give the help and advice he will require.

3.11 CONCLUSION

The venture capital industry is itself one of the success stories of the 1980s and without doubt a large number of new businesses have been born as a result. It is bound to stay under governments of all potential colours. However, a reverse of the trend whereby the entrepreneurial risk takers are becoming more adequately compensated would reverse the flow of the venture capitalists' life blood — the motivated, successful managers.

The industry will have to reassess its objectives over the next few years to move away from investing in lower risk management buy-outs where the potential returns are reducing and be innovative in finding exciting opportunities. Management buy-ins and corporate venturing are examples of probable popular areas of investment. If the venture capital industry continues to raise more money than it invests the enthusiasm of investors is bound to wane.

APPENDIX: ILLUSTRATIVE LIST OF MAJOR PROVIDERS OF VENTURE CAPITAL

London

3i (Investors in Industry)
Advent
Alan Patricof Associates
Alta Berkeley Associates
Barclays Development Capital
Baring Brothers Hambrecht & Quist
Candoor Investments
Charterhouse Development Capital
CIN Industrial Developments
Citicorp Venture Capital
County Development Capital
Development Capital Group
ECI Ventures
Electra Candover Partners
Electra Investment Trust
Fountain Development Capital
Gresham Trust
Guinness Mahon Development Capital
JMI Advisory Services
Kleinwort Benson Development Capital
Lloyds Development Capital
Midland Montagu Ventures
MTI Managers
National Westminster Growth Options
Schroder Ventures
Thomson Clive & Partners
Venture Link

Regional

3i have a regional network of 21 offices outside London.
Avon Enterprise Fund
Birmingham Technology
Cambridge Capital
Centreway Development Capital
Clydesdale Bank Equity
Hodgson Martin Ventures
Industrial Development Board for Northern Ireland
Lancashire Enterprises
Merseyside Enterprise Board
Murray Johnstone
Northern Investors
Scottish Development Agency
Summit
Ulster Development Capital
Welsh Development Agency
West Midlands Enterprise Board
West Yorkshire Board.

CHAPTER 4

Management buy-outs

D. Carter
Peat Marwick McLintock

4.01 INTRODUCTION

Management buy-outs (referred to in this chapter as MBOs) have been a major agent for corporate change in the UK in the last decade. Virtually unknown in the UK before 3i pioneered the concept in the late 1970s, the MBO is a particularly British variant of the longer-established US leveraged buy-out (LBO), said to have been invented by leading practitioners Kohlberg, Kravis, Roberts & Co as long ago as 1965. The difference is not merely the product of linguistic chauvinism. Whilst both have many features in common, an MBO crucially involves the managers as owners, whereas an LBO is often achieved over their dead bodies and is in essence a sophisticated mathematical miracle, whereby a company is bought over a period out of its own cash flow, through the temporary artifice of unconventionally high borrowings.

An MBO usually involves three parties: the management team, preferably with some years' experience in all the key roles, the vendor and the financiers. They generally arise from:

(a) a reassessment by the parent of the contribution of an otherwise viable business to the overall group strategy, enabling the concentration of management and financial resources on the main group business; or
(b) a sale by a receiver of a business as a going concern; or
(c) a sale of a privately-owned company by shareholders wishing either to retire from the business or to diversify their investments.

A suitable business will usually have a history of profits, the prospect of future profits and a positive cash flow, to give reasonable certainty that the financiers' investment will be repaid. Proven management, solid assets, a spread of products, a significant market share and relative immunity to sudden technological change all help to reassure the financiers.

The main steps involved in a successful MBO are to:

(a) identify the prospective buy-out by considering whether the interests of the three parties, vendor, management and its supporting financiers, can broadly be met;
(b) assess the viability of the buy-out in a memorandum identifying:
  (i) proposed management structure;
  (ii) market;

58

(iii) sources of supply;
(iv) profits and cash flow record and forecasts;
(v)   potential sources of short- and long-term finance;
(vi) potential tax considerations; and
(vii) proposed share structure;
(c) reach agreement in principle with the vendor;
(d) obtain financial backing, requiring an update of the initial plan to reflect the agreed financing arrangements;
(e) identify the best structure for taxation and financing for the transfer; and
(f) draft legal agreements and complete the purchase.

4.02 MBOS TO DATE

1 Numbers

In the absence of authoritative statistics, an estimate of the number and value of UK MBOs is shown in Table 4.1 below.

Table 4.1 Estimate of total UK MBOs

	Number	Value £m
1980	100	40
1981	170	120
1982	190	230
1983	200	230
1984	190	260
1985	230	1,030
1986	270	1,230
1987	300	2,820
	1,650	5,960
Annual average	210	750

The estimate of numbers relies in part on the conventional wisdom that 3i does half of all MBOs and an extrapolation of their own published figures. In fact the 3i proportion up to 1981, when there was little competition, was probably more than half; but since 1983, when the potential management team has had a considerable choice of financial institutions interested in MBOs, it must have been lower, falling to perhaps a third by 1985 as shown by research by Messrs Coyne and Wright of Nottingham University.

Whatever the true numbers, and many small buy-outs due to their very private nature are likely to remain uncounted, it is clear that we have a vital new economic force. 200 MBOs per annum is certainly significant.

More important than the number of MBOs has been the substantial increase in the size of the larger ones over the last decade. Here the approach has been to aggregate the larger and better publicised MBOs, providing a good, if not precisely accurate, measure. Whereas the total value for MBOs in 1980 is estimated at £40m, the totals for 1982–1984 were about six times greater; 1985 and 1986 both exceeded £1b and 1987 has set a new record at £2.8b.

The growth in the size of MBOs is illustrated by Table 4.2 below which stratifies the larger MBOs (taken as those with total funding at over £10m in current values). Both the annual totals and emerging buy-outs at over £100m clearly underline this growth. The names of the 100 MBOs of this size to date may also be of interest, and they are shown in Table 4.3 below.

Table 4.2   Larger MBOs 1981–1987 by size (total funding in £m)

	1981	1982	1983	1984	1985	1986	1987 (to date)
£m							
10–15	4	4	4	4	13	17	11
25–50		1	3	2		6	5
50–100		1		1	5	4	5
100–250						2	5
250+					1		2
Total	4	6	7	7	19	29	28

2 Trends

Analysis suggests some trends, especially regarding the sources of suitable MBOs. The majority are divestments of non-core businessess by UK listed companies although there have been several large divestments by overseas groups, such as Parker Pen, United Machinery and Wickes. For example Lawson Mardon came from BAT Industries, which has been concentrating its major recent acquisitions upon the financial services sector; Premier Brands (food manufacturing) was seen as outside Cadbury Schweppes' redefined mainstream activities; Mecca and Compass (leisure) were out of Grand Met; Mallinson-Denny (timber importers) was an earlier diversification of Brooke Bond, now seen as non-complementary by its own more recent acquirer, Unilever (detergents and food); while Caradon (building products) came from Reed (publishing and packaging).

There is a solitary purchase from receivership (Stone International). Although this is quite a common source of smaller MBOs, £18m was quite a lot to pay for the electrical division of the bankrupt textile machinery group, Stone Platt. This was bravely underwritten by Electra, without the benefit of normal due diligence procedures, but its courage was amply rewarded by the flotation of Stone in 1984.

There are several MBO products of the Government's privatisation programme: National Freight Consortium (1982) and Victaulic (1983); two shipbuilders (1985 and 1986); various National Bus subsidiaries, which were offered for sale separately; and most recently three parts of British Leyland which the Government was prepared to sell. The two earliest were in fact employee buyouts, as also Vickers/Cammell Laird, where no less than 80% of the employees applied for shares at an average cost of £600. The evidence does seem to show, however, that employee buy-outs need plenty of time; a management with a crusading zeal, such as that of Sir Peter Thompson at NFC, where the share price has risen from an original £1 to £46; and a little generosity from the vendor, which, therefore, probably has to be the Government.

Further progress towards wider share-ownership is to be expected. Larger

Table 4.3 Larger MBOs 1981/87 (total funding in £m)

£m	1981	1982	1983	1984	1985	1986	1987 (to date)
Under 25	Famous Names (8) Hornby (10) Gleneagles (13) Ansafone (14)	Isis (8) Stanley Gibbons (9) Stone (18) Amalgamated Foods (21)	SPP Group (9) E & Am Ins (10) Thermalite (12) Victaulic (15)	Evans Halshaw (9) Westbury (12) DRI (22) Paragon (24)	Brymon Airways (9) Bison (10) Willis Faber (10) Tibbet & Britten (10) Essanelle (11) MENCC (12) Record Ridgway (13) Secure Homes (13) Royco (13) Ellerman Lines (15) Vosper Thornycroft (19) Wades (19) Bradstock Group Inc (20)	Trend Communications (10) Exacta (10) Leyland Bus (10) KDG Instruments (11) Jeyes Hygiene (11) Maccess (11) Furmanite (12) Gomme (12) European Industrial Services (12) Partco (13) Intercraft Designs (15) Cundell Corrugated (15) Nestor ENA (15) Computing Devices (19) HUS Deposits (19) Technitron (21) Berkertex (22)	RFS Industries (10) Tilbury Plant (11) Porth Decorative Products (12) Holliday Dyes (12) Janson Green (13) AVO (14) RCA Service (14) Gold Crown Foods (15) Aqualisa Products (16) Aynesley China (17) Richard Sankey (24)
25–50		First Leisure (44)	Hugin (26) Timpson (42) Collier (47)	Wordplex (28) Simplex (29)		Haleworth (25) GBE International (25) Evans Healthcare (27) Bowater Paper (38) City Merchant Developments (40) Norwest Holst (45)	Istel (26) United News Shops (27) Clares Equipment (29) Crown House Engineering (36) Rentco (43)
50–100		NFC (53)		Target (50)	St Regis (52) Haden (60) Caradon (66) Mallinson–Denny (93) Mecca Leisure (95)	Unipart (52) TIP Europe (60) Parker Pen (74) United Machinery (86)	BTA (50) Fairey (51) Pontins (58) Associated Fresh Foods (68) Moores Furniture (80)
100–125						Vickers Shipbuilders (100) Premier Brands (102)	Wickes (120) International Leisure (156) Compass (160) Allied Steel & Wire (181) Humberclyde Investments (205)
250+					Lawson Mardon (280)		Hays (255) MFI/Hygena (718)

MBOs often include quite a wide spread of managers in addition to the key team and the inclusion of 170 managers in the Mallinson-Denny deal is an example of this. There is also increasing use of the three government-approved share incentive schemes, usually installed when the MBO is complete and the need for secrecy no longer applies. There are also signs that initial union hostility may be softening. Unity Trust (owned by the Cooperative Bank and 40 trade unions) is keen to take stakes in MBOs on behalf of the employees in the range of 10–25%, without board representation which is seen to conflict with the trade union role. Unity Trust is apparently working on the principle that every employee has a right of ownership, not just those with the money and inclination to invest.

There have been four successful bids for listed companies to date (International Leisure Gomme, Haden and Raybeck), but a well-publicised bid for Molins failed, presumably because the premium offered over the share price was considered too small by many institutions. There are two obvious difficulties in bids for listed companies: to rationalise how the directors can recommend the existing shareholders to sell to themselves, given their existing duty to the shareholders; and to get control, so that we can expect increasing use of schemes of arrangement requiring 75% approval, as compared with applying the pre-emption rights available with 90% acceptance.

Although the history of these large MBOs is short, many of them have already achieved an exit route. There have been several full listings, such as Stone, Wordplex, First Leisure, Westbury, SPP, Bradstock, Vickers/Cammell Laird, Caradon and Mecca. National Freight Consortium has its own informal market and Isis is quoted on Granville's OTC. There have been successful takeover bids of Collier by Burtons, Famous Names by Imperial, Thermalite by Marley, St Regis by David Smith and Mallinson-Denny by Hillsdown Hunter. Given that 50 of the 82 larger MBOs did not exist about two years ago, this is quite considerable activity, which will certainly continue.

3 A wider perspective

One can gain a wider perspective of the importance of MBOs by considering them in the context of mergers and acquisitions generally. DTI statistics show peak years of £1.9b (1968), £2.5b (1972) and £7.1b (1985); although in 1985 prices those two earlier years would each have been about £11.0b. MBOs at around £1b per annum are by no means insignificant in comparison and it is perhaps rather surprising that merchant banks, which have been so active in the merger field, have to date been less prominent in the MBO market.

4.03 MOTIVES

The key factors motivating each of the key participants in an MBO-vendor, managers and financiers are considered below:

1 Vendor

As already noted, an MBO may be the result of a sale by a retiring owner or of a receivership. More usually, however, it is due to a policy of divestment, typically due to one of six reasons:

1 the subsidiary or division just does not fit; for example, after acquiring a conglomerate there is a need to sell off the non-complementary divisions;
2 some acquisitions prove disappointing and a demerger by MBO allows the correction of past mistakes, in particular those of the previous managers as perceived by the present ones;
3 the profitability of the subsidiary may have deteriorated due to a change in market or technology;
4 the parent may need cash and the sale of a subsidiary may be the easiest source;
5 the vendor may simply be re-arranging its asset portfolio, perhaps to concentrate on its core businesses (those it perceives as having the best prospects); and
6 the subsidiary, although profitable, may be perceived as having poor profit growth prospects and its presence in the group may depress its stock market rating.

For whatever reason, group management now often identify the possibility of an MBO to subsidiary or divisional management, as this has the benefit of at least increasing the potential market by one. The vendor has an obligation to obtain the best price, but experience shows that an MBO can often produce this. There seems to be a tendency for vendors to favour the management, provided that other things are equal. Thus we have recently seen the management of Premier Brands given two, and that of Thorn EMI Screen Entertainments three, attempts to over-bid corporate purchasers, although in the latter case management were unable to raise sufficient finance.

2 Managers

For managers, an MBO offers both risks and opportunities. On the negative side, managers proposing an unsuccessful MBO run a risk of losing their jobs, if they upset parent management. Even if they succeed, they will be asked to make an investment which it would hurt them to lose, raised largely by second mortgages on their homes. They will also regret the removal of the parent's ability to finance capital expenditure programmes and shortfalls in working capital.

On the positive side an MBO may be the only real opportunity a manager has in his working life of achieving a significant capital sum. The management team have a unique inside knowledge of the business and the parent company board and any potential corporate purchaser have to rely on the willingness of the management team to share this knowledge. Whatever the reality, the vendor must always fear that the managers could walk away, if a realistic offer from them was thwarted by a competing bid, possibly leaving little but the residual assets to sell. Sometimes an MBO may provide the managers with their only serious alternative to redundancy: if so a heavy discount on the book value of the assets should be available, as the vendor will wish to avoid the costs of such redundancy and any tax claw-backs. It usually proves possible to buy services more cheaply from external sources than the cost of the much resented head office management charge. Most importantly even part-ownership provides an entrepreneurial motivation. Whereas most British managers already work much longer hours than nine to five, experience suggests that an MBO team will typically use those hours much more effectively than before.

3 Financiers

There is plenty of evidence of the rewards of MBOs for financiers and, thus, there is no shortage of lenders and equity investors in a good project. MBO equity investment is, however, characterised by low failure rates. Whereas 3i have admitted to 18 failures out of a population of 300 MBO investments, this compares with their typical experience of one failure out of three with start-up investments. The MBO investment is also characterised by good compound returns. US research indicates average annual returns of 30/40% compound, which is a good return where the risk of failure is relatively low. I understand that research by 3i into deals it had been offered and had rejected led it to conclude that it should have made even more MBO investments than it in fact did.

4.04 NEGOTIATING THE PURCHASE

One of the most delicate steps in an MBO is the negotiation of the terms of sale between the divesting company and the management team. The financiers will also have an interest in the outcome, and all three parties will require professional advice if a satisfactory agreement is to be reached. The main matters for negotiation are agreement in principle to an MBO; identification of the price range and likely terms of sale; and the sale and purchase contract. Factors likely to affect the price are set out in Table 4.4 below.

Table 4.4   Factors determining the agreed price of an MBO

The divesting company	*The management team*	*The financial backers*
Strategic policy	Assessment of own skills	Possibility of positive cash flow
Competing purchase offers	Potential for profitable growth	Growth potential
Rationalisation or closure costs	Effect of freedom from group	Quality of management team
Motivation of management	Assessment of value of operation	Reasons for any current problems
Effect on working capital	Transfer of pension rights	The product and the market
Accounting implications	Financial backing available	Management's share of equity

1 The financial arrangements

Assembling a financial package will be part of the process of negotiating price and terms. There are various ways of giving the financiers a stake in the buy-out and the managers will wish to give the financiers as small a percentage of the share capital as possible, while not leaving the new business too dependent on borrowings.

Among the options for financing the MBO are the following:

(a) ordinary share capital — sometimes a minority holding to leave control with the management team;
(b) convertible preference shares or loan stock — with the right to convert to ordinary share capital at a future date (the conversion terms often reduce as performance improves, to give an additional incentive to the management team);
(c) options to subscribe for a specified number of shares at a future date;
(d) a straight loan; and
(e) a bank overdraft.

In practice, a combination of these forms is often selected, with varying rights to voting, dividends, capital and redemption and different tax implications. Table 4.5 below gives a simplified balance sheet of a company which has emerged from an MBO.

Table 4.5 Simplified balance sheet of an MBO company

	£000	£000
Assets		
net operating assets:		1,000
Financed by:		
ordinary share capital — managers	200	
— financiers	100	300
Preference or loan capital		300
Bank overdraft		400
		1,000

2 Conclusion of the negotiations

A carefully-worded legal document will seal the buy-out, as with the sale or purchase of any business. Each party will require legal advice independently for this important stage.

Normally an agreement to sell a business includes a section on warranties and indemnities against unforeseen liabilities and tax assessments. With a buy-out, the seller may be unwilling to give the warranties and indemnities which a corporate purchaser might require, taking the view that existing management should be aware of problem areas and potential difficulties. The management team will often have no alternative but to accept this; thus a searching investigation is required by the financiers to check that there are no undisclosed onerous obligations or commitments; tax affairs, in particular, should be subject to close scrutiny.

3 Companies Act considerations

The directors may have a conflict of interest between their duties to the company and their personal interests as potential purchasers; the statutes require:

(a) each director to declare his interest in any proposed contract at the first board meeting to consider the contract (Companies Act 1985, s 317);

(b) directors to consider the interests of employees (Companies Act 1985, s 309); and

(c) the approval in advance by EGM of the disposal of the lower of £50,000 or 10% of the net assets of the company (Companies Act 1985, s 320).

In the case of private companies, the vendor company is entitled to assist the management team by lending part of the purchase consideration (Companies Act 1985, ss 155–158); but public companies may assist only where the loan can be shown to be part of some larger purpose, made in good faith and not merely to reduce the consideration. If a listed company sells part of its business to a director, The Stock Exchange's *Yellow Book* designates this as a Class IV transaction requiring a circular to shareholders and approval in AGM.

4.05 RAISING THE FINANCE

The management team will usually be unable to raise all the finance necessary to purchase the business from their own resources. Outside backers must be sought who are prepared to invest often the major part of the finance. While many conventional sources of finance are happy to invest in MBOs, there are also institutions which specialise in this particular type of enterprise. Objective advice from a professional adviser, such as an accountant, without a direct interest in the outcome of the deal, will often prove invaluable in finding the best source of finance.

Where the majority of the ordinary share capital may be controlled by the management team, much of the other finance will be in the form of preferential or loan capital. The business will have to generate cash to pay preference dividends and loan interest and repayments from the start. The investor will want to be assured that the business can generate sufficient positive cash flow to fund these payments before making any commitment.

1 Clearing banks

All the major clearing banks have specially designed financial packages to meet the needs of private business as they see them. These differ in many respects, but all are able to offer loan finance — for high risk propositions. Finance may possibly be provided at a premium rate of interest under the Government's Loan Guarantee Scheme. Packages involving a stake in the business are also available, usually from the bank's merchant banking arm or its specialist venture capital company. The latter, in particular, are also more likely to be prepared to consider propositions where the ratio of loan finance to share capital (the gearing ratio) is as high as 5:1 — as is often the case with buy-outs. Clearing banks will also provide overdraft finance, if required, for working capital.

2 Dedicated funds

During this decade several dedicated funds have emerged, outstanding amongst which is the £260m Electra Candover fund, which aims to apply the considerable experience of these two institutions on larger deals to even larger ones with minimum equity-type funding of £10m (leveraged to perhaps £50m of total funding) and upwards. Other funds include Charterhouse Development Capital (£100m), Schroder Ventures (£72m), Foreign and Colonial (£20m) and Granville (£10m).

3 Overseas players

The latest development in the market has been the arrival of many of the bigger players from the US LBO market, in particular Bankers Trust, First National Boston, Security Pacific, Merrill Lynch, Citicorp, and, most recently, Manufacturers Hanover. Some are keen on senior debt; others on higher risk mezzanine or other unsecured borrowings; others on equity; and some on a complete 'strip' of all these types of financing. Collectively they are offering new concepts of lending, either against cash flows or against imaginatively evaluated assets, and this could lead to much higher levels of gearing than hitherto. Mezzanine finance is a novelty in the UK, being debt rewarded for lack of security by an above average interest rate and usually some option to subscribe for equity.

Given London's cosmopolitan banking community it is not surprising that other international banks are also interested in buy-outs, including Standard Chartered and Scandinavian to name but two.

4 Other sources of finance

The following additional sources of finance should be considered:

(a) deferred purchase terms agreed with the vendor;
(b) sale and leaseback — buildings can be sold to financial institutions under arrangements that permit continuing occupation under lease, thus releasing capital;
(c) leasing of plant and machinery which may be less costly than purchase if the business has insufficient taxable profits to benefit from the available capital allowances;
(d) pension loan-back — where a pension fund is set up for the new company, or the directors take out retirement annuities, it is often possible for part of the funds so invested to be lent back to the company (at normal commerical terms);
(e) factoring — the 'sale' of trade debts at a discount to professional debt factors reduces working capital requirements;
(f) trade financing — local businessmen, major suppliers or customers may be prepared to provide finance to maintain the business;
(g) internal cash generation — an efficient financial management system can improve internal cash flow and reduce the need for outside cash;
(h) government grants — available selectively for investment projects or for projects in the assisted areas, government factories for lease or purchase on attractive terms or finance from EEC sources.

4.06 PERSONAL TAX PLANNING

Although individuals' tax positions vary, the principal personal tax considerations of the management are normally:

(a) the financiers will require the managers to make a cash investment which is significant to them (albeit entitling them to a disproportionately high share of the company) to ensure their commitment, and the managers may accordingly need to borrow. In order to obtain tax relief for interest paid the borrowings must be in the form of a loan (and not an overdraft) to acquire ordinary share capital in a close company (Finance Act 1974, Sch 1, paras 9 and 10) and the managers must:

(i)   work for the greater part of their time in the actual management or conduct of the company at the time the loan is made and while the interest is paid (Finance Act 1982, s 49); or

(ii)   have at least a 5% interest in the company; and

(iii) the company must either be a trading company, a member of a trading group or receive, in each accounting period, more than 75% of its income from, in practice, interest or dividends from its trading subsidiaries.

The company must also be close at the time the managers' investment is made. Close company status can be achieved at the outset by forming 'Newco' as the vehicle for the acquisition and issuing shares to the management in priority to the investors. If Newco later ceases to be close, interest relief should technically continue to be available but the Inland Revenue has shown signs of challenging this if there was no intention for the company to remain close, as is often the case with larger MBOs. The management should, in any event, subscribe as early as possible and before there is any contract for the investors to do so;

(b) care must be taken to avoid the growth in the value of the management shares being taxed as income (Finance Act 1972, s 79). There are two main exemptions which prevent an income tax charge from arising, provided that the shares are not subject to special restrictions:

(i)   if the majority of the available shares of the same class were acquired by employees or directors who are together able as holders of those shares to control the company; or

(ii)   if the majority of available shares of the same class were acquired otherwise than because of an opportunity offered to the holder by reason of their employment.

Although a requirement to dispose on cessation of employment is not a special restriction (provided the disposal price does not exceed market value), generally these are widely defined and include restrictions affecting transferability, dividend and voting rights and even restrictions in a related loan agreement;

(c) the use of an approved share option scheme for employees may now be tax efficient as gains will only be subject to capital gains tax; and

(d) if the MBO proves successful, substantial gains could arise in the value of the managers' shares, therefore personal tax planning should be considered at the outset: for example cash gifts to enable children to acquire the shares or the use of an offshore trust.

4.07 PURCHASE OF SHARES OR ASSETS

It is usually a matter for negotiation whether the business is bought by acquisition of shares or the underlying assets. An assets purchase avoids the uncertainty of warranties and indemnities. The vendor has to pay tax on:

(a) the automatic claw-back of reliefs hitherto obtained on plant and stock, though this may be mitigated if the vendor has trading losses available;

(b) the capital gain arising on the disposal of any chargeable asset (e g premises and goodwill) at more than original cost; and

(c) the profit on the sale of any trading asset.

Conversely the management team will be able to claim capital allowances on the value attributed to the plant acquired; and obtain a higher capital gains base cost for any assets acquired for more than their original cost to the vendor. The purchase consideration will require apportionment between assets in the agreement and frequently the interests of the parties will be opposed.

Where the shares of a target company are acquired by Newco, the vendor will be taxable at 30% on any gain and the purchase price of the shares will represent the capital gains base cost to Newco. The benefit of any trading losses and surplus ACT brought forward by the company will be available against future profits of the trade provided that there is no major change in the conduct of, or major reduction in, the trade within three years before or after the change in ownership (Taxes Act 1970, s 483). Also, the availability of losses is now restricted to the extent that the losses have been funded by creditors (Finance Act 1986, s 42 and Sch 10). Otherwise the disadvantages of an assets sale for the vendor are only partially compensated for by the advantages to the purchasers.

4.08 HIVE-UPS AND -DOWNS

Many MBOs involve the acquisition either of one of several trades carried on by the same company or of a subsidiary from a group. The buy-out is often preceded by either a 'hive-down' of the business to be acquired or a 'hive-out' of all assets other than the business to be acquired. The separation of the vendor's trades can be carried out without any immediate taxation consequences, subject to the following:

(a) the hive-down or hive-out company must be 75% owned by the vendor company, or all such companies 75% commonly owned (Taxes Act 1970, s 252);

(b) capital gains tax liabilities can crystallise on any intra-group transfers of assets held by the company leaving the group (Taxes Act 1970, s 278);

(c) any write-off of trading (as opposed to capital) intra-group debts constitutes a taxable receipt (Taxes Act 1970, s 136);

(d) the hive-down company may have a small share capital so as to minimise capital duty;

(e) stamp duty may be payable if a hive-up company is used;

(f) the acquisition of one of a company's businesses will kill any trading losses, although using divisional accounts or some alternative basis may enable apportionment to be negotiated with Inland Revenue agreement;

(g) the Inland Revenue may counteract any tax advantage arising from certain transactions in securities (Taxes Act 1970, s 460), unless made for commercial reasons without tax advantage as their main aim. Clearance should be sought by the vendors;

(h) in the longer term there can be problems in a non-trading holding company getting tax relief for interest and management expenses as the receipt of investment income will be subject to close company apportionment rules. This can be avoided by subsequently hiving-up the trading subsidiary into Newco; and

(i) trading losses that have been funded by creditors, including intra-group creditors, but excluding loan stocks, will not now be available to the hive-down company (Finance Act 1986, s 42 and Sch 10).

4.09 THE FUTURE OF MBOS

There is clearly plenty of finance available for the right MBO. Dedicated funds probably total £500m, but these represent perhaps only a third of the total equity available for investment in MBOs. It is reasonable to assume that this investment will be spread over the next three years and thus the market has about £500m available for investment per annum. On a modest gearing of 1:3, this would imply an annual capacity for MBOs of £2b.

We have no recent UK experience of a prolonged bear market and it could be that lower price earnings ratios generally would depress the urge to divest non-core or low-growth activities if the divesting company is unlikely to win a higher rating as a result of the sale. On the positive side a break in the market would involve more distress selling of viable divisions pre- or post-receivership and less competition from corporate purchasers no longer able to issue paper at favourable price earnings ratios. Most importantly, given similar interest rate levels to those currently prevailing, price levels will be more accessible to largely debt-financed MBO vehicles. In any event the market value of smaller and medium-sized unquoted investments is less volatile than their quoted brethren, where The Stock Exchange invariably exaggerates trends at the top and bottom of cycles. None of the bigger MBOs has yet failed, but the high interest rates of a recession could be beyond the means of some of the newer MBOs, which would have had too little time to reduce their high gearing to manageable levels.

CHAPTER 5

Take-overs, mergers and acquisitions

A.D. Macaulay
Herbert Smith

5.01 INTRODUCTION

Over the last four years there has been a remarkable increase in the number of take-over bids and in the degree of public interest generated. In the year to March 1983 the total number of published take-over offers amounted to 121. In the following year the comparable figure was 163 and in the year after a total of 202 bids was announced. In the year to March 1986, the comparable number was 206, while the figure for March 1987 was 280.

Although this represents a rapid increase, the level of activity in terms of numbers of bids does not begin to approach that of the early 1970s. Table 5.1 below shows the number of announced bids in each year since 1969, from which it might be deduced that the low level of activity in the early 1980s was perhaps the aberration.

The most significant aspect of the recent wave of activity has been the sheer size of the target companies, which have sometimes been significantly larger than the predators. This aspect reached a peak in late 1985 with Elders' £1.5b bid for Allied Lyons and Argyll's £1.8b bid for Distillers. At about the same time there were competing bids of around this value by Hanson and United Biscuits for Imperial Group. This last battle was won by Hanson with a bid worth £2.7b. In fact, the bids announced in the last two months of 1985 had a value which totalled more than the value of all the bids in the previous 12 months.

Another interesting feature of this series of mega-bids is the size of the increase between the opening offer and the level at which the offer was successful. For example, the increase in value between the opening Argyll bid for Distillers and the successful Guinness bid was some £800m, nearly equal to the previous highest bid ever in the UK, BAT's £950m take-over of Eagle Star in December 1983.

A number of factors has fuelled the recent wave of take-overs. The long bull market has pushed up the value of many companies' shares, making them attractive bid currency. The shake-out of British industry over the last few years has also provided many opportunities; companies which have been slow to react to economic changes become vulnerable to attempts to change the management by means of a take-over; it is normal practice for the offeror to try to persuade the target's shareholders that the offeror's management can do a better job than the incumbents.

The growth in the level of institutional shareholdings in British companies has not caused this factor to reduce in importance. It might have been expected that a comparatively small number of professional shareholders would have the ability

Table 5.1   Take-over bids and merger proposals

Year to March	Number of announced take-over and merger proposals
1969	575
1970	392
1971	331
1972	436
1973	388
1974	286
1975	151
1976	148
1977	199
1978	225
1979	167
1980	142
1981	147
1982	147
1983	121
1984	163
1985	202
1986	206
1987	280

Note: The above figures include cases where rival offers have been announced for one company and also include offers and schemes of arrangement made or proposed by the controller of a company to acquire the outstanding minority.
Source: Annual Reports of The Panel on Take-overs and Mergers 1969–1986.

to realise when their investments were performing badly, would understand the reasons for such performance and would have the power to take action accordingly. Experience has suggested that this is not the case. It is rare for fund managers to want to rock the boat by participating in a proxy battle to depose the existing management. Instead, with one or two exceptions, they have preferred to sell their shares to a predator with more highly regarded management, very often taking the predator's own shares as consideration rather than cash. The institutions have also promoted take-overs in their capacity as members of the underwriting circuit; they have been willing to provide the cash to finance take-overs and thereby to continue to fuel the growth in such activities.

Further, a company sometimes carries out an essential major restructuring which results in profit performance suffering for a period. Such companies are often at their most vulnerable at such a time and an offer made just before the benefits of the restructuring come through can be very dangerous for the existing management; their recent record may, on paper, not be very impressive and shareholders may be tempted to recoup their apparent losses by accepting an attractive offer.

Recent events have suggested to some that the tide of opinion may be turning against the predator. Dixons failed to take over Woolworths in the middle of 1986, and unsuccessful bids in the engineering sector (the subject of substantial recent restructuring) for McKechnie Brothers and APV have suggested that the odds are now in favour of the defence. The most spectacular failure was that of

BTR to acquire Pilkington in January 1987; BTR's bid was withdrawn some two and a half weeks before the last possible closing date.

There has also been academic research which suggests that successful take-overs are often not in the interest of the offeror; the task of digesting the target is often greater than anticipated and the hoped for benefits often fail to materialise. It is, however, fair to say that this research is somewhat controversial and is unlikely to deter the board of a potential offeror which believes that the take-over which it intends to mount will, if successful, be of benefit to the offeror.

Another factor which now gives potential offerors more pause for thought, especially in the case of a large target company, is the cost of failure. While a failed offeror very often covers its costs, or even makes a profit from the sale of the stake which it has built up in the target on the course of the bid, Argyll's net loss of some £34m on the failure of its take-over bid for Distillers represented a sizeable sum for a company whose profit before tax and before the expenses of the bid amounted to £64m.

Politically, too, the climate of opinion has turned against take-overs. There are moves to require the offeror to prove to the Monopolies and Mergers Commission that his proposed take-over would be in the public interest, at least in the case of large bids. This reversal of the present situation, where the onus of proof is on those trying to show that the bid is against the public interest, could well result in major problems for offerors; it would also, some would argue, be wrong to take the decision out of the hands of the shareholders, whose money is involved, and constitute a significant interference with the freedom to dispose of one's property.

5.02 DEFINITION OF A TAKE-OVER

At this stage, it is probably helpful to explain what is meant by the terms 'take-over' and 'merger'.

A take-over is a transaction whereby one company or, occasionally, an individual (or group of individuals) ('the offeror') acquires control of another company, or the assets of another company. This chapter will restrict itself to take-overs involving the obtaining of sufficient voting shares in a public company ('the target') (which may or may not be listed on The Stock Exchange) to enable the offeror to control the target. Control is exercised, in the last analysis, by the ability to decide the outcome of a general meeting of the target's shareholders and hence to determine the composition of the target's board. It is often not necessary, for this purpose, to obtain more than 75% of the voting rights attaching to the target's shares or more than 50% of the voting rights, although those are the percentage majorities needed to pass a special and an ordinary resolution respectively. In many companies it is unlikely that a sufficient number of shareholders will be found of like mind and willing to vote to prevent one shareholder, with appreciably less than the required number of shares under his control, from securing that the meeting produces the result he wants. In the UK it is considered by the Take-over Panel, and probably generally accepted, that the holder of 30% or more of the voting rights of a public company can in practice usually secure the passing of an ordinary resolution and can therefore control the composition of the board of that company. In practice, it is most unusual for a take-over offer in the

UK to end in anything other than the achievement of total control of the target or in failure. In this respect the UK is very different from the USA and Australia where it is common for take-over offers to be made with the objective of obtaining only a majority of the voting rights.

A merger is any transaction whereby the shareholders of two companies become fellow shareholders in one company, perhaps one of those two or perhaps a new, third, company formed for the purpose. The expressions 'take-over' and 'merger' are often, however, used in a way designed to distinguish the commercial substance of the transaction. A take-over is usually seen as one company acquiring control of another in a commercial sense. A merger, on the other hand, is seen — or at least presented — as the coming together of two equal companies for the greater good of both. Experience shows that, however described or effected, transactions involving the combination of two companies result in the board of one company becoming dominant and, to the extent, one company takes over the other.

5.03 METHODS OF EFFECTING A TAKE-OVER OR MERGER

1 The general offer

This is an offer for the entire issued voting equity capital in a company and is the most common form of take-over. An offer document is posted to the shareholders in the target. Under the City Code on Take-overs and Mergers (see below), this offer must remain open for at least 21 days. The Code also requires that the offer may not remain open for more than 60 days unless it has been accepted in respect of a majority of the voting shares and has become unconditional as to acceptances or in certain other limited circumstances (for example if there is a competing offer).

Such a take-over may provide as consideration shares in the offeror, or other securities such as debentures, or loan notes, or (unusually) cash alone or, (commonly), shares or other securities with a cash alternative offer. Such a cash alternative is not normally provided by the offeror out of its own resources; instead, the offeror arranges for (usually) a merchant bank, or stockbroker to underwrite (or 'underpin') the offer by offering to buy from accepting shareholders, at a fixed price, the consideration·shares (or other securities) to which they will become entitled if they accept the offer.

The offer may be recommended by the board of the target, in which case it will usually be successful; or it may be opposed by the target board, in which case there is often a fierce battle with the outcome often unknown until the last day of the bid.

2 The partial offer

This is similar to a general offer. The main difference is that the offer is for less than 100% of the issued voting shares in the target. Each shareholder may accept the offer in respect of more than the requisite percentage of his holding, but if he accepts for more than the requisite percentage his acceptance will be scaled down unless other shareholders have accepted for less than the requisite percentage (or have not accepted at all).

A distinguishing feature of partial offers in the UK is that where the offer is for more than 30% of the voting rights it can, under the Take-over Code, only succeed if a majority of the voting rights of the target is separately voted in favour of the offer. Thus, a shareholder who does not want the offer to succeed but, if the offer does succeed, wishes to sell his shares at the offer price, can accept the offer but at the same time vote against it.

This rule helps to explain why partial offers are so rare in the UK compared with the US and Australia, where they are common. There has only been one partial offer in the UK in the last three years and that was unsuccessful. Experience in the US and Australia shows that partial offers there present shareholders with a difficult decision. The level of the offer is often carefully pitched above the current market price but not sufficiently above it to justify, in the minds of shareholders, the transfer of control of their company to the offeror. In other words, the control premium may be seen as inadequate. However, a shareholder who does not accept the partial offer runs the risk that if the offer succeeds, he will be left with a minority stake which may well be less valuable than if the company had remained independent. There is, therefore, a considerable incentive to accept the partial offer, not because it is necessarily a good offer (although it may, of course, be so) but out of the fear of being left in as part of a minority. The effect of the incentive to accept is that the very result often comes about which the shareholder does not really want, namely the sale of his shares and the change of control. This is, of course, attractive to a potential predator. The Take-over Code's rule providing for a separate vote as to whether the offer should succeed ensures that shareholders are not faced with this dilemma, and can vote against the offer if they do not regard it as good enough but at the same time decide to accept it in case (against their wishes) it should succeed.

3 Schemes of arrangement

There are two sets of procedures covered by the term 'scheme of arrangement': that governed by the Companies Act 1985, ss 425–427; and that governed by the Companies Act 1985, s 582.

A scheme of arrangement under s 425 involves the holding of general meetings by the 'offeror' and the 'target' to pass resolutions approving the scheme, and the approval of the scheme by the High Court. In effect, the shares in the target held by its shareholders are cancelled and those shareholders receive instead new shares in the offeror or, sometimes, both companies' shares are cancelled in exchange for shares in a new holding company. Sometimes, the shares in the target are exchanged for shares in the offeror. A particular advantage of a scheme of arrangement is that only a simple majority in number, representing 75% in value, of the shareholders present and voting at a general meeting is needed for the scheme to be effective in respect of all of the issued capital of the 'target'. Thus, shareholder apathy can work in favour of the scheme. In a general offer, it is necessary for the offeror to achieve acceptances in respect of 90% of the shares for which the offer is made before it can compulsorily acquire the outstanding balance under the Companies Act 1985, s 428 (see below). On the other hand, such a scheme must comply with rules which allow less flexibility to respond to market developments than is the case in general offer.

A scheme of arrangement under s 582 involves the liquidation of the two merging companies and the transfer of their assets to a new company. The shareholders in the two liquidated companies receive shares in the new company in compensation. Such a procedure is only likely to be effective where there is known to be little, if any, dissent on the part of the shareholders, as s 582 gives dissenting shareholders powers to require the liquidator to purchase their interests, which could seriously affect the whole scheme. There are also complications in that the claims of creditors against the two liquidated companies are not transferred to the new company.

4 Issue of new shares by the 'target'

One company can sometimes take control of another, not by means of a general offer to buy the shares already in existence, but by means of an issue of new shares by the target company direct to the new controller. Sometimes this is in exchange for cash and sometimes in exchange for some other asset. This is a popular way in which the owners of a flourising private or unlisted public company can acquire control of a listed company, by 'reversing in' their own company in exchange for the issue of shares. Such a transaction normally requires the approval of the target's shareholders. This is necessary under the Take-over Code if the new shareholders are to be left with more than 30% of the shares in the target and if they wish to avoid the obligation under rule 9 of the Take-over Code (see below) to make a general offer for the remaining shares. Such a transaction is colloquially known as a 'whitewash' because the target's shareholders approve (or 'whitewash') the new controller and thereby relieve him of the obligation to make an offer for their shares. It should be noted that the whitewash procedure is only available if the new controller obtains control by means of the issue of new shares. If he obtains more than 30% of the target by means of a purchase or by means of a purchase connected with an issue of new shares by the target, then shareholders are not permitted by the Take-over Panel to 'whitewash' this (other than in wholly exceptional circumstances) and a general offer will be required.

The Stock Exchange also has requirements for shareholder approval in relation to listed companies where it is proposed that an acquisition is made which is regarded as a Major Class 1 transaction. This is defined as one where the acquisition represents 25% or more of the offeror company involved, based on a series of tests. Similar rules apply in relation to companies dealt in on the Unlisted Securities Market.

5 Reverse take-over bid

This is a species of take-over involving the issue of shares by the 'target' whereby the target makes an offer to the shareholders in a larger company to acquire their shares in exchange for new shares in the offeror. The result is that the shareholders in the company receiving the offer become the majority shareholders in the company ruling the offer. Sometimes, in a 'classical' reverse take-over the board of the larger company becomes the controlling element on the board of the new holding company. Sometimes (a recent example is the Guinness take-over of Distillers) the board of the smaller company has control. The Stock Exchange treats both such examples in the same way, and from the point of view of shareholders' approval and of listing requirements there is no practical difference. However, the 'classical' case is the one which would more generally be regarded as a reverse take-over.

5.04 THE REGULATORY BACKGROUND

1 The Take-over Code

The UK is unique in the importance of non-statutory regulation in relation to take-overs. It is remarkable when one considers that many take-overs are hotly contested that the participants are prepared to comply with the Take-over Code and the rulings of the Take-over Panel, despite the fact that the Panel has no statutory authority or powers.

The origin of the Panel lies in the inadequacy of the statutory regulation of the financial markets in dealing with the conduct of take-overs in the 1950s and 1960s. Those principally involved in take-overs whether as advisers to offerors or target companies, as investing institutions or as major companies came to feel (as did politicians and the public) that the existing law was inadequate both to protect the interests of shareholders facing a take-over offer and to control the conduct of the parties to a bid. After a number of take-overs, which, it was generally felt, had been conducted in an unsatisfactory manner (by the offeror, or by the board of the target, or both), the Bank of England took a leading hand in forming the Take-over Panel in 1968.

The Panel consists of representatives of:

the Accepting Houses Committee;
the Association of Investment Trust Companies;
the Association of British Insurers;
the Committee of London and Scottish Bankers;
the Confederation of British Industry;
the Council of The Stock Exchange;
the Financial Intermediaries, Managers and Brokers Regulatory Association;
the Institute of Chartered Accountants in England and Wales;
the Investment Management Regulatory Association;
the Issuing Houses Association;
the National Association of Pension Funds;
the Securities Associations;
    and
the Unit Trust Association.

It thus represents the main associations whose members are involved in take-overs, whether as advisers, shareholders, regulators, or potential targets.

The Take-over Code is promulgated and administered by the Take-over Panel. The Code does not have the force of law, but reflects what those most closely associated with take-overs regard as best practice in the conduct of take-overs.

Despite the Panel's lack of legal powers, it does have sanctions by which it can enforce its authority. For example, it can and does issue public reprimands to offenders. This may seem to be a mild sanction in a take-over where hundreds of millions of pounds may be involved. Further, there are countries where the receipt of such a public reprimand of this nature may be seen as some sort of badge of honour, perhaps as indicating how far an adviser, say, is prepared to go for his client. Nevertheless, in the UK the circle of those actively involved in take-overs is comparatively small, and practitioners and companies are keen to preserve their reputation for fair dealing, if for no other reason than that criticism by the Panel can harm a party's case in a take-over, and thereby cause it financial loss. In the case of a financial adviser, this could result in long-term loss of business. The effectiveness of this sanction is shown by the fact that the Panel has rarely had to use its ultimate sanction, the request that its members withdraw the facilities of the City from an offender who refuses to comply with a Panel ruling.

When Parliament debated the Financial Services Bill, which was passed in late 1986, the decision was taken to leave the Panel out of the new system of regulation.

The decision to leave out the Panel was a matter of some controversy, particularly amongst members of the opposition in Parliament, who took the view that, to be effective, the Take-over Panel required the same sort of statutory backing as the Securities and Investment Board ('the SIB'). The Panel argued strongly against this view. In particular, it considered that the nature of its relationship with its members would be changed if the ultimate sanction was to be some form of recourse to law rather than the peer group pressure which had applied in the past. It also pointed out that the Take-over Code provides far wider protection for shareholders than is provided in countries with a statutory (and hence, arguably, less flexible) system of regulation. It argued that once the law was involved in an area as competitive as the conduct of the parties in a take-over, the Panel would find itself subject to frequent challenge in the courts. This would inevitably hinder the smooth operation of the take-over process, which relies heavily on the Panel's ability to respond flexibly and quickly as circumstances require. This ability only exists, and the Panel is only able to deal with the hundreds of points on the Code which arise in a typical week, because practitioners share responsibility for the promulgation, application and enforcement of the rules, and therefore have an interest in seeing that those rules are applied sensibly and flexibly. The Government accepted that the Take-over Panel should not be brought within the new framework although it has indicated that should the City wish this to change, then it would consider such a request favourably.

Since then, the Panel has been challenged in the courts for the first time in an application for judicial review. In this case, which arose out of the controversial take-over of McCorquodale by Norton Opax in November 1986, the Court of Appeal ruled that the Panel was subject to judicial review by the Court, notwithstanding that it had always regarded itself as a self-regulatory body. The Court refused to grant the application for judicial review in that case, and went on to express the view that it would be rare for a Panel decision to be overturned.

Recent public revelations about the Guinness take-over of Distillers, and other contentious take-overs, have resulted in an upsurge of criticism of the Panel, and in demands for its role (whether performed by it or some other body) to be brought within the statutory system.

In May 1987 it was announced that the SIB would take non-compliance with the Code as indicating that a person might not be 'fit and proper' to carry on investment business; and the government announced that the Panel would be allowed access to certain information obtained by other persons under certain statutory authorities.

The Take-over Code sets out a number of General Principles, from which are drawn the Rules which follow and the Notes which amplify and explain the Rules. The General Principles, Rules and Notes are interpreted by the Panel in accordance with their spirit, not their letter; this means that they can be (and frequently are) extended to cover situations not precisely covered by the words of the Code, or relaxed in circumstances where the justice of the case requires.

The first and most important General Principle is that all shareholders must be treated equally. This is interpreted to mean that not only must all receive the same offer, but that if the offeror buys shares in the market it must increase the value of its offer to not less than the price paid in the market. This principle is reflected in many of the Code's Rules. An example is rule 16, which prohibits an offeror from acquiring shares in the target, whether as a result of purchases or otherwise, in circumstances in which he treats one shareholder more favourably than another. A 'side deal' of this nature is prohibited except in certain restricted circumstances. In one recent case, for example, the offeror acquired some shares from a shareholder and at the same time entered into an agreement with that shareholder which was likely to lead to the sale to that shareholder of certain assets of the target company. The Take-over Code provides that such a transaction is acceptable provided that a general meeting of the target company's shareholders is held to approve it and the transaction is recommended by the independent adviser to the target company. In the case in question, the target company's adviser was not prepared to recommend the transaction and the Panel therefore ruled that it could not proceed.

General Principle 7 prohibits the board of a target — or potential target — company from taking action which might frustrate a bona fide offer without the approval of the shareholders in general meeting. This effectively prevents the target's board from taking a number of defensive measures which are available in the US. For example, in the US, it is often possible for a target company to buy in some of its shares (often including those of the predator, which is known as 'greenmail') as a defensive measure. Another possible defence is the sale of one of the key assets of the target to another company so as to induce the offeror to withdraw its offer on the grounds that the transaction is no longer worth pursuing ('the Crown Jewel Strategy'). There may also be handsome compensation payments ('golden parachutes') in the event that the take-over is successful.

General Principle 7 effectively prevents these and other strategies. It is interpreted, however, as only applying to the sort of frustrating action which makes the target company less attractive to the creditor, or which effectively results in the directors of the target providing some benefit for themselves should the offer succeed.

The Code also requires proper disclosure of information to shareholders to enable them to reach an informed decision. It requires the board of a target to obtain competent independent advice on the merits of a take-over bid and to disclose that advice to shareholders. It lays down a timetable to ensure that shareholders have adequate time for their decision and, of considerable importance, to ensure that once an offeror has won, the offer must remain open for at least a further 14 days to enable previously undecided shareholders to accept rather than remain locked in as a minority. The only exception to the 14-day rule is in the case of a cash underwritten offer provided principally by a third party.

Also of considerable importance is rule 9 of the Code. This provides that where a person, either alone or jointly with others acting in concert with him ('a concert party'), acquires 30% or more of the voting rights of a company, he must make a general offer to the outstanding shareholders to acquire their shares for cash at not less than the highest price paid by him (or the members of the concert party) in the previous 12 months. If a shareholder already has between 30% and 50% of the voting rights of a company, then an offer is similarly required if his holdings (including any concert party) increase by 2% or more per annum. The philosophy behind this rule is that 30% is, in practice, the level at which a shareholder can be reasonably sure that he can procure the passing of an ordinary resolution at a general meeting of the company, given shareholder apathy and the usual lack of co-ordination of shareholder action. In effect, therefore, a person who acquires 30% or more has made a take-over and he must therefore treat all shareholders equally by extending an offer to them. Rule 9 therefore prevents the acquisition of 'creeping control' and usually ensures that control is only obtained by means of an offer at a price which shareholders find attractive. As mentioned above, one of the exceptions to this Rule is the 'whitewash' procedure.

2 The rules governing substantial acquisitions of shares ('the SARs')

These rules are promulgated and administered by the Take-over Panel, but are not part of the Take-over Code. One effect of this distinction is that the SARs do not apply to companies which are not listed or quoted on the Unlisted Securities

Market, or dealt in under Stock Exchange rule 535.3 (under which The Stock Exchange provides a dealing facility for certain unlisted companies). The SARs restrict the speed at which a shareholder may increase his holding between 15% and 30% of the voting rights of a company and require the disclosure of shareholdings above 15% on the day following certain increases in shareholding — as opposed to the period of five business days provided by the Companies Act 1985. The rules were originally introduced following controversy over a series of 'Dawn Raids' in 1979 and 1980, in which major shareholdings were built up in companies within a matter of hours, before the board of the company had time to react or advise its shareholders. The SARs are of considerable importance in relation to the planning of the tactics of a bid (see below).

The SARs also provide a mechanism known as a 'tender offer' which is, in effect, a seven-day partial offer for up to 30% of the shares in a company. It was originally anticipated that there would be a number of tender offers but in practice, there have been only two or three a year since the facility was introduced. The level of success on the part of offerors has been comparatively low. This is in part due to the fact that tender offers are sometimes used tactically and partly because shareholders who receive a tender offer often assume that the offeror is merely using the tender offer to build a substantial stake to be followed by a full offer at a higher price.

3 The Companies Act 1985

There are two main areas (apart from those discussed above) where this Act is particularly relevant to take-overs:

(a) Section 151

The Companies Act 1985, s 151 prohibits a company from providing financial assistance for the purchase of its own shares except in certain circumstances. Section 155 mitigates the effect of this considerably in relation to a private company. An offeror which is hoping to finance the offer, directly or indirectly, out of the assets of the target company needs to consider these provisions carefully. Financial assistance may be given by a public company when the assistance is given in good faith and is incidental to some larger purpose of the company. Financial assistance by way of payment of dividends is also permitted. If these routes are unavailable for whatever reason, then another possible route is for the offeror to convert the target company into a private company and then follow the route provided by s 155. The offeror does, however, face some difficulty if the target is not a wholly-owned subsidiary of the offeror, as the minority shareholders would be likely to object to their company's funds being used in this way. This means that the s 428 procedures discussed below need to be completed first, and this may cause unwelcome delay to an offeror with financial commitments to meet.

In practice, most offerors take the view that once they have achieved more than 50% of the voting rights of the target company, then they are likely to achieve the necessary 90% level. For this reason, while virtually every offer has as a condition that the offeror acquires control of 90% of the shares for which the offer is made, it is almost invariably the case that the offeror reserves (and usually exercises) the right to reduce this 90% level down to mere a majority of the voting rights. There have been few occasions in recent years when an offeror has not chosen to reduce this 90% level in order to secure voting control. In the case of Bristow Rotorcraft's offer for Westland in 1985, the offer lapsed because of failure to achieve the 90% condition despite the fact that Bristow had received acceptances of some 65% and the board of Westland had changed its views and decided to recommend share-holders to accept the offer. Concern about the financial position of Westland may have been a factor here; Westland was subsequently subject to competing rescue schemes, from Sikorsky of America and from a European Consortium. More recently, in the autumn of 1986 the offer by Sears for Blacks Leisure was recommended by Blacks' Board, who advised shareholders that receivership was likely if they rejected the offer. In fact, although more than 50% of the shares in Blacks were assented to the Sears offer, the offer was not declared unconditional as to acceptances because Sears required 90% to ensure that they could obtain total control.

(b) Sections 428–430F

The Companies Act 1985, ss 428–430F, have been amended and rationalised by the Financial Services Act 1986. In broad terms, they provide for the compulsory acquisition of the shares held by the outstanding minority following a successful offer in which the offeror has acquired not less than 90% of the shares for which the offer was made. Section 429 gives the offeror the right to require the minority to sell their shares in certain circumstances. Where the offeror has acquired 90% or more of the shares of a class the minority holders of that class can, under s 430A, require the offeror to buy their shares.

These provisions are of considerable importance. With almost any public company it is virtually impossible for an offeror to guarantee that he will receive acceptances in respect of all the shares of a given class, however attractive his offer. One reason for this is shareholder apathy. Further, shareholders may have moved or died without the company being aware of this. There is also the prospect of a small outstanding minority which will reject any offer, however good. In order to facilitate the completion of mergers the Act allows the minority of holders of shares of a given class to be bought out compulsorily once 90% of the shares of that class for which the offer has been made have been assented to the offer. It is considered that 90% support shows that the offer is likely to have been at a reasonable level.

Conversely, it is considered that the position of a minority with less than 10% of a company can be difficult and therefore that if an offeror has obtained acceptances in respect of 90% of the shares of a class (whether under the offer or by purchases) he should be required to buy out the minority if they wish to be bought out.

4 The Prevention of Fraud (Investments) Act 1958 and the Financial Services Act 1986

The Prevention of Fraud (Investments) Act mainly affects take-overs by prescribing who may issue offer documents. In practice, unless the consent of the Department of Trade is obtained, offer documents can normally only be issued by banks, stockbrokers and licensed dealers. This structure has been replaced by the Financial Services Act 1986 and the whole organisation of the financial markets has been affected by this new Act.

In essence, the Financial Services Act sets up a new system of regulation, described as self-regulation in a statutory framework. The main body controlling the financial markets is the SIB which can delegate certain of its powers to what are described as self-regulating organisations. These self-regulating organisations are composed of practioners representing various sectors within the financial services industry and lay down and enforce rules to be followed by their members. The rules must fall within certain guidelines laid down by the SIB.

The main area of the financial services industry left untouched by the Financial Services Act is the Take-over Panel.

The direct impact of the Financial Services Act on take-overs is therefore comparatively limited, other than for the amendments to the Companies Act 1985, ss 428–430F discussed above.

5 The Fair Trading Act 1973

Sections 57–75 of this Act provide for the Secretary of State for Trade and Industry, having received a recommendation from the Office of Fair Trading, to decide whether or not to refer a take-over or merger to the Monopolies and Mergers Commission. Other than in the case of newspaper mergers (which must be referred except in minor cases), a take-over or merger can only be referred if it involves a combination of 25% or more of the relevant market or where the book value of the assets being acquired amounts to £30m or more. The Monopolies and Mergers Commission is required to report on as to whether the take-over may be expected to operate against the public interest and, if so, may make recommendations for the protection of the public interest. A report on a reference must be made within six months but this can be extended for up to a further three months at the request of the Commission. If the Commission thinks that a take-over could be expected to operate against the public interest, the Secretary of State then determines whether or not the take-over should be allowed to proceed.

On a reference to the Monopolies and Mergers Commission, the Take-over Code requires that the offer must lapse unless the first closing date of the offer has passed and the offer has become unconditional as to acceptances. Considerations of a possible reference to the Monopolies and Mergers Commission therefore form a major part of the calculations of both the offeror and the target company; the offeror naturally tries to persuade the Office of Fair Trading that a reference to the Monopolies and Mergers Commission is not necessary or justified. The target board normally seeks to achieve the opposite result. It might be considered that such action on the part of the target board — which might frustrate the wishes of a majority of the target shareholders — could amount to frustration of an offer in breach of General Principle 7 of the Code. However, the Take-over Panel takes the view that General Principle 7 should not be interpreted in this way and lobbying the Office of Fair Trading has become an accepted and regular feature of all large contested take-overs.

The parties involved are, however, in some difficulty when deciding on the approach to adopt in relation to the Office of Fair Trading. Government policy over the years has fluctuated, not always because of a change of government. The overriding concern of the Secretary of State when determining whether or not to make a reference on the advice of the Office of Fair Trading is the public interest. In 1984 Norman Tebbit, then the Secretary of State, announced that references would only normally be made on the grounds that competition might otherwise be adversely affected. However, the reference of the Elders IXL bid for Allied-Lyons was made because of quite different considerations.

Elders IXL is a major Australian brewing group whose best known product is Foster's Lager. In October 1985, it announced an offer for Allied-Lyons, a major food and drinks conglomerate. Allied-Lyons was larger than Elders IXL and the offeror's intention was to acquire the core brewing business of Allied-Lyons and dispose of many other parts of it. The offer was financed by a very high level of borrowing from a number of international banks and concern was expressed as to the desirability of a major British company being acquired on such a basis. There was also concern over the exceptionally complex corporate structure set up by Elders IXL with a chain of companies some of which were not, in a strict sense, subsidiaries of Elders IXL. The bid appeared to give rise to no significant competition aspects but nevertheless was referred because of wider concern about the effect on the public interest of the financing of the bid. The Monopolies and Mergers Commission reported in September 1986 that the bid should be allowed to proceed on the grounds that the take-over should not be expected to operate against the public interest. In fact, although Elders IXL then had, under the Take-over Code, three weeks within which to renew its bid, it chose not to do so and instead acquired the Courage brewing business from Hanson Trust (which had itself recently acquired this on its take-over of Imperial Group).

It was reported in the press that the board of Allied-Lyons had faced something of a dilemma in relation to the possibility of a reference to the Monopolies and Mergers Commission. On the one hand, a reference was likely to be a very effective defensive move. On the other hand, to be seen to be lobbying too hard for a reference would damage the company's credibility, especially if the Secretary of State eventually decided that a reference was not justified. This dilemma is one which is not unknown to other target companies.

Another reference on grounds other than competition was that of Hillsdown Holdings' bid for S & W Berisford (which owns British Sugar Corpn) in May 1986. In that case, the reason was the special position of British Sugar Corpn in the UK sugar market.

Yet another reference on non-competition grounds was made at the end of 1986, when Gulf Resources' bid for IC Gas (which owns Calor Gas) was referred. The concern in that case was the high level of borrowings by Gulf Resources needed to finance the bid.

In the light of recent history there must be some sympathy with the position of those who have to advise clients whether or not a reference of a bid is likely.

6 The Stock Exchange

Where a listed company is involved in a take-over, it is required by The Stock Exchange to comply with certain rules in relation to the contents of documents. Further, as discussed above, a Major Class 1 acquisition must be subject to the approval of the offeror's own shareholders. Approval is also required if the target is connected with a director or substantial shareholder of the offeror. Where an offeror is issuing shares as consideration and those shares are to be listed, the offeror must normally issue listing particulars which comply with the rules laid down by The Stock Exchange under powers delegated to it by The Financial Services Act.

Unlike the Take-over Panel, The Stock Exchange examines proofs of all circulars before despatch to ensure that they comply with The Stock Exchange's rules and it is important that advisers ensure that advance proofs of circulars are presented to The Stock Exchange for their consideration without delay.

7 The Capital Gains Tax Act 1979

Under this Act, certain disposals of securities are subject to tax on the gain realised. Tax is not, however, charged where shares are disposed of in exchange for other shares in the context of a general offer (whether partial or for all of the target's shares). This general exemption does not apply to holders of more than

5% of the shares in the target unless clearance is specifically given by the Inland Revenue. It is therefore important that the offeror should apply for such clearance at the earliest possible stage in order that the tax position of large shareholders in the target is not prejudiced, which might result in their being less willing to accept the offer. Where shares are exchanged for cash (or consideration shares are disposed of, for example, under a cash underwritten alternative) this relief from capital gains tax is not available.

8 The Company Securities (Insider Dealing) Act 1985

This Act (inter alia) prohibits a person who has received confidential price sensitive information about an offer or contemplated offer from a person connected with a company from dealing in shares in the target company on The Stock Exchange or through an off-market dealer.

It was not until 1981 that insider dealing as such became a crime in the UK although it has been a crime in the US for many years. Before that, the only control over the misuse of confidential information, whether generally about a company or specifically about an anticipated take-over bid, was exercised by The Stock Exchange and the Take-over Panel. These self-regulatory bodies both had (and still have) rules designed to prevent a person in possession of confidential price sensitive information from using that information to make a profit by dealing with others who are not in possession of the same information and therefore deal to their disadvantage. For a number of years a steady trickle of insider dealers was reprimanded by The Stock Exchange or the Take-over Panel, and in many cases, required to pay to charity the profit made by the misuse of confidential information. It was hoped that once insider dealing became a criminal offence, the law would punish those responsible and that the deterrent effect of criminal sanctions would lead to a decrease in its incidence. However, these hopes have not entirely materialised. This is in part due to the difficulty in securing a conviction. The courts require proof of guilt beyond reasonable doubt and the Department of Trade and Industry is understandably reluctant to prosecute except when it feels it has a strong case. The result has been remarkably few prosecutions since 1981 and even fewer convictions. This does not compare favourably with the record of The Stock Exchange and the Take-over Panel before then.

The Financial Services Act has attempted to alleviate this problem by requiring those questioned by inspectors appointed by the Department of Trade and Industry to answer such questions, even if the answers would tend to incriminate the person questioned. This removal of the 'right to silence' is justified on the grounds of the difficulty of establishing that insider dealing has taken place. Nevertheless, it is the case that persons suspected of far more serious crimes have the right to remain silent, and these new provisions may well involve a disproportionate weakening of the rights of the accused. The political climate is undoubtedly hostile to insider dealers, and the recently announced proposals by the Government to extend the maximum sentence from two years to seven years may be an over-reaction to political pressure.

It is not unusual for the price of the shares of a potential target to rise shortly before the announcement of a bid. This is not necessarily, however, as a result of dealings by people with inside knowledge of a likely bid at a price higher than the current market price. In many cases the price rise is not out of line with a general advance in the relevant sector. Sometimes a rise follows an announcement of a potential bid or the taking of a significant share stake by a person who is generally considered to be a predator.

Difficulties sometimes arise because the coverage of insider dealing by the Take-over Panel and by the Insider Dealing Act is somewhat different. In particular, the Act permits insider dealing away from The Stock Exchange or an off-market dealer; the Code prohibits it in both such cases. Further, the Code does not allow members of a consortium to deal in advance of the announcement of a consortium offer, other than on the basis that any profit or loss on the dealing will be for the account of the consortium as a whole. There is no such requirement in the Act, and members of a consortium are, under the Act, free to deal if they do so to promote their offer whether or not all profit or loss is for the account of the consortium as a whole.

Similar considerations apply in relation to buying by the potential offeror's advisers prior to the announcement of the offer. Here again, the Take-over Code is arguably stricter than the Insider Dealing Act in that such buying can only be on the basis that no profit arises for the offeror's adviser and any such profit must be for the account of the potential offeror as if the potential offeror had himself made the purchases.

Accordingly, any purchases of shares in a potential target company prior to the announcement of the offer should be considered with care if the sanctions of the law and of the Take-over Panel are not to be incurred.

5.05 WHY MAKE A TAKE-OVER BID?

The reason behind the decision to make a take-over bid vary in each case. However, major factors include:

1 Increasing the offeror's share of a market

The offeror hopes that increasing the size of its business in this way will lead to greater efficiency and economies of scale and possibly valuable cross-fertilisation of ideas from the new personnel who will join the offeror's group. Such offers are particularly at risk of a reference to the Monopolies and Mergers Commission.

In January 1987, Sir Gordon Borrie, the Director-General of Fair Trading, expressed some scepticism as to whether UK companies needed to have a dominant position in the UK in order to compete effectively abroad; the argument of international strength through dominance in the UK may therefore not be persuasive to the Office of Fair Trading.

2 The desire to obtain assets which are undervalued

Where this is followed by the sale of those assets it is sometimes known as 'asset-stripping'. This derogatory term is sometimes unfair if, as is often the case, the ultimate acquirer of those assets is prepared to pay a high price because he believes he can (and often does) use them more effectively than the original owners. To this extent the offeror may be seen as performing a valuable service in freeing assets from inefficient management.

3 Diversification

An offeror who operates in only one area of business is vulnerable to any change affecting that business. It can therefore make considerable sense to acquire some unrelated business in order to provide strength through diversity.

4 Acquiring valuable assets in exchange for shares

Sometimes this can simply involve a strengthening of the offeror's asset base. However, a specific type of take-over where this is a factor involves a take-over bid for an investment trust company by, say, an industrial company. The objective is to issue shares in the offeror to shareholders in the target investment trust and, on obtaining control of the investment trust to realise its portfolio as rapidly as possible and use the proceeds in the business of the offeror. Such a procedure is often (perhaps somewhat misleadingly) known as a 'disguised rights issue'. It is not of course, a rights issue as such, as the shares in question go to outsiders not to the company's own shareholders. There has been a recent spate of bids for investment trusts but such trusts continue to be formed and are far from being an endangered species.

5 Forming a conglomerate

The offeror may seek to acquire a wide range of entirely unconnected businesses and in this way build a group of strength and flexibility. While acquisitions do not always bring the benefits hoped for, some conglomerates have been remarkably successful. The current political climate is significantly less favourable to conglomerates.

6 To acquire a valuable asset

The offeror may seek to obtain a specific business, or a particular strength in a specific area of the country or of the industry. If the acquisition can be made for shares, rather than cash, then, provided that the offeror's earnings are not diluted, such an acquisition can seem very attractive.

7 As a defence against a predator

It is sometimes felt that if the target company makes itself substantially larger, it might become indigestible for a predator. Elders IXL tried to argue that Allied-Lyons' proposed acquisition of Hiram Walker was intended to make Allied-Lyons too big and complex for Elders IXL to take over. This charge was strongly denied by Allied-Lyons, who pointed to considerable industrial logic in the acquisition. This acquisition was, as required by General Principle 7 of the Take-over Code (which continues to apply during the period of a Monopolies and Mergers Commission reference), subject to the approval of the shareholders of Allied-Lyons. They could therefore decide whether they wanted the Hiram Walker acquisition or the Elders IXL offer. This seems to leave the decision in the right place, namely with those whose financial interests are involved.

5.06 PLANNING A BID

The importance of good research cannot be over-emphasised. The potential offeror must discover all it can about the potential target's business, management and financial performance. Normally, the only sort of information is in the potential target's published figures but these are often expanded upon by research carried out by stockbrokers and others, or by general knowledge of the industry. All the available information needs careful consideration by financial experts to ensure that the meaning behind the various statistics is ascertained.

The offeror also needs to consider carefully what it will do with its acquisition should this succeed. It is essential that the offeror should be able to take effective control immediately its offer succeeds, to avoid the risk of a leaderless acquisition losing efficiency and market share. The offeror should not have to spend too long after the completion of the acquisition in learning enough about the business to enable it to take sensible management decisions. The offeror also needs to consider whether it has the resources in terms of personnel to enable it to devote the necessary amount of senior executive time both to running the new acquisition and to integrating it with the existing structure of the offeror.

The strategy and tactics of the bid must also be planned carefully although these must not override the all important commercial considerations. It is essential that professional advisers are selected who are familiar with the world of take-overs. The rules are complex and not always easy to apply. Events can sometimes move very fast, and experienced advisers are needed to ensure that problems are dealt with rapidly. The stock markets are not prepared to wait while an offeror's advisers formulate their plans to deal with new developments.

A team should therefore be assembled at an early stage consisting, preferably, of a merchant bank, a stockbroker, a solicitor, an accountant and a public relations adviser. It is important that all those involved should be aware of what is proposed at every stage so that they can contribute most efficiently. This is an area where close co-operation between the offeror and its advisers is essential and those involved must all be capable of working together as a harmonious team. It is likely that this teamwork will be tested on more than one occasion in the course of the bid as matters develop.

The offeror needs to consider not only itself and the potential target but also the likely reaction of other companies. It is quite common for the announcement of one offer to precipitate another offer, whether at the volition of the rival offeror or at the request of the target board as a defensive manoeuvre ('the white knight defence'). Even an agreed bid can sometimes collapse on the intervention of a third party. In Spring 1985, Charterhouse Petroleum and Saxon Oil announced an agreed merger. This was to be accomplished by offers for each by a new holding company incorporated for the purpose. The merger was generally favourably received and was proceeding to a conclusion when Enterprise Oil announced an offer for Saxon Oil which offered a higher price to Saxon shareholders than they would be likely to obtain if they took shares in the new holding company. In due course, Enterprise's offer was successful and the plans of the boards of Charterhouse Petroleum and of Saxon for a merger failed.

Similarly, United Biscuits and Imperial Group announced an agreed merger in late 1985. This was frustrated by Hanson Trust, which made an offer for Imperial Group which was ultimately successful.

The offeror must therefore consider whether it will be possible to achieve 'a shut-out' on or immediately after the announcement of its offer. A shut-out arises where the offeror has, from the outset, the certainty that it will obtain voting control of the offeror, either because it has purchased more than half the offeror's shares or because it has obtained binding irrevocable commitments to accept the offer from the holders of more than half of the target's shares. Sometimes it is not possible to achieve this level of certainty and in practice, a figure of perhaps 40% should normally be sufficient. There are, however, hurdles to be overcome in that both the SARs and the Take-over Code endeavour to restrict the ability of an offeror to acquire a large stake in a target in a short period of time without the assent of the board of the target company.

Again, an offeror needs to analyse very clearly its objective in making a take-over bid and must weigh up the potential benefit against the costs involved and the risk of failure. It is particularly important for the offeror to have a clear idea of the maximum price which it is prepared to pay. There is a risk, in the heady and often emotional atmosphere of a hotly contested take-over bid, that the offeror may pay too much to ensure success.

As discussed above, the offeror and its advisers also need to anticipate the likely reaction of the Office of Fair Trading to the proposed offer. However, all is not necessarily lost even if the Secretary of State refers the offer to the Monopolies and Mergers Commission. In both the United Biscuits/Imperial and the Guinness/Distillers take-over bids there was a reference to the Monopolies and Mergers Commission on competition grounds. In each case, the parties were able to arrange for the disposal of certain assets, conditional on the success of the bid, and thereby as a result allay the fears of the Office of Fair Trading and the Secretary of State in relation to competition.

A recent development in relation to the Monopolies and Mergers Commission has been the instigation of litigation against the Commission itself. Argyll Group took legal action in relation to the arrangements between Guinness and Distillers which led to the withdrawal of the original reference to the Commission and Matthew Brown took action in relation to the Commission's clearance of the bid by Scottish and Newcastle Brewers for Matthew Brown. Both attempts to overturn decisions by the Monopolies and Mergers Commission were unsuccessful.

The offeror must appreciate that, under the Take-over Code, the announcement of the firm intention to make an offer results in the offeror's being obliged to post a formal offer document unless a rival offeror posts a higher offer or in wholly exceptional circumstances (which do not include general economic changes). The announcement of the offer must include all the relevant terms and conditions to which the offer is subject and the drafting of these for the press announcement requires care.

5.07 DEFENDING AGAINST AN UNWELCOME BID

The target board is required by the Take-over Code to obtain competent independent advice on the merits of the offer. It is required to advise its share-holders, and to inform them of the substance of the advice from the independent adviser, within 14 days of the posting of the offer document.

If this advice is to reject the bid, the target board needs to consider possible defences.

As indicated above, a target board facing an unwelcome offer has open to it far fewer defences than its counterpart in the US. General Principle 7 of the Take-over Code severely restricts its room to manoeuvre. Nevertheless, there is much that a defending board can do:

(a) The best form of defence is to ensure that the perception of shareholders, the market and the press is that the existing board is doing a good job. This defence is, however, unlikely to be effective unless the board has already established good communications with shareholders and the press and has kept them fully informed of the company's progress. Even then, the mere creation of a good image is unlikely to be sufficient in itself unless accompanied by actual performance in terms of delivering good financial results or in clearly organising the company's affairs so as to improve its ability to deliver good financial results.

(b) Considerable importance is frequently attached to the making of a forecast of the results of the target for the current financial year. The Take-over Code has strict rules (which apply equally to the offeror) designed to ensure that profit forecasts are made responsibly and reported on by independent financial advisers. These rules have helped to ensure that profit forecasts are rarely made unless they can be met, except in unforeseen circumstances.

(c) A revaluation of the target's assets can sometimes show that the offeror is seeking to acquire them too cheaply and may therefore help to push the target's share price beyond the offeror's reach. It may, however, have the unwanted effect of showing that the return on assets obtained by the existing board is inadequate.

(d) As indicated above, target boards often lobby the Office of Fair Trading with a view to securing a recommendation of a reference to the Monopolies and Mergers Commission. This is often accompanied by intensive political lobbying. Unless the offeror can restructure its offer so as to escape from the reference, the result of a reference to the Commission has the effect of driving the offeror away for at least six months, in which period the target board may have the opportunity to take steps to improve the company's performance.

(e) If a board decides that market sentiment is such that its company is bound to be taken over, it sometimes seeks a more acceptable offeror ('a white knight'). Once the board institutes such a search, and this is publicly known, the company's days of independence are likely to be over. It is also sometimes the case that the white knight turns out to be less than friendly following the change of control. This is, however, a tactic which can result in a series of increased bids and counter bids by the rival bidders, which is normally to the financial benefit of the target's shareholders.

(f) A tactic which rarely works is the appeal to shareholder loyalty. This is a rare commodity in a listed company. The recent failure of Dixons' bid for Woolworths may be an exception to that principle. Woolworths Holding plc was formed in 1982 by a consortium of institutions with a view to acquiring F W Woolworth plc and injecting new management. There were strong indications that the members of the original consortium felt that, having put the new management into its position, they were morally bound to continue to support that management until it had had the chance to do the job to which it had appointed.

More unusual was perhaps the case of Lloyd's Bank's offer for Standard Chartered. This failed narrowly, leaving Lloyd's with purchases and acceptances totalling some 42%, insufficient to declare its offer unconditional as to acceptances largely because of substantial market purchases by major shareholders loyal to Standard Chartered.

Debt

CHAPTER 6

Sources of UK short-term and medium-term debt

G. L. Wynne
Watson Farley & Williams

6.01 INTRODUCTION

For most companies and individuals the traditional source for funds required for a business remains a bank or banks, and this is the case even with the availability, to certain of them, of alternative forms of fund raising through access to the world's capital markets and the general 'securitisation' of financing. In this case, borrowers of substantial size who meet certain specified criteria (sometimes legally required or otherwise dictated by the market) are able to obtain funds by the issuance of securities (for example bonds and notes) either on a long-term basis (in the case of bond issues), or on a short-term revolving basis in the case of note issues commonly known as RUFs (revolving underwriting facilities) and NIFs (note issuance facilities). The method of utilising this market is dealt with more fully elsewhere but it is worth contrasting this type of arrangement where the relationship that the borrower has to the provider of funds (ie the noteholder) is comparatively weak with the general relationship that exists with a bank providing finance where such relationship is invariably closer and stronger during the life of the facility. For this reason the flexibility in relation to both the borrowing and its repayment is that much greater. This area and its various refinements form the basis for this chapter.

It is still the case that the most common form of short-term financing remains the overdraft facility. This is made available (generally speaking) by the bank which provides the day-to-day banking for the borrower concerned. Similarly, in looking at medium-term financing (that is to say five to seven years) a term loan arrangement is again the most common source of finance. In this latter case there are variations in the manner in which the funding can be provided to permit the borrower with his bank supporting him to obtain attractive financing packages.

This chapter looks at these two specific forms of financing and their various developments. In addition, it notes innovations in the market and in particular the availability of short-term notes and sterling commercial paper to certain large corporate borrowers. A review of financing opportunities would not be complete without also looking at the raising of finance through trade related activities.

6.02 OVERDRAFTS

1 General

The simplest definition of an overdraft would perhaps be an arrangement which a customer has with a bank whereby the bank allows, on a revolving basis, the borrower to borrow funds which are repayable on demand. It is the 'demand element' of this financing that enables the granting of it to be comparatively simple although, from the borrower's perspective, the uncertainty of the continued availability invariably presents a problem. The borrower has the flexibility of obtaining funds up to its maximum limit when required, safe in the knowledge that it can simply repay those funds when it has surplus cash and re-draw them as and when required.

Quite often the borrower is able to use these funds by issuing cheques drawn on the bank concerned. A variation would be to require funds to be transferred at the borrower's discretion. Interest is usually charged at a percentage above the bank's base lending rate (or a cost of funds calculation perhaps using the London Interbank Market rate (LIBOR)). The interest is sometimes merely added to the overdraft account by a debit from the bank or, alternatively, the borrower is required to pay the interest directly.

It is possible to refine the overdraft arrangement so that the only 'true' element that remains is that it is payable on demand. Thus, within the overdraft facility the interest rate can sometimes be calculated by using LIBOR funding but with interest payable quarterly or even six-monthly. The overdraft can also be used to support receivables financing or factoring (see below).

The cost of establishing an overdraft facility should be comparatively small (possibly an arrangement fee with the bank) and, while the cost of borrowing itself may be slightly higher than with the other forms of financing to be considered, the flexibility of controlling the cost by only utilising the overdraft when funds are required gives the borrower the greatest amount of flexibility. In addition the funds should be available immediately or on very short notice and little (if any) formality is required once the facility is established.

2 Types of security

It is normal when a bank provides an overdraft facility for that bank to require, particularly from a company, security for the amount outstanding. In the UK the normal way in which a bank protects itself is to obtain from the borrower a charge (normally a fixed and floating charge) over all of the assets of the borrower to support the overdraft facility. The charge is expressed to be a fixed and floating charge in that it would normally be a fixed charge on the premises of the borrower and its plant and machinery, but would 'float' over the rest of the assets enabling the borrower to continue to recycle its assets (most importantly its stock in trade and/or work in progress) without being unduly hindered. Given the existence of such a wide charge, the bank would then not be interested to any great extent in restricting the borrower's other activities, but the borrower may of course be constrained from any other borrowing in that it cannot provide any security which ranks in priority, or equal, to the charge given to its overdraft bank without the consent of such bank. Thus, a borrower embarking on a fund raising activity for a new venture would undoubtedly be restricted in this by a fixed and floating charge securing its overdraft.

If the overdraft facility is supporting a specific part of the borrower's business (for example financing its trade receivables) then it may be possible to structure the facility on the basis of the security being limited to those particular assets.

Whilst the above overcomes what would otherwise be a major problem (the lack of availability of accessible future security to a new lender) the overdraft, as previously intimated, contains no continued certainty for the borrower. It is in law repayable on demand which, for this purpose, gives the borrower no direct right at all to its continued availability although, for practical purposes, most banks tend to review a satisfactory account only on an annual basis.

In the above circumstances a borrower wishing to achieve more certainty as to the medium-term availability of finance may well wish to look at a medium-term financing instrument such as a term loan.

6.03 TERM LOANS

1 General

A term loan is normally established by a commitment from a bank to make funds available to a borrower by way of drawing in specified amounts which can then be outstanding for a period normally of between three and seven years. Within this framework provisions are inserted regarding the terms of the repayment, particularly as to when the repayments must start and how they are dealt with during the term of the loan.

2 Common provisions

The most common repayment schedule leaves a period at the commencement of the facility when no repayments are required (the grace period) and this might perhaps be two years whilst the borrower utilises the funds to achieve an income generating arrangement. During this grace period interest only is paid. At the end of the grace period repayments are normally made in equal periodic instalments at six-monthly intervals over the balance of the loan period. However, variations on this can be negotiated to reflect the projected cash flow of the borrower so that, for example, part of the loan can be repaid over the period of the loan, but a substantial balance is then repayable at the end of that period (the 'balloon' payment). Alternatively, where specific circumstances so dictate the whole of the loan can remain outstanding for the period with a repayment of the full amount at the end of the loan term (the 'bullet' payment). In any of these variations where a substantial portion of the loan remains outstanding it may well be that the bank requires some certainty as to availability of funds to meet what would then be a substantial repayment obligation or security in respect of this obligation whether by way of assets or a guarantee.

In negotiating the provisions to be contained in a term loan there are a number of specific considerations relating to the mechanics of the transaction in add .on to repayment which have to be considered and dealt with. The first point relates to how the money is to be available, whether in a single lump sum or in multiple drawdowns. Much will depend on the purpose of the facility. For example, if the funds are for the purchase of an asset then a single advance will normally be required. If, however, the funds are for the construction of a particular project or working capital purposes then availability in instalments would be required. In this latter case a drawdown period is normally agreed (from one month to periods in excess of one year, depending on the circumstances). Any funds not drawn during this period are normally cancelled. It is usual for a lender to require a fee (commitment commission) payable on the undrawn amounts for his agreeing to keep funds available. The mechanics for drawdown should be contrasted with the overdraft where funds are available throughout the facility period up to the maximum permitted amount. It should be noted that the sophisticated drawdown procedure of a term loan is a necessity for the lender bearing in mind that the lender is committed to advancing funds if a series of pre-agreed conditions are and remain met. In an overdraft, as mentioned above, the lender can simply cancel the arrangement and not be obliged to advance further amounts.

In a term loan it is usually possible to negotiate for the right to prepay all or part of the loan in advance of the repayment schedule but it is common for prepaid funds not to be made available again. Prepayments are applied against the repayment schedule in inverse order of maturity (thus shortening the facility life). However, a 'revolving element' may be negotiated. A revolving arrangement in a term loan can, in its simplest form, simply mean that any amount prepaid can, during a specified period, be redrawn. The effect of this is that the drawdown period may well continue for the life of the loan but the available amount reduces (so that there is either a lesser amount for drawing or a repayment required on each reduction date). If the facility is either secured on a particular asset or assets or repayments are dependent on continued cash from the exploitation of a project the ability to redraw is often controlled by a test related to the value of assets secured or future anticipated revenue.

It may also be possible to have some flexibility in relation to the payment of interest. The borrower can sometimes have the right to select different lengths of interest periods in an attempt to reduce the interest cost and to protect cash flow. This can even be on the basis that different lengths of interest period apply to different portions of the loan. Thus, whilst the margin (or profit) to the lender over LIBOR (or other cost of funds) will be constant the borrower can select the funding period which may well alter his borrowing rate. The interest periods are usually periods of one month up to a year. Interest is paid at the end of the period although where the interest period exceeds six months it is usually also paid six-monthly.

As mentioned previously the term loan is evidenced much more formally than the overdraft and the documentation will provide not only for the mechanics of the borrowing, interest and repayment provisions already covered, but will also contain a series of obligations imposed on the borrower as to how its business should be conducted and, more importantly, a series of events (the events of default) pursuant to which the loan could be repaid earlier if the bank so required. This should be contrasted to the overdraft facility where the loan is repayable on demand. The reason for this is that in order for a term loan to have attraction to a borrower, it must have the certainty of finances for the agreed period if and so long as it complies with its obligations specified in the document and none of the specified events of default occur.

To be more specific regarding further provisions, it is normal that the borrower in a term loan is required to covenant with the lender matters over and above the mere servicing of the debt. The types of covenant will depend quite often on the purpose for which the loan is intended and the credit standing of the borrower. A number of standard provisions regarding the maintenance of appropriate consents and the continuation of its business in a prudent manner tend to be common to most arrangements, but other restrictions, for example, like the creation of security (the negative pledge) and the transfer of assets will very much depend on the negotiated position. As well as covenanting to do and not to do certain things the borrower will also make a series of statements (representations and warranties) about itself and its business and these statements are expressed not only to induce the lender to make the funds available but as the pre-conditions for the obligation of the lender and for the continued availability of the funds. The representations and warranties again may be subject to negotiation but will also run to the credit worthiness of the borrower so that, for example, statements regarding the payment of taxes and the status of litigation will be relevant.

A lender may well decide in a term loan that the 'ideal financial position' of the borrower can best be reflected by requiring the borrower to comply with pre-determined financial ratios which are tested (usually) annually against the audited accounts. These ratios tend to restrict borrowings and/or liabilities unsupported by assets, and two more common ones are a debt to equity ratio and a current ratio (current assets to current liabilities). Failure to comply with these is normally a basis for termination (being an event of default referred to below) although it is possible to require shareholder funds to adjust the ratio (see below in references to types of security).

The most usual remedy for a breach by the borrower of any of the representations or covenants mentioned above will be two-fold: namely that the lender can refrain from making further funds available; and/or can require the earlier repayment of funds which have already been lent. In addition to these events of default there would naturally be the failure by the borrower to make payments of principal, interest and other amounts on their due date. Further events of default would be matters running to the creditworthiness of the borrower (its insolvency, appointment of a receiver, etc) and its failure to pay other debts on their due date (the cross-default clause) and also specific circumstances relating to the borrower and the means selected for the repayment of funds, for example for the project concerned.

It is not uncommon for a term loan to be unsecured but quite often in early discussions with the lender concerned an important question is whether or not the term loan should be secured on the assets of the borrower and, if so, on which assets.

3 Types of security

Whereas the overdraft facility if it is secured tends to be secured on all of the assets of the borrower it is quite normal in the case of a term loan for the security to be limited to specific assets or project being financed. Thus, for example, a term loan provided to finance the acquisition of a property (for perhaps the building of a factory) would have the security limited to the property concerned, the assets thereon and the revenues generated thereby.

Within the framework of this could well be provisions to value the security being offered and possibly to require that the security be maintained at a margin over the amount of the loan, to provide the bank concerned with protection in the unfortunate case of enforcement or the reduction in the value of the asset. The effect of requiring a security margin would then require the borrower to prepay the loan to preserve the margin or to furnish more security. In all of these circumstances the borrower is losing flexibility in relation to all or part of its business, so it is important for the borrower to negotiate a position whereby the greater the amount of security he provides to the lender the fewer the restrictions should be on the parts of its business which are not subject to that security. This could ultimately be reduced to the lender being required to look only to the asset concerned for its source of repayment (limited recourse lending).

Where limited recourse lending is involved then there are a number of differences in the structure of the transaction and possibly in the obligor itself. Quite often the borrower will be a company specifically established to undertake the project concerned, when it is easier to structure the nature of the risk for the lender, which is that it ultimately has no support from the other assets of its customer (which are then held in another company or companies). In exchange for this risk the lender will naturally require a tightly-drawn agreement restricting the special purpose borrower to running only the project. In addition, all of the assets will normally be secured in favour of the lender together with the proceeds from their exploitation. It may well be, particularly with a development (for example the building of a factory), that the customer will be required to support the early stages of construction either with finance or expertise or a mixture of both on the basis that completion of the project as a viable unit is achieved. In this way the lender bears only the risk of the project failing to produce sufficient revenues rather than a poorly built or abandoned project in its entirety. The return to the lender in an arrangement such as this may well exceed the interest return referred to above but care has to be taken to ensure that the transaction does not infringe laws such as the Partnership Act 1890; this could make the lender and borrower 'partners' and turn the lender's provision of finance into a provision of equity so that the lender is, in effect, subordinated to all other creditors.

Instead of providing security from its own assets a borrower may find it more convenient to obtain a guarantee from a third party to provide to its bank. If the borrower is a subsidiary of a larger company then such a guarantee may well be provided by that larger company, but alternatively the guarantee could be provided by other interested parties including the individual shareholders or a third party bank. In this latter case the third party would invariably charge a fee. (As will be seen below the provision of guarantees by a bank may well form part of a term loan facility.)

Other forms of comfort can be provided to a lender to improve the credit standing of a borrower or a particular project and these all tend to have an effect on the flexibility contained in the principal document. For example, the shareholders of a borrower may well be prepared to support any shortfall in the borrower's funds to enable continued debt service to proceed. This type of arrangement (often called a cash deficiency arrangement) would require shareholders to provide funds by way of increased equity participation or subordinated lending to enable the borrower to meet its obligations. Less formal (and generally less binding) arrangements are also possible by use of letters of comfort from a substantial shareholder. This could cover matters like control of the borrower or the continued availability of intra-group resources. A number of disputes may often arise in these 'so-called' letters of comfort as to whether they are legally enforceable. It is much better at the outset for the parties to agree on whether this additional 'support' is meant to be binding, and therefore actionable, should a problem arise.

The structure established for a term loan, namely a well drawn regime giving 'certain availability' to the borrower against restrictions on its business may well be applied to similar facilities which do not necessarily result in the lender providing medium-term funds itself, but instead enable the borrower to have some selectivity in this. Some of these are considered below.

Before completing a review of the type of security it is worth noting (in the case of a UK company) that the provisions of the Insolvency Act 1986 may well cause a re-thinking by lenders on how to structure secured transactions and possibly even unsecured transactions. This Act imposes a regime whereby a borrower can seek the protection of the courts by means of an administrator, who could control the business of the borrower and devise a 'rescue plan' for its assets and liabilities. The net effect of such an arrangement is to restrict the secured lender's rights in certain circumstances to realise on its secured assets and to prevent petitions for the winding up of a borrower whilst a survival plan is under consideration. The appointment of the administrator can be defeated by the appointment of an administrative receiver under a floating charge by a lender so that it is quite likely that in future charges taken by lenders would include a floating charge. To achieve this purpose, the floating charge must be over all, or substantially all, of the assets of the borrower so that it may well be that special purpose companies emerge, not only on a purely project basis, but to provide to the lender the above right.

6.04 GUARANTEE FACILITIES

It is quite possible that a borrower may wish to establish a number of banking relationships with other lenders (not being its normal banker), particularly in the case where they have access to low-cost financing which can be made available to the borrower subject to satisfying certain conditions. An example would be fixed-rate ship financing provided by foreign yards and/or their banks. One common requirement of these financings is that the borrower provides its own bank guarantee of its obligations. In these circumstances the borrower may well negotiate that instead of receiving funds directly from its lender, the lender provides its own guarantee to third parties who will then make loans on 'advantageous terms' to the borrower. These terms are often a lower direct borrowing cost and/or achieve an extended maturity. The lender acting as the guaranteeing bank will charge a fee for its guarantee and this must be added to the cost to establish whether the overall cost is worthwhile.

With the bank guarantee the direct lender should require very little by way of restrictions from the borrower and the arrangement may well be evidenced by promissory notes alone. It will be for the lender/guarantor to require a similar document to the term loan containing covenants and other restrictions. It should be noted that, unless the guarantee provides for a prepayment of obligations, it may well be that the direct lender will remain content to receive payment from the guarantor even with financial difficulties on the borrower's side so that the lender/guarantor may well see its remedy as being the provision by the borrower of cash collateral to support the unmatured contingent liabilities rather than early repayment as mentioned above. However, since this subsidised financing is more often at a fixed rate, the borrower should try to negotiate from the direct lender of this finance a prepayment right in case market rates change.

An extension of the guarantee facility may well be used in a mixed arrangement where the lender provides loans and also guarantees to enable the borrower (particularly in a project) to pay for local expenditure with subsidised local funds from local banks who are protected by a bank guarantee. The lender then is able to control all security and the borrower's obligations are unhindered.

An extension of this mixed facility has been adopted by lenders in an attempt to make their own provisions of finance more attractive to borrowers.

6.05 MULTIPLE OPTION FACILITIES (MOFs)

Using the structure of the term loan type document referred to above the lender may be prepared to permit the borrower greater flexibility in the types of financing which can be made available within an overall maximum amount. Thus, the borrower may take a mixture of term loans (and these may be on a revolving basis) and conceivably an overdraft facility by way of direct financing. In addition, the borrower may have the right to require the lender to issue guarantees, letters of credit and other bonds under the umbrella of this document to enable the borrower either to obtain lower-cost financing (see above) or to expand/develop its business. The possibilities of direct financing instruments are almost endless and other instruments and facilities mentioned in this chapter (for example, the acceptance credit facility referred to below) can be made available. All of the above involve the lender in direct credit responsibility so that provisions regarding repayment or reduction of the maximum amount of the facility will be included. Thus, in all of the above arrangements the structure of the term loan tends to be observed but, as mentioned in relation to guarantees, the borrower can find itself with an obligation to provide cash collateral for the contingent or third party obligations as well as repayment of the loans concerned.

Within this overall facility, and if the borrower meets the relevant criteria mentioned below (primarily relating to being a listed company on The Stock Exchange), the borrower may be permitted, through the lender, to issue short-term notes and sterling commercial paper (see below). This can sometimes involve other parties (such as underwriters of a tender panel) and some of these structures are considered elsewhere. The overall purpose can be that a single document has the ability to cover the borrower's short-term and medium-term needs together with special access to the financial capital markets on a short-term basis. There has been a significant increase in the use of MOFs by UK listed companies since they gained access to these new capital markets.

6.06 TO SYNDICATE OR NOT

In discussing all of the above an assumption has been made that the borrower will deal directly with an individual lender who will provide all of the financing (other than in the case of the MOF where some of the following may well apply. If the amount or the arrangements justify it a lender may instead bring together a group of banks (a syndicate) who will advance on an individual basis a portion of the facility available. In these circumstances one bank (normally drawn from the syndicate) will act as agent for the remaining banks to hold the day to day negotiations with the funds coming from the group itself. The advantage to the borrower is that it can obtain (within one document) a substantially greater amount of funds, but its disadvantage is the loss of day-to-day contact with its lenders as a whole and also the potential inflexibility of having a group of lenders who are required to agree to one specific course of action.

It should, however, be noted that apart from the additional complications of having a group of banks the structure from the borrower's point of view still remains that access to its funding should still be guaranteed throughout the life of the facility, subject to the usual restrictions regarding the running of its business and its own financial condition.

6.07 ASSET FINANCING

1 General

For certain borrowers it may be desirable or useful for them to raise finance either through their existing assets or to use such financing for the purpose of acquiring a specific asset. Whilst these fund raising activities are considered elsewhere in much greater detail mention is made of them here for sake of completeness.

2 Leasing and hire-purchase

Both the leasing and hire-purchasing of assets enable the acquirer to obtain the use (and for accounting purposes the value) of an asset even though the financing is being provided by another party. In the case of leasing the availability of capital allowances to the legal owner (the financer) can often mean that the cost of the financing is reduced once the benefit of these allowances are taken into account.

Whilst it is easy to see how these methods can assist in the financing of an acquisition of an asset it is also worth noting that they can be used as a method of generating cash flow and/or to finance a borrower's own leasing or renting activity.

3 Sale and 'buy-back'

Where a borrower already owns an asset it may be possible for that asset to be sold to a bank or other lending institution for a cash sum (thus improving the borrower's cash flow), on terms that the asset is immediately 'returned' to the borrower under an arrangement whereby the borrower then pays periodic amounts for the use of the asset, and included within this is a financing charge. The tax implications of sale and lease-back transactions (where the tax advantage of capital allowances is involved) is again considered elsewhere so that for this purpose consideration is only given to the fund raising advantage and cost.

Thus, the borrower would then under its on-going arrangement with its financer agree to make payments (whether by way of lease, hire-purchase or otherwise) in much the same way as it would under a lending arrangement and quite often the provisions of the lease/hire-purchase agreement resemble a financing agreement, particularly in relation to events of termination. It should, however, be noted that the right given to the financer is to recover his asset and to claim a termination sum which, generally speaking, is the balance of the outstanding payments discounted for early receipt. The major risk for a financer would be that whilst in a loan arrangement his principal is recoverable quite easily, in a leasing/hire-purchase arrangement there may be questions of the receipt of an excessive amount being challenged for being a penalty as a matter of English law.

As mentioned above the use of sale and buy-back, particularly by way of a hire-purchase agreement is often a satisfactory means for a party to acquire assets which it can then lease on to its own customers. The effect of this is that the 'borrower's' customers provide the financing to service the purchase of the asset and a profit element for the borrower for the difference between its own financing cost under the lease/hire-purchase agreement and its income under its own lease.

If the financer is prepared to accept exclusively the credit risk of the borrower then, as previously discussed, the documentation for this arrangement will be similar to the term loan containing events of early termination, undertakings regarding the maintenance of the equipment and indemnities in favour of the owner of the equipment (ie the financer), to ensure that the transaction is as risk free as possible to him. On the other hand, if the transaction depends for its success on the underlying sub-lease it is possible to deal with the transaction by way of the creation of a security interest in the sub-lease and provisions to ensure that the lease payments under the sub-lease are received directly by the financer. The rights of the financer may again be limited in recourse to the sub-lease. In this event the arrangement is not dissimilar to the limited recourse financing mentioned above.

It is quite possible to structure the asset financing in exactly the same way as a loan financing, so that the same cash flow results are achieved and, in summary, asset financing, particularly where the asset is not part of a greater project, can easily be dealt with within this structure.

One element that has been mentioned in discussing asset financing has been the availability of income produced by the asset concerned, which could, in certain circumstances, be made available to a financer to assist in the structuring of the transaction. The use of debts to generate cash flow is itself a form of financing although here it should be noted that, other than in the factoring arrangement described below, the financing raised by use of book debts or receivables (as they are sometimes called) merely accelerates receipt of moneys which would in any event be receivable by the borrower.

6.08 TRADE FINANCING

1 The financing of book debts

There are two distinct ways of financing the company's book debts. The first way is the sale of those book debts for a cash sum and this is generally called factoring. The alternative is to finance those book debts by, in effect, giving the book debts as security, and this can be termed 'invoice discounting' or 'receivable financing'. Both of these topics are dealt with elsewhere, but again it is worth noting a few points, particularly from the point of view of a bank financing the arrangement.

Generally speaking, true factoring services tend to be offered by specialised companies rather than banks, in that this arrangement involves the purchase by the company of all of the trade debts due, coupled with a debt collection service. By arrangement with the factoring company concerned the risk of bad debts must be dealt with, but a full factoring arrangement would enable a company to receive cash for its sales ledger on terms that the factoring company then looked exclusively to the debts for recovery of its funds.

By contrast, in a receivables financing the financer receives by way of assignment all, or a pre-determined number, of the debts by way of security, and based on the value of these debts a proportion of funds are made available to the borrower. Upon payment of the debts by the borrower's customers the cash is then applied by the financer in satisfaction of the borrowing and interest thereon and the balance is then ultimately received by the borrower once the debt obligation has been repaid.

It is possible within the framework of a receivables financing for funds to be advanced on a revolving basis using the security of the unpaid and unmatured debts from time to time on a rolling formula basis. Thus, on a weekly or a monthly basis the amount of the debts would be valued and funds advanced to the borrower in respect thereof.

In this type of receivables arrangement it is quite common to have extensive documentation to deal not only with the complex mechanics, but also with matters like representations and warranties, undertakings and events of default, which have all been discussed under the heading of term loans earlier in this chapter. The financer would then have the right to cancel the availability of the facility and/or to declare all amounts due and payable. The effect of such a declaration would be to enable the financer to step in and recover the debts directly from the customers as and when they fall due.

It should be noted that there are defects in the security arrangements particularly in light of the Insolvency Act 1986. As was mentioned above, the fact that an appointment of an administrator will prevent the enforcement of a fixed charge and, in the case of a floating charge, would permit the substitution of security. Thus, a bank financing receivables by way of an assignment of the receivables as security may well find that it is unable to enforce its charge upon the insolvency of the borrower. Thus, financing on this basis may well be adjusted in the future.

In addition, in a normal receivables financing the borrower's customer may well be unaware of the underlying documentation and will consequently not have received notice (which in legal terms perfects the charge) from the financer, and consequently there may be the legal, as well as practical, difficulties for the financer collecting the money directly. From a practical point of view much of the problem can be overcome by ensuring that all of the debts are initially paid into a pre-agreed account for application in discharge of the borrowing.

2 Forfaiting

A forfaiting transaction can be seen, to a certain extent, as a variation on the factoring of debts referred to above. Its value is primarily to a borrower who is the seller of goods (or conceivably services) to a third party who resides abroad and in circumstances where that third party (the purchaser) wishes, or requires, that it be permitted to pay the purchase price in instalments.

In order to achieve a forfaiting transaction the seller needs to arrange with the purchaser that the purchase price be evidenced by either bills of exchange or promissory notes, each payable in a fixed amount on a pre-agreed future date, so that the aggregate purchase price is evidenced in a series of bills of exchange or notes (for this purpose references are to notes). In many cases the credit risk of the purchaser may be insufficient for a forfaiting transaction and consequently there would be a requirement that the obligations of the purchaser be guaranteed by a commercial bank in the jurisdiction of the purchaser. This guarantee is evidenced either by a separate guarantee or by a guarantee endorsed on the note itself. The legal requirement in the appropriate jurisdiction must be met to ensure that the guarantee (or aval, being the specific term applicable to an endorsed guarantee) are dealt with.

One final pre-condition is that the notes must contain no reference to the underlying commercial transaction so that they stand alone as evidencing an obligation to pay a definite sum of money on a definite date. Thus, the purchaser will always be obliged to make payment under the notes although he would still have any rights against the seller if, for example, the goods supplied were defective.

If the above situation can be achieved then the seller has all of the elements necessary for a forfaiting transaction. The seller will approach a forfaiting company (which could be its own bank) and raise finance based on the discounted value of the notes. The financing bank would evaluate the rates of interest over the life of the transaction, the creditworthiness of the purchaser and its guaranteeing bank and its own requirements for a rate of return, and would then quote a purchase price (which in other circumstances would be the equivalent of loan proceeds) to the seller. The major point from the position of the seller is that the financing bank would then agree to purchase the notes on terms that it had no recourse to the seller if the notes were subsequently not met. It is this without recourse element that distinguishes most forfaiting arrangements from any receivables discounting facility. Indeed one derivation of the word 'forfaiting' is that the bank forfeits its rights against the seller.

The financing documentation for this arrangement is accordingly quite simple. The form of the promissory note must, as stated above, be clear and simple and the purchase agreement between the financing bank and the seller/borrower is also surprisingly simple, and merely sets out the terms of the purchase. The seller may be asked to make some limited warranties regarding the underlying transaction, but essentially it is the purchasing bank that has the responsibility for checking the documentation. Whilst the explanation given relates to an individual transaction a forfaiting facility for a number of transactions involving the seller can be set up on the same basis.

It is also possible for the financing bank to arrange for a syndicate of banks to support the transaction either on a strictly syndicated basis (along the lines discussed above) or with the bank concerned then sub-financing to the syndicate. The complexity of these arrangements need not concern the seller who is interested in only the funds raised. However, the purchaser (and perhaps more importantly the guaranteeing bank) may be reluctant to see the notes in the hands of too many people, particularly if the end acquirer is not a bank, and restrictions may well be inserted to prevent this occurring.

6.09 ACCEPTANCE CREDIT FACILITIES

An acceptance credit facility is not a loan facility but an alternative method of raising money through the discounting of bills of exchange.

In simple terms the borrower issues a bill of exchange drawn and accepted on a bank. The bank discounts the bill, either itself or in the market and the discount value is paid to the borrower in return for the obligation of the borrower for the reimbursement of the full value of the bill on its presentation to the bank on maturity. There is therefore no security for the bank other than the creditworthiness of the borrower, who will generally be a company of good standing.

In practice, acceptance credits are often made under a facility agreement which is similar to a loan agreement and may incorporate an option for the borrower to receive cash advances or acceptance credits. The bank (or banks if a syndicated facility is arranged) granting the facility will usually charge an acceptance commission on the face value of each bill drawn by the borrower. The facility may be a revolving one allowing the borrower to issue bills up to a maximum aggregate amount at any time. When the borrower wishes to make a drawing under the facility it will forward bills to the bank for the full amount of the intended drawing. The bank will attempt to discount the bills but is usually under no obligation to release any money to the borrower if it fails to do so and in these circumstances the bills will be cancelled and returned. The discounted value of the bills, less the acceptance commission charged, will then be made available to the borrower. It is usual to provide that the aggregate proceeds receivable by the borrower should be no less than the equivalent receipt of loan proceeds (less interest) in a loan facility.

The agreement will contain the usual type of representations, warranties, and events of default referred to in the term loan facility; the latter of which will include failure to provide cash cover for any bill on its maturity (the equivalent of a failure to pay). The bills are normally short-term, that is, between 30 and 180 days' maturity. If the borrower is of high standing it is unusual for additional security to be provided by a borrower but if the facility is closely related to the purchase of goods the banks may take letters of hypothecation on the goods.

Bills of exchange may be discounted to other banks or discount houses or in the London Discount Market. Discount houses only may discount bills to the Bank of England, provided they are 'eligible bills'. This means they must have an eligible name as acceptor (there are currently some 150 banks, both foreign and British, who qualify) and the bill must represent a real underlying transaction. The advantages of an acceptance credit facility are that funds are provided by the purchasers of bills and not the bank and consequently the effective cost of borrowing to the borrower may well be less than in a loan transaction.

6.10 STERLING DEBT SECURITIES

1 General

The above sources of finance are generally (apart from acceptance credits) provided by banks or the financial community as a whole. The effect of this is obviously a restriction on where funds can be obtained and at the same time a comparatively expensive form of borrowing in that banks and other financial institutions naturally require a return on their investment and, as they themselves have to pay interest on funds raised, the borrowing base is that much higher. A natural further source for raising sterling would, therefore, be the non-banking part of the community. This could well result in cheaper borrowings.

Whilst UK companies have been able in the past to raise foreign currency funds in the euro-currency markets (by way of bond issues, note issues, etc) the raising of funds in the UK on a regular basis for short-term funds was restricted, particularly since the Banking Act 1979. This restriction was based on the problem that the obtaining of funds on a regular basis could amount to 'carrying on a business which is a deposit taking business for the purposes of this act' (Banking Act 1979, s 1(2)) which required authorisation from the Bank of England.

In order to assist companies in raising short-term funds two provisions have been enacted which enable companies who meet certain pre-determined criteria to raise short-term sterling funds.

2 Short-term notes

As a result of the Banking Act 1979 (Exempt Transactions) (Amendment) Regulations 1985, companies which meet the following conditions may issue sterling debt securities (which as defined include bonds, notes, debentures and debenture stock payable only in sterling). The conditions for exemption are:

(a) the issuing company must have its shares listed on The Stock Exchange or traded on the Unlisted Securities Market or be a wholly-owned subsidiary of such a company;

(b) either an application must be made for the securities to be admitted to official listing and listing particulars complying with the requirements of The Stock Exchange must have been published or a prospectus satisfying the requirements laid down by the Companies Acts must have been published in relation thereto;

(c)   the securities may be issued and transferred in denominations of £100,000 or more; and

(d)   the securities must have a maturity period of at least one year.

The securities to be issued may have either fixed-rate or floating-rate interest. One further condition must be met and that is that if the issue raises £3m or more Bank of England permission must be obtained as to the timing of the issue in accordance with the Control of Borrowing Order 1958.

As a result of the above, certain companies can issue short-term sterling notes which can be used either to increase their capital base or to finance ventures on a more short-term basis. However, in view of the minimum size of the securities and the type of company concerned this is not a market that is available either to small companies or to small investors. It does, as mentioned above, at least permit a company to decide on its own rate of interest rather than being controlled by the borrowing rate of the bank concerned.

It should be noted that since there are further restrictions regarding the obtaining of investors and finding investors who are prepared to underwrite an issue the banking community, at least from the investment banking side, will still be very much involved in the pricing and timing of such issues.

As can be seen from the above the short-term note addressed one particular sector in the market but, since its minimum term was one year, it did not help the company that wanted to raise its sterling for a shorter period to meet its shorter-term funding requirements.

This was addressed by the Bank of England in April 1986 and changes were made with effect from May 1986.

3 Sterling commercial paper

As mentioned above it was the Banking Act 1979 which again prevented the raising of short-term funds on a regular basis. As a result of the Banking Act 1979 (Exempt Transactions) (Amendment)·Regulations 1986 which came into operation on 20 May 1986 companies which met the specific criteria laid down were permitted to issue sterling commercial paper (defined as a sterling debt security which may not be redeemed in whole or in part until after seven days beginning with the date of issue but which must be redeemed within one year beginning with the date of issue). Thus, it finally permitted those companies to issue short-term bearer notes denominated in sterling. However, the type of issuer who is permitted to utilise this market must meet the following criteria:

(a)   the issuer (or in the case of a wholly-owned subsidiary its guarantor) must be a company with net assets of not less than £50m; and

(b)   the company must have its shares listed on The Stock Exchange.

It should be noted that the Bank of England does not wish recognised banks or licensed deposit takers (or 'generally' their subsidiaries or holding companies) to issue sterling commercial paper and this market is also not available to building societies. Changes are, however, anticipated in this area.

Sterling commercial paper, as well as having the maturity listed above, must be issued in bearer form, but in a minimum amount of £500,000. The paper must also bear on its face a statement that it has been issued in compliance with the Regulations.

If all of the above provisions are met then sterling commercial paper will be exempt not only from the Banking Act but also from the Control of Borrowing

Order 1958 mentioned above. The effect in this latter case is that timing consent from the Bank of England will not be required which, of course, is essential if sterling commercial paper is to meet its objective: namely immediate access for companies to sterling on a short-term basis. The immediate access and the short-term nature will thus enable companies to meet immediate requirements and also seasonal variations in their business for funding purposes.

When the regulations took effect there were still significant problems for companies seeking to meet the above criteria and primarily as a result of the prospectus requirements contained in the Companies Act 1985. The effect of this was that companies were required to issue prospectuses which would again have made it impractical (for reasons of updating of information) for issues to occur at short-term notice. Since the position regarding the prospectus requirements was less onerous where the issuer is incorporated outside Great Britain (even if the paper is guaranteed by a British company) this was the means adopted for raising the funds. The exemption relates to securities offered to 'professional people' but in view of the minimum size of the notes (£500,000) this is perhaps not a problem.

Section 195 of the Financial Services Act extends the above prospectus exemption for overseas issuers to companies incorporated in Great Britain. When Part V of this Act comes into force further and wide exemption are anticipated.

4 Mechanics of issue

For both short-term notes and sterling commercial paper the major source of issuing will certainly be through managers/dealers and thereafter to professionals in the market. Certain issuers may elect to have a particular issue 'underwritten', thus making certain of the funds, although in order to encourage competitiveness from those in the market the mechanics of a tender panel (where the best price from the tenderer will prevail) may be advantageous to the issuer at the appropriate time.

Whilst there is a limited market of issuers who can take advantage of the above devices they do represent progress in the armoury of a company wishing to have available immediate access to funds.

A number of substantial groups have taken advantage by establishing either sterling commercial paper programmes or a form of multiple option facility which includes a sterling commercial paper option. It is not always easy to ascertain the size of any particular market, but since the Regulations took effect it is thought that in excess of £6,520m in facilities have been arranged although only a small portion of that amount (£1,655m as at June 1987) was actually in issue.

6.11 SUMMARY

In addition to the financings listed in this chapter there are other, more specific, means for companies to raise finance, including the stock market and other sophisticated forms of project financing, leasing and venture capital. For smaller companies it still appears to be the case that for the vast majority of them in the UK the means of raising short-term and medium-term debt remains by negotiation with either their own clearing bank or with the substantial number of foreign commercial banks that have representation in the UK.

For the more sophisticated raising of finance, whether this be a larger amount through a syndicated arrangement or alternatives to pure loans (such as acceptance credits), the investment banks and merchant banks are involved and when the larger public companies are involved for the securitised part of the market, the investment and merchant banks play an even greater role.

It is arguable that at this stage (mid 1987) a two-tier market exists with larger companies able to take advantage of the securitised and bearer issue side of the market whilst smaller companies are restricted to the pure banking sector. It may well be that more and more companies will find comfort in the closer relationship with the banking community, and revert to more conventional means of borrowing directly from banks but taking advantage of the 'risk transfer factor', and will utilise limited and non-recourse forms of project financing.

CHAPTER 7

Sources of UK long-term debt

J. Rutterford
Alexanders Laing & Cruickshank

7.01 INTRODUCTION

This chapter concentrates on the alternative source of long-term debt finance available to companies in the UK. We restrict ourselves to UK sources of debt, although we refer to commonly used alternative sources of sterling debt finance, such as the eurosterling market, also referred to in Part C below on international finance.

Historically, the UK banking sector viewed itself as a provider of short-term debt, to finance companies' needs for working capital. Since banks obtained their funds through retail current and deposit accounts and had relatively small amounts of capital, they were vulnerable to sudden demands for repayment by depositors. This led them to avoid lending long and to make loans repayable on demand, mostly in the form of overdrafts. Thus, UK companies, if they wished to borrow money for capital investment, were forced to turn to long-term investors via the capital markets. This attitude of the banks explains the early development of capital markets in both the UK and the US, compared to countries such as Germany, France and Japan. In these countries, banks were encouraged, usually by central government, to offer long-term debt to companies in the form of long-term bank loans.

By the 1960s, most UK companies had a wide variety of types of loan capital on their balance sheets, for example, debenture stock, unsecured loan stock, and convertible loan stock. These had either been issued via the stock market to investors or placed privately, perhaps with one or more insurance companies, say as a mortgage debenture secured on a property. The majority of these debt issues were fixed interest, with maturities of between 15 and 30 years, very different from the variable interest rate, repayable on demand, overdraft.

The loan capital markets flourished in the UK until the early 1970s, when uncertainty about future inflation and interest rates in the wake of the oil crisis made investors wary of investing in long-term, fixed-interest debt securities. The decline in importance of this form of finance can be seen in the new issue statistics, shown in Table 7.1 below. For example, in 1964, £222m of long-term debt was issued by companies in the capital markets, with even higher issue totals in 1965 and 1966 (under a new tax system) of £442m and £464m respectively. This compares with a mere £43m, before adjusting for inflation, in both 1973 and 1974.

Table 7.1 New issues by companies by type of security (including eurosterling and bulldog issues)

	Debt			Preference	Ordinary	Total
	Convertible	Other	Total			
	£m	£m	£m	£m	£m	£m
1963	35.3	229.0	264.3	14.7	163.9	442.9
1964	60.2	161.8	222.0	10.7	168.9	401.6
1965	28.1	414.3	442.6	3.7	45.5	491.4
1966	38.4	425.8	464.2	16.4	142.5	623.2
1967	29.7	313.8	343.5	5.7	72.6	421.9
1968	128.3	161.3	289.6	3.1	363.7	656.4
1969	231.7	144.8	376.5	—	195.0	571.5
1970	101.3	183.0	284.3	17.2	51.9	353.4
1971	96.7	243.7	340.4	12.8	310.4	663.6
1972	96.4	199.2	299.6	10.9	649.9	956.4
1973	21.6	21.3	42.9	14.0	153.6	210.5
1974	25.6	17.2	42.8	—	119.3	162.1
1975	117.0	95.8	212.8	44.8	1320.7	1578.4
1976	14.8	77.7	92.5	44.5	1023.9	1160.9
1977	2.0	91.8	93.8	33.9	816.6	947.3
1978	2.4	6.4	8.8	41.3	612.5	662.5
1979	26.8	34.6	61.4	34.6	786.2	885.1
1980	215.7	1.5	217.2	37.1	853.6	1107.9
1981	373.5	66.9	440.4	113.1	2110.8	2664.3
1982	71.3	1044.8	1116.1*	32.5	1165.3	2313.9
1983	64.4	694.5	758.9*	80.7	2370.1	3209.7
1984	118.1	2135.7	2253.8*	78.4	1947.5	4279.7

*Of which £860m in 1982, £420m in 1983 and £447m in 1984 was *domestic* bond issues by *UK* companies.

Source: Midland Bank Quarterly Review.

The relative importance of bank lending and the debt capital markets as sources of finance for UK companies has therefore varied substantially over time. Undistributed income naturally provides the major source of funds, but bank lending has provided as much as 69% of outside sources of finance (in 1974) and as little as 15% (in 1966). Conversely, long-term debt raised on the capital markets has ranged from 0% of external sources of finance for the UK corporate sector (in 1974, allowing for repayments) to 36% in 1966.

So, rather than issue what appeared to them very expensive fixed rate long-term debt, companies preferred to borrow short-term from the banks (in the hope that interest rates would go down) or turned to the eurobond market where innovations and the traditionally shorter term maturities of the bonds meant that there was still demand from investors for corporate debt securities. Since then, the UK corporate bond market has never fully recovered, partly because of the success of the eurobond market, where UK companies can borrow in sterling or in foreign currency, partly because the UK banks have begun to lend longer term, and partly because of the 'crowding out' effect of the UK gilts market. This 'crowding out' effect can be explained by the substantial increase during the 1970s of the amount of government debt issued, which, with its cheaper transaction costs and tax advantages, was designed to appeal to precisely those long-term investing institutions which had been the major purchasers of long-term corporate debt securities. Also, UK governments were careful during the 1970s to introduce innovations in the gilts market, such as convertible and variable rate gilts, to encourage investment during times of uncertainty, whilst the Bank of England discouraged UK companies from equivalent types of innovation.

This negative attitude towards the corporate bond market has been relaxed in the 1980s with, for example, moves by government not to overcrowd the long maturity end of the yield curve. The differences in taxation of government and corporate bonds have also been substantially reduced. For example, liability to capital gains tax on gains made on disposal of corporate bonds held for more than one year was removed by the Finance Act 1984 for investors acquiring corporate bonds after the 1984 Budget. Also, transfer stamp duty on purchase of corporate debt securities was removed in 1976 whereas it has not been payable on gilts since the nineteenth century. Innovations in the corporate bond sector such as deep discount and index-linked bonds have also been encouraged: for example, the same 1984 Finance Act allowed a slight deviation from complete symmetry in taxation for investors and issuers in corporate deep discount bonds, yielding a small tax advantage. Previously, only government deep discount bonds had had any tax advantages.

This chapter now goes on to describe the alternative forms of long-term debt available in the UK market and the factors which a company should take into account when deciding whether to issue any of these types of debt.

7.02 TYPES OF DEBT

1 Debentures

A traditional form of debt raised before the 1970s by companies such as Marks & Spencer, with substantial property in the form of shops, was the 20- or 30- year mortgage debenture, issued in a private placement (not through the stock market) to an insurance company. Debenture stock is a similar form of debt, but in this case the loan is divided up into securities and sold via the stock market to a variety of investors. Debenture stock holders normally have a trustee, acting on their behalf, who will check that the company is adhering to the provisions laid down in the trust deed, for example, that the company pays the interest and principal as and when laid down. The trustees will probably be an insurance company or professional firm who will charge a fee for acting as trustee.

A debenture or debenture loan stock is usually secured on the company's assets, either with a fixed charge on a particular asset such as property (when it is called a mortgage debenture) or with a floating charge or both. Note that, in the UK, the term 'stock' as in 'debenture stock' refers to a debt security, whereas in the US 'stock' refers to equity. Debt securities are often called 'bonds' in both countries. In addition, in the US, debentures refer to general *unsecured* obligations of the company, whereas in the UK there is almost invariably some form of charge. The floating charge, in particular, is a peculiarly British phenomenon.

A floating charge is a charge attached to all the present and future assets of the company without any particular assets being specified. The company is free to deal with the assets in the normal course of business without constantly referring to the debenture holder. However, if the company is wound up or if it defaults on the debenture agreement and the debenture holder steps in, the floating charge crystallises and becomes a normal fixed charge on all the present and future assets of the company as at the date of crystallisation (except that there are other fixed charges in existence and subject to payment of preferential creditors such as the Inland Revenue and employees). It is normal at this stage for the debenture holders to appoint a receiver to act on their behalf, to sell the company's assets as he sees fit, either as a going concern or piecemeal.

2 Unsecured loan stock

As its name suggests, this type of debt has no charge on the company's assets, either fixed or floating, and so ranks below debentures in a winding up of the company. Thus, the interest rate or coupon (the latter term deriving from the days when debt securities were in bearer form with the certificates having detachable coupons used to claim interest payments) on such debt will be higher than on a debenture stock issued by the same company. As with a debenture, it is normal for the loan stock to have a trust deed with a trustee appointed to act on behalf of the loan-stock holders. Typical covenants in the trust deed in this case are likely to refer not to charges on the assets of the company but to the amounts and types of other debt which the company can issue. Loan-stock holders will want to protect their position by limiting the amount of debt which ranks above them or equally with them ('pari passu'). It can do this in several ways, for example, by means of a 'negative pledge' which prohibits the company from issuing more secured debt without giving the loan-stock holders equal rights; or by imposing a maximum limit on a debt to net assets ratio where the debt is defined to be all debt ranking above or pari passu with the loan stock. This latter condition would not prevent the company from issuing debt which ranks below this loan stock, for example, additional 'subordinated' loan stock, although subordinated loan stock is more commonly issued in the US where companies today have the wide range of debt securities not commonly seen in the UK since the 1960s.

The relative default risk of debt securities will affect the coupon at which they can be issued, and their risk can be measured by such ratios as pre-tax interest coverage, cash flow/long-term debt, long-term debt/market capitalisation, and so on. More formally, credit rating agencies can give a rating to each issue, as occurs

Table 7.2   Corporate Bond Rating Categories*

Standard & Poor's Rating Categories†	Description
AAA (Aaa)	Bonds rated AAA have the highest rating assigned by Standard & Poor's to a debt obligation. Capacity to pay interest and repay principal is extremely strong.
AA (Aa)	Bonds rated AA have a very strong capacity to pay interest and repay principal and differ from the highest rated issues only in small degree.
A (A)	Bonds rated A have a strong capacity to pay interest and repay principal, although they are somewhat more susceptible to the adverse effects of changes in circumstances and economic conditions than bonds in higher-rated categories.

*Table 7.2 Cont'd**

Standard & Poor's Rating Categories†	Description
BBB (Baa)	Bonds rated BBB are regarded as having an adequate capacity to pay interest and repay principal. Whereas they normally exhibit adequate protection parameters, adverse economic conditions or changing circumstances are more likely to lead to a weakened capacity to pay interest and repay principal for bonds in this category than for bonds in higher rated categories.
BB (Ba) B (B) CCC (CCa) CC (Ca)	Bonds rated BB, B, CCC and CC are regarded, on balance, as predominantly speculative with respect to capacity to pay interest and repay principal in accordance with the terms of the obligation. BB indicates the lowest degree of speculation and CC the highest degree of speculation. While such bonds will likely have some quality and protective characteristics, these are outweighed by large uncertainties or major risk exposures to adverse conditions.
C	The rating C is reserved for income bonds on which no interest is being paid.
D	Bonds rated D are in default, and payment of interest and/or repayment of principal is in arrears.
Plus(+) or Minus(–):	The ratings from 'AA' to 'B' may be modified by the addition of a plus or minus sign to show relative standing within the major rating categories.

*These Standard & Poor's corporate bond rating categories also apply to municipal bonds.
†The ratings in parentheses refer to the corresponding ratings of Moody's Investors Service, Inc.

Source: Standard & Poor's Corporation.

in the US with the agencies Standard & Poors, Moody's, Duff and Phelps, and Fitch & Co. The exact credit ratings will depend on the agency but, for example, a Standard & Poors rating will vary from AAA to D and a Moody's rating from Aaa to C. Table 7.2 above describes the meaning of each of the ten ratings accorded by Standard & Poors.

Although ratios are used by the rating agencies to accord these rankings, they maintain that the ratios are only guidelines. For example, the *medians* of the pre-tax interest coverage ratios for the AAA, AA, A, and BBB categories were 12.82X, 9.50X, 6.65X, and 4.41X respectively for US corporate bonds rated by Standard & Poors in 1980. Other, less quantitative factors are taken into account before giving a rating, at the company's request and for which the company pays between $5,000 and $20,000 per issue. For example, Moody's places emphasis on the issuer's total debt burden and the cash flow position and Standard & Poors considers the issuer's economic environment to be of importance. This may lead to different relative rankings from these two main rating agencies.

Any debt issue ranked at or above BBB by Standard & Poors and Baa by

Moody's is considered to be 'investment grade'; certain US investing institutions are only allowed to invest in this type of corporate debt. Debt issues (and note that each individual issue is ranked rather than the company issuing the debt) ranked non-investment grade are termed 'junk bonds', a somewhat emotive term. Until recently, issuers informally accorded a junk bond rating for a potential issue by an agency would either improve the quality of the bond (through, say, increased security for the debt) or renounce the issue altogether. Junk bonds were therefore primarily investment grade bonds which had fallen on hard times.

Recent interest in junk bonds has stemmed from the view (based on an analysis of past performance) that the yield premium on junk bonds when compared to investment grade bonds has more than compensated for the increased default risk, as measured by the actual defaults which occurred and the compensation obtained. The required premium on long-term corporate US bonds over long-term US Treasury bonds has been estimated at only 0.17% to compensate for credit risk, a premium much less than the premiums observed in the bond markets. This has led investors, in particular those limited to bonds but yet seeking high yields, to invest in existing junk bonds and in new issues of junk bonds used to finance the leveraged buy-outs which have become popular in the US. There has been no equivalent development in the UK.

The main US rating agencies have begun to turn their attention to the non-US bond markets. For example, Standard & Poors now rates issues, on the request of the issuer, in the eurobond and sterling commercial paper and bond markets. However, as yet, there is not the blanket coverage achieved in the US.

3 Preference shares

The relative position of debt securities in a winding up is obviously important as far as the risk of each type of debt security is concerned. Preference shares, although in many ways similar to fixed interest debt, always rank below all forms of debt in a winding up and, indeed, can never put the company into liquidation or appoint a receiver if the company defaults on its preference dividends. For this reason, preference shares should always yield a higher income than unsecured debt securities. For the issuer, debt interest is deductible from pre-tax income for tax purposes, whereas preference dividends are payable out of after-tax earnings. However, this tax advantage of debt is no longer as significant under an imputation tax system for dividends and in an environment in which the corporate tax rate and the basic rate of personal tax are close. An additional advantage of preference shares relative to debt is that, for financial companies such as UK banks and insurance companies, non-redeemable preference shares may be treated as capital for reserve ratio requirements. Also, corporate investors in preference shares can offset the ACT deducted from their dividend receipts against the ACT which they are required to pay on their own dividend payments.

Some of the perpetual floating rate notes issued by UK banks in the eurobond markets (and these issues have all been in US dollars) have effectively been issues of preferences shares. The status of this debt (for example the National Westminster Bank plc Series C issue of 5 November 1985) has been defined as unsecured, subordinated debt with no negative pledge and equivalent to preference shares in the event of the winding-up of the issuer. The coupon, in the case of the National Westminster issue payable quarterly, does not have to be paid if no share dividend has been declared by the issuer in the previous six months. Any arrears of interest do not accrue interest and can be paid at any time at the option of the issuer.

The attractions to investors, especially foreign banks, of such notes are that they provide a form of investment which is linked to inter-bank rates and is very liquid. However, if they are viewed *not* in comparison with short-term bank deposit rates but in comparison with yields on corporate preference shares and bonds, their return is less attractive.

4 Convertible unsecured loan stock

A form of loan stock commonly issued in recent years is convertible unsecured loan stock: for example, RTZ 9.5% 1995–2000. This security is exactly like an ordinary loan stock except that the holders have the option to convert their stock into a fixed number of ordinary shares of the company at a predetermined rate, in this case into 20 ordinary shares for every £100 nominal of stock. This conversion ratio is protected against new issues of shares, for example, rights issues.

The conversion dates are also pre-set, in the RTZ case, every June between 1984 and 1995. The stock was issued in 1980. It is normal for convertible loan stocks issued in the UK to have a period of several years between the issue date and the first possible conversion date. In this way, the company can be sure that it will pay interest rather than dividends for at least those first years. In the US, equivalent issues are normally convertible immediately. However, by setting the conversion price at a premium over the existing share price, it will not be in the holders' interest to convert in the early years. Conversion will take place when the holders can convert into more valuable securities, either because they will receive more income or because the capital value of the shares has become worth more than that of the loan stock.

The attraction of convertible loan stock from the issuer's point of view is that the company can issue convertible loan stock at a lower interest rate than the equivalent 'straight' loan giving reduced servicing costs in the early years. Investors, on the other hand, value the protection against high interest rates and inflation afforded by the opportunity to convert into equity.

5 Bank debt

As mentioned in the introduction, UK banks have been reluctant in the past to lend long-term. 1986 statistics from the Committee of London & Scottish Clearing Bankers show that 30.0% of their lending is now for maturities greater than three years, with 17.5% of that being for mortgages to the personal sector. The bulk of the remainder is doubtless to the corporate sector, in the form of both foreign currency (for example, export credit loans) and sterling loans. No information is available on exactly how 'long-term' these loans are. The definition of 'long-term' is obviously subjective, but is normally considered to be for over 15 years in the gilt-edged market and seven years in the eurobond market. Recent issues in the sterling eurobond market, for example, have been for eight to twelve years, thus falling into the category of 'long-term'. Bank loans are not, it would appear, a major source of sterling long-term debt for UK companies.

7.03 TYPE OF PAYMENT

The traditional corporate debt security was fixed interest, with semi-annual payments of interest and a final 'balloon' payment of principal on maturity. The maturity date might be one date in the future or a series of dates spread over several years. The issue might also have a sinking fund set up to finance repurchase of the stock at maturity.

More recently, to reduce interest-rate risk, inflation risk, and default risk, the coupon and principal payments have been adjusted to suit investor demand. Most of these innovations have taken place in the eurobond market which has lower issue costs and transaction costs and which is not subject to control by the Bank of England and the UK Stock Exchange.

1 Fixed and floating interest rates

When interest rates rise, the value of fixed interest stock falls. In times of uncertainty about future inflation and interest rates, investors may be unwilling to lend long term in the fear that their actual return in real terms will be below their expected real return. One way round this problem is to issue long-term debt where the coupon is linked to short-term interest rates. In the eurobond market, the coupon is usually linked to three- or six-month London Interbank Offered Rate (LIBOR), bid rate (LIBID), or the mean of the two (LIMEAN). For example, the Standard Chartered Bank £150m issue of floating rate perpetual notes offers a coupon of three-month LIBOR plus 0.1875%.

The corporate issuer will now look at both fixed- and floating-rate debt when making a borrowing decision. His preference will be determined by the relative initial cost, by his view of future interest rates, and by whether the firm wishes to know the cost of the debt in advance or whether it prefers to pay the prevailing rate of interest. The development of the swap market has also meant that the first consideration, relative cost, need not affect the choice between fixed- and floating-rate debt. The issuer can raise debt in the cheapest market and, if he wishes, swap into a preferred form of interest payment. Also, throughout the life of any long-term debt liability, the company can take a view on future interest rates and swap between fixed and floating interest rates and, indeed, between interest rates in a variety of currencies. According to his view of interest rates, the corporate treasurer can therefore take a passive or an active role in the management of the long-term liabilities on his company's balance sheet. As well as choosing between fixed and floating rate on issue, he can switch between the two at any time. He is thus no longer forced to live with the original debt decision.

In addition to cost, a major consideration for the company is the likely cash flow profile of the interest and principal repayments. If the issuer prefers to have fixed debt costs, he will choose fixed-rate debt. In this way, he is protected from rises in interest rates. However, floating-rate bonds may have a 'cap' or 'floor' (or both, known as a 'collar') attached, in which case interest rates will not be raised above a pre-set maximum (a 'cap') or fall below a minimum (a 'floor'), thus reducing the uncertainty associated with floating-rate interest payments. On the other hand, some issuers prefer floating-rate debt; for example, banks can in this way match the interest rate risk of their loan assets with their debt liabilities.

It is worth recognising that the existence of the swap market derives from different perceptions of credit risk in each of the capital markets: for example, poorer credit risks are required to offer higher yields relative to good credit risks on fixed-rate eurobonds than is the case in the floating-rate market. The normal swap, therefore, consists of the more highly rated company issuing fixed-rate debt, the lower-rated company raising floating-rate debt, and both parties then entering into a swap agreement.

2 Deep discount stock

The relative tax advantages of different types of debt security for issuers and investors can also be exploited to minimise the cost of debt. For example, if fixed interest debt is issued with a coupon substantially below prevailing interest rates, it will be priced well below par (the nominal value of £100). The return to investors will therefore be more in the form of capital gain when the debt is redeemed at £100 on maturity and less in the form of income than on a conventional debt security issued at around par. If the tax on capital gains is less onerous than on income, there will be attractions to investors in buying deep discount stock. This can, however, be counterbalanced by a reduction in attractiveness to corporate issuers who, with a low coupon issue, will have less tax-deductible interest.

The success of US dollar corporate 'original issue' deep discount or even zero coupon bonds was due to the fact that US companies were allowed to deduct for tax purposes the difference between the issue price and par value of their bonds on a straight line depreciation basis, whereas Japanese investors, who bought these bonds, were able to treat the price difference as capital gains for tax purposes, not taxable in Japan.

Zero coupon bonds, where the entire return is in the form of one payment on maturity, have added advantages for investors. They reduce interest rate risk, since there are no coupons during the life of the bond which have to be reinvested at prevailing, as yet unknown, interest rates. Investing institutions, with future liabilities fixed in nominal terms, can exactly match their liabilities with zero coupon bond assets.

For the issuer, the cash flow costs of deep discount debt are lower than for conventional high coupon fixed interest debt or floating rate debt. Deep discount debt therefore has a longer effective maturity than traditional fixed interest debt with the same number of years to redemption, thereby increasing the risk of default. The credit risk of corporate zero coupon bond issuers, in particular, must be good, although risk can be reduced by shortening the life of the bond. For example, the first zero coupon bond issue in the eurosterling market was a seven-year bond by Redland in March 1985. Overall, the maturities of sterling zero coupon bonds issued by companies in the eurobond market in 1985 and 1986 have ranged between three and ten years, a somewhat lower range than observed for conventional eurosterling issues.

3 Index-linked debt

One innovation in the UK gilts market which has not as yet been adopted in the corporate bond market is the index-linked bond. With index-linked gilts, all the coupon payments and the principal repayment are linked to the Retail Prices Index, so that the amounts are more or less protected against inflation.

The reason why there is not exact index-linking is because there is a lag of eight months between the monthly RPI figure and the payment to which it is linked.

In the US, some companies have linked coupon payments to commodity prices to which their profits are closely related, for example Petro-Lewis has linked the payments on a bond to the price of oil. In the UK, before it was decided to privatise British Telecom, a proposal to issue British Telecom bonds with payments linked to the sales revenues of British Telecom was seriously considered. The French railway company, SNCF, has a bond whose payments are linked to the price of rail travel.

As with deep discount debt, the cash flows on such debt securities are low in the early years, with the typical coupon on the UK government index-linked securities being 2.5%. Consequently, a high proportion of the repayment is at the end of the life of the bond, in the form of the index-linked repayment of principal. This may be unattractive to companies in that the tax allowable element is small and the major part of the repayment is unknown until redemption.

4 Call and redemption provisions

The original sinking fund was a fund of money, amassed by the company during the life of the debt issue, which was sufficient at the end to repay the entire loan. This reduced the credit risk of the loan as far as the investors were concerned and protected the company from having to refinance the entire amount of the loan at redemption, possibly at a time of high interest rates.

Such corporate debt issues as are made on the UK markets no longer have these sinking fund provisions. The issuers are normally large, as in the case of Barclays Bank issuing a 16% coupon £100m unsecured loan stock in 1982, and have no need to reassure investors that there will be sufficient to repay the principal in n years' time.

However, in the US corporate bond market, the majority of industrial corporate bonds do have sinking funds. These are not actual funds in which cash is amassed, untouched, until redemption; instead, they are provisions whereby each year the company repurchases with current earnings a proportion of the bonds, so that at maturity there may only be a fraction or none at all outstanding. The price at which the bonds are repurchased is a predetermined amount, most often the par value if the bonds have been issued at par.

In addition to the sinking fund repurchases designed to protect *investors* from default risk, US corporate bonds also have call provisions for the issuer to repurchase the entire issue early. These are designed to protect the *issuer* from adverse changes in interest rates.

For example, if interest rates fall during the life of the bond, the issuer would like to refund at a lower rate. Investors, on the other hand, will not wish to sacrifice any capital gain they may have made from the bond trading at above par. Call provisions of this type usually prevent the issuer from calling the bond early for the first five or ten years of the life of the bond and then set the call price at above par, so that investors do not lose all benefit from falling interest rates. In such cases, it is therefore crucial for investors to look at the prospective yield to first call as well as yield to maturity, and take the minimum of the two as the likely return on investment.

At times when investors are reluctant to invest in long-term, fixed-interest bonds, for fear of rising interest rates and falling bond values, the opposite type of provision can be included: namely, that the investors have the right to 'put' or sell the bond back to the issuer at a predetermined price around par. Both types of provision have been used in the US and eurobond markets, but neither innovation has had success in the UK. In the UK, the investing institutions dominate the long-term debt securities market and these insurance companies and pension funds prefer known redemption dates both for gilts and corporate debt.

7.04 ISSUE CONSIDERATIONS

1 Method of issue

UK corporate bonds are issued via either a public offer for sale underwritten at a fixed price or a private placement. This is different from the eurobond issue system in which a group of investment banks will form a syndicate to place the issue with their international clientele. In these cases, preliminary interest in the issue is ascertained *before* the final price and terms of the issue are determined.

The UK corporate bond market is subject to control by the Bank of England. One of the ways in which this market is regulated is by the queueing system. Companies wishing to make a domestic bond issue are required to notify the Bank and are given a date on which the issue can be made, as much as six months in advance. If market conditions are not suitable on that date, the issuer must either cancel the issue or rejoin the queue. The eurobond system, with no queueing system, allows for quicker advantage to be taken of 'bond windows' (types of bonds for which there is current demand and insufficient supply).

2 Costs

The underwriting costs of a UK issue of, say, over 2% are typically higher than in the eurosterling market where competition can lead to finer rates being charged.

3 Interest and tax

No transfer stamp duty is payable on either type of bond trading. When interest payments are made to investors, no withholding tax is payable on eurosterling bonds issued by UK companies since the 1984 Finance Act and on eurosterling bonds issued by UK building societies since April 1986. This contrasts with interest payments on domestic issues which are subject to the witholding of ACT at the basic rate of personal tax (currently 27%), although investors can apply for exemption from this rule.

Interest payments are normally semi-annual with accrued interest on a 365-day basis for domestic UK corporate bonds (as in the gilt-edged market). In the eurosterling market, however, interest is paid annually and accrued interest determined on a 360-day year, 30-day month. Although all prices are quoted clean of accrued interest, UK corporate bonds, again as with gilt-edged securities, are quoted both cum-div and ex-div before the interest payment date.

4 Investor considerations

UK corporate bonds are registered securities whereas eurobonds, including eurosterling issues, are normally in bearer form. UK investing institutions, the pension funds and insurance companies, have adapted only recently to the settlement and holding systems necessary for bearer bonds. Investors in euromarket bearer bonds become members of a clearing system, such as Euroclear or CEDEL, with settlement using a book entry method via these systems. Some eurosterling issues, however, are available in registered form.

Prior to 1979, when UK exchange controls were abolished, UK investors were obliged to purchase investment currency (paying a premium over normal exchange rates) to purchase eurobond issues, even if these were in sterling. This major disadvantage no longer applies.

CHAPTER 8

Project finance

N. Sabin
P. Addison
PK English Trust Company Ltd

8.01 INTRODUCTION

The term 'project finance' has become common banking jargon in recent years, often employed to describe transactions which are in fact quite conventional from a financial point of view; at the same time financing techniques have been developed for some projects which represent a dramatic departure from the normal requirements of banks and other providers of finance and it is these developments which are discussed in this chapter.

The particular characteristic of project financing is the procurement of finance on terms which recognise that some or all of the risks associated with a particular project will be accepted by the providers of the finance and not by the project sponsors. The extent to which project finance may be arranged on this basis varies considerably and depends on particular on the nature of the project.

The principal factors which project sponsors and their financiers take into consideration are described below, but it is important to remember throughout that project financings are very much tailormade to the needs of individual projects; for that reason and because they are sometimes the last resort in financing terms, they have often prompted innovative financing techniques.

Project financing is particularly appropriate for capital intensive projects which may be expected to generate a strong and reasonably assured cash flow and which can therefore support a high level of debt. For instance, many oil companies which are small relative to the sums involved in the development of major discoveries are able to sell or take a 'production payment loan' on an existing field already in production to pay for the further development of a new field, just as property developers can sell or mortgage existing properties to pay for new developments.

Such production payment financings tend to be on a limited recourse basis; that is, if the field fails to produce sufficient revenue, the lender has no recourse to the oil company except in limited circumstances such as failure of the oil company to operate the field competently. In this way the company sheds much of its risk on its old field and yet is still able to retain the long-term benefits of its new discovery.

It is rare, however, for such limited recourse finance, and rarer still for true non-recourse finance, to be offered on a project during the development phase.

8.02 FUNDAMENTALS OF NON-RECOURSE AND LIMITED RECOURSE PROJECT FINANCE

The process of structuring a workable financing package for a project with limited recourse to the project sponsor often involves splitting the total project risk into more manageable pieces. This might involve:

(a) reducing the size of that part of the project which requires immediate financing to an absolute minimum by considering phased investment and the reduction of the scope of the project to the minimum necessary to produce revenue. The extent to which this is possible obviously depends on the nature of the project;

(b) finding structures for the various contracts which allocate acceptable parts of the total risk to contractors, takers of product or to commercial insurers; again, the extent to which contractual parties might be prepared to accept a part of the risk would depend on the project and the level of competition for the contracts concerned; and

(c) exploring the extent to which risk may be covered by risk-sharing between various sources of commercial or other finance (e g regional grants, export or development credits, new equity, etc). It is in this area that the greatest scope for risk-sharing often lies and where the majority of developments in project financing have taken place. It is important to consider the potential sources of finance in detail, and this we do in the sections following.

8.03 EQUITY

In many projects it is attractive and appropriate to undertake the project in a company formed for that purpose: this may have the advantage of isolating the extent of recourse to the original project sponsor in the event that the project should fail and of increasing the amount of external finance available to the project. A joint venture or operating company might be formed to undertake the project and the construction and installation of the plant and to arrange the necessary financing. The company might also arrange marketing of the end product on which the financing would in part be secured.

As many of the interested parties as possible would take shares in the company, in proportions to be determined by reference to their interest in the project, e g buyers of the end product may be prepared to take substantial equity. Some parties might take nominal amounts of equity initially, with provision for a gradual increase in their equity stake when the commercial and technical viability of the project has been established. In some cases a stock exchange quotation might be arranged to provide a further source of equity.

Determination of the amount of equity which is available and necessary for the project to succeed is normally the first phase in establishing a viable financial structure. Lenders will not support the project unless they are satisfied that the available equity is 'adequate': unfortunately, there is no firm rule as to the minimum level of equity which is necessary to induce loan support — obviously this depends on the nature of the project, ie the risks involved and the anticipated level of return on the funds invested.

As a very rough guide a debt : equity ratio of 85 : 15 would be the absolute minimum for a development project and a more common and comfortable figure has been 75 : 25 or 70 : 30. In addition lenders would require additional assurances from some or all of the shareholders: these are discussed below.

8.04 LOAN FINANCE

The extent to which loan finance may be available for a project depends on the risks which lenders are being asked to take. There is a wide variety of loan sources and a corresponding variation in the degree of risk which they are prepared to accept.

The areas of risk in which lenders will require to be satisfied are discussed below; the sources of loan finance fall broadly into the following three categories:

1 Concessionary loans

In the UK, subsidised loan finance, grants and other forms of incentive are available on a regional and selective basis in the assisted areas; the extent of the assistance available is often at the discretion of the government officials involved. In addition the European Investment Bank will provide up to 50% of the gross investment cost of qualifying projects by means of loans repayable in instalments over up to 20 years; grants and loans are also available under the auspices of the European Regional Development Funds and dedicated bodies such as the European Coal and Steel Community.

2 Fixed-rate finance

The attraction of fixed rate funds in a project financing is that they enable an important aspect of future costs to be quantified; depending on the nature of the project, fixed rate funds may be raised by the issue of loan stock, by borrowing in the commercial banking markets and on a concessionary basis as described above.

It may also be possible to obtain fixed cost finance from suppliers of equipment to the project: for example, many foreign suppliers will be able to offer government subsidised fixed interest rate export finance in support of their products. It is particularly important in this context to examine the quotations received in detail: whilst the interest rate quoted may appear attractive, the price quoted by the supplier may include premium and fees paid to export credit agencies and banks in order to procure the low interest rate finance.

An equally important consideration is exchange exposure if the finance offered is in a foreign currency: the extent to which it is possible to cover forward, or hedge the exposure by other means, may be limited, particularly where the drawdown and repayment of the loan is geared to construction and/or revenue schedules. The true cost of a foreign currency loan can only be determined after taking into account the cost of forward cover and related considerations.

3 Commercial funds

It should be possible to secure commercial loan facilities on a floating interest rate basis to cover any portion of the cost of the project which is not financed by equity and loan capital. Whilst lenders in this market are most flexible as to security requirements, the fact that their loans are on a floating interest rate basis can have a very damaging impact on the cash flow of the project. It is therefore normal to minimise utilisation of this form of finance, keeping it in reserve for e g cost overruns and other contingencies.

8.05 LENDER'S REQUIREMENTS

The arrangement of finance for a project on a limited or non-recourse basis is extremely complex, particularly when it involves private and public sector interests. Lenders will try to achieve the basic position that the whole of the project return should be available to them until they are repaid in full, and they will want to be insulated as far as possible from the many separate risks that could affect that return. To achieve a successful financing, the sponsors must go a long way towards satisfying those requirements, many of which also apply to the providers of equity, grants and the other potential sources of finance which have been discussed.

The risks involved can be analysed in several ways. At its most simple, the question is one of cost and return, but it is more convenient to approach the problem from the standpoint of the lenders, identifying the risks on which they will require to be satisfied, which include those discussed below.

1 Completion risk

Lenders will analyse the project to ascertain whether it will be successful in producing an end product which meets design specifications of quality and quantity within estimated cost and time limits. This is one of the aspects of a project which lenders will examine most carefully.

(a) Lenders will look for assurances from the operator on the contractual arrangements under which construction of the various facilities will be undertaken. While such contractual arrangements may take different forms, lenders will typically prefer to see one major contracting firm responsible for each section of the project working under a lump-sum fixed contract with a fixed completion date, penalties for delay and turnkey responsibility for the commissioning of that section. A clear definition of tasks and the division of responsibilities is of particular importance for projects in which several companies, especially from different countries, are involved.

(b) Lenders will expect to receive the following information, prepared or endorsed by independent consultants:

    (i) a feasibility study, evaluating the technology and confirming that the project can be completed to meet technical specifications at estimated cost. Lenders will need to be satisfied from a production history of such plants that the facilities do in fact produce the products in the quantities and in the quality for which they are designed; and

    (ii) an economic projection forecasting the production, sales, operating costs and earnings generated over the life of the project. Lenders will measure both the ability of a project to cover the required payments in each year and the average of the debt service over the repayment period. Lenders will further assess the reserves and the future net revenues remaining when the loan is due to be finally repaid.

(c) Lenders will seek a guarantee from another party that the project facilities will be completed on time. The financial strength of the party giving this completion guarantee will be essential to the success of a project financing.

The terms of the guarantee are likely to include the following:

(a) it will be necessary to define precisely what constitutes 'completion'. The definition will depend on the apportionment of the risk between the lenders and the operator and can range from the physical completion of certain key facilities to the meeting of production targets over a stipulated period, once completion is achieved. In the latter instance the guarantee would cover the continuous operation of the facilities at the designed capacity so as to produce the quantity and quality envisaged;

(b) lenders will need to be satisfied that the party giving the completion guarantee will meet any cost overrun incurred up to the point of completion and that it will have the ability to do so. The guarantor will be obliged to arrange for completion by a certain date and to subscribe equity to meet any overrun costs;

(c) there may be a continuing obligation on the guarantor to meet debt service requirements on the loan prior to defined completion;

(d) if repayment of the project debt is accelerated prior to completion, the obligation to pay under the completion guarantee may also be accelerated;

(e) if the guarantor defaults under another agreement, the obligation under the completion guarantee may be accelerated regardless of progress on the project;

(f) there may be a requirement that the guarantor will not sell its equity interest (if any) in the project; and

(g) operators will naturally seek to obtain back-to-back guarantees from their main suppliers in the form of performance guarantees in order to offset any potential liability to which they may be exposed from project delays to deficiencies in the contractually specified performance of equipment supplied.

2 Operating risk

Lenders will need to be satisfied that the project facilities will operate successfully at all times so that the end product will be produced in the quantities and qualities required. They will accordingly analyse the following factors:

(a) the record of the operator of the project over a number of years in the operation of plants of its kind together with the extraction/processing/ transportation technology to be employed;

(b) the availability of management of proven ability and of a trained workforce;

(c) the quality of the financial plans and projections of management, including its ability to monitor expenditure during the construction period and to control operating expenses thereafter;

(d) the availability of all necessary governmental consents; and

(e) the location of the project, including the infrastructure and transport facilities currently available or planned, and its potential environmental impact. The lenders will relate the costs of the feedstocks and power required by the project to the economic projection. It is preferable that both feedstocks and power should be covered by long-term, fixed-price contracts.

These factors are relevant to the risks associated with the failure of the plant to perform as well as anticipated, and its breakdown or interruption after start-up. An appropriate insurance policy with a loss payable clause in favour of the lenders, can cover on an 'all risks' basis the construction and operation period and may cover loss of profits due to delay resulting from force majeure risks. However, loss of profits as a result of break-down may not be recoverable and such a loss may jeopardise the ability of the project to meet its debt service. It is necessary in these circumstances to establish which party will bear such losses and the ability of such a party to meet them.

3 Marketing risk

A major factor governing the attitude of lenders to a project will be the ability of the operator to sell sufficient volumes of end-product to generate the required revenues to meet debt service. Lenders are very unlikely to accept the risk that an undefined quantity of product will be sold to undefined buyers at some date in the future.

Particular attention will be paid to the agreements which the operating company seeks with potential purchasers of the plant's production from a date realistically related to completion. The contracts into which the operating company enters for the sale of production will have to provide lenders to the project with enforceable claims against the purchasing entities in the event of production being delayed or the purchaser not fulfilling his commitment to buy the product at a specific date and price. The identity of the purchaser and the enforceability of the claims against such a purchaser will be of vital importance in satisfying lenders. Consideration will have to be given to the manner in which the product is allocated between different categories of purchasers and the lenders will need to be satisfied that any new projects, whose implementation is directly linked to the supply of the end product, will be completed in step with the project which they are financing.

Lenders will accordingly expect the operator of the plant to enter into off-take commitments for the sale of the product with a party or parties who can not only reasonaly be expected to meet such commitments but who are also sufficiently strong to meet any judgment for damages that might be awarded against them. The lenders will seek to be protected by the allocation of a substantial proportion of the output of the plant under sales contracts, running well after final repayment of the financing, with acceptable parties at a minimum price.

Such off-take commitments take different forms. A 'take and pay' agreement is one under which the buyer of the output undertakes to purchase the product on its being offered to him. The most attractive form of an off-take commitment for an operator is a 'take or pay' agreement under which the purchaser agrees unconditionally to make payment for the delivery of defined quantities of the product at defined prices irrespective of whether delivery is made or not and regardless of events of force majeure.

In examining off-take commitments lenders will generally look at the following elements in each agreement:

(a) the strength and creditworthiness of the buyer;
(b) the period of the commitment;
(c) the proportion of the designed capacity or stated quantities of the plant covered;
(d) requirements for the quality of the product in the off-take agreement;
(e) force majeure provisions;
(f) the conditions under which the buyer can refuse to accept the product;
(g) the sales price. Lenders will compare this price with that used in the economic projections and the feasibility study, and will also prefer to see provision for price escalation to cover increases in operating costs; and
(h) the currency of payments. If payments are expressed in foreign currency, lenders will assess the impact of fluctuations in exchange rates on the project cash flows.

The assurance provided to lenders by off-take arrangements is considerably strengthened if the purchasers have a real financial commitment to the project in the form of direct loans to, or a significant equity holding in, it.

An operator will find it easier to negotiate more attractive off-take commitments, including provisions for the passing on of cost escalations to purchasers, if the products are likely to be in strong demand over the foreseeable future.

The above considerations apply generally to off-take agreements and the security which they constitute to lenders in limited recourse financing. The manner in which lenders are provided with direct access to the sales contracts and whether they would regard all the project's clients as equally credible remains to be seen. Only a careful analysis of the different off-take agreement will enable the project sponsor to assess whether lenders would be satisfied with an arrangement whereby the debt service of the project was met by the totality of its sales or whether the product sales agreements would need to be divided in such a fashion as to provide varying degrees of access to the contracts to the lenders.

4 Political risk

Political risk can never be wholly excluded. However, lenders will want to be satisfied not only that all necessary consents and authorisations have been granted before disbursements, but also that there is every possible assurance that they will continue to be in force so that the project can be consistently operated according to plan. It may be necessary to obtain undertakings covering such diverse matters as supply of essential services (power, water, etc), tax and duty, and maintenance of all relevant consents. Lenders may try to insist that if the government in any way alters the basic political and regulatory foundations on which the project was originally devised, then it should automatically become a full guarantor of all project debt.

CHAPTER 9

Leasing and factoring

M. D. Evans

T. G. Hutson
Association of British Factors

PART I LEASING

9.01 INTRODUCTION

A leasing transaction is a commercial arrangement whereby an equipment owner (the lessor) conveys the right to use the equipment in return for the payment by the equipment user (the lessee) of a specified rental over a pre-agreed period of time.

Leases can either be operating leases or financial leases. Probably the single factor distinguishing most clearly a 'finance lease' from an 'operating lease' is the lessor's view of his activity. Does he regard himself as lending money in order to make a profit in the form of a return on funds invested or does he regard himself as operating an asset in order to make a profit from its use?

In the UK there are three types of contracts which entitle the 'lessee' to have use of the asset in question. These are as follows:

(a) finance lease;
(b) operating lease; and
(c) hire-purchase or instalment sale.

There is no distinction between a finance lease and an operating lease for either UK tax or company law purposes. In both cases, the lessor will be treated as the owner of the leased asset and entitled to the relevant capital allowances. For UK accounting purposes, however, there is a distinction and this is contained in the Statement of Standard Accounting Practice (SSAP 21). It is necessary under SSAP 21 for lessees to capitalise assets held under finance leases and record in the balance sheet both the asset and the obligation to pay future rentals. In 1982 these types of lease were defined in the International Accounting Standards Committee ('IASC') standard on accounting for leases (IAS 17).

IAS 17 classifies a 'finance lease' as a lease under which: 'the lessor transfers to the lessee substantially all the risks and rewards incidental to ownership of an asset. Title may or may not eventually be transferred'. In such a lease the rentals payable are normally sufficient to enable the lessor to recover the capital cost of the equipment and, additionally, provide a return on funds invested.

An 'operating lease' is defined by IAS 17 as any lease, other than a finance lease. Thus, in an operating lease some of the risks and rewards of ownership are retained by the lessor. The term 'operating lease' encompasses the short-term hire of equipment such as televisions, motor cars, or aircraft, etc over a period which is less than the asset's economic life.

A 'hire-purchase contract' is a contract for the hire of an asset which contains a provision giving the hirer an option to acquire legal title to the asset upon the fulfilment of certain conditions stated in the contract. Such agreements are distinguished from other leasing contracts for both legal and tax purposes. Under UK tax law, a contract of this type will enable the lessee, and not the lessor, to obtain the relevant capital allowances on the capital cost of the equipment. The capital allowances should be available to the lessee in full as long as it shall be, or may become, the owner.

9.02 A TYPICAL LEASE TRANSACTION

When a company wishes to acquire a new piece of equipment it has the choice of purchasing the equipment or arranging to acquire the asset by means of a lease.
   Under the purchase alternative:

(a) the company owns the equipment and finances the purchase either from its own resources or by borrowing; and
(b) the company claims capital allowances and interest costs as tax deductions.

Under the lease alternative:

(a) the company negotiates the lease with a financial institution (the lessor) which buys the equipment nominated by the company; and
(b) the company pays to the lessor lease rentals, which incorporate both interest expense and reductions of principal. The full amount of each rental is an allowable tax deduction. At the maturity of the lease, the lessee would normally act as the lessor's agent for the sale of the equipment, receiving a rebate of rentals or sale commission equal to almost the whole of the sale proceeds. By this route, the lessee participates in the residual value of the equipment.

There are many ways in which lease rentals may be structured. A typical lease would be at a fixed or floating interest rate over a period of five years with rentals payable quarterly in advance. The lease is considered as an amortising loan on an annuity basis being fully paid out by the end of the five-year period, during which time the lessor will have earned its anticipated return.

The lessor seeks to maintain a pre-agreed after-tax rate of return from the transaction. There are usually variation clauses in the lease documentation which enable changes to be made to the rental to take account of various factors such as changes in the lessor's cost of borrowing, monetary controls, tax rates, capital allowances, timing of expenditure and other factors which may affect the lessor's cash flow. Below we consider the calculation of rentals based upon a standard formula given the following assumptions:

Asset cost:	£1,000,000
Length of lease:	5 years
Lessor's cost of funds:	11% per annum
Frequency of rentals:	Quarterly in advance
Effective cost to lessee:	10% per annum

based upon the following formulae:

$$P = \frac{C}{a}$$

$$\text{and } a = \frac{1 - \left[\dfrac{1}{(1 + i)^{n - x}}\right]}{i} + x$$

where:

a = rental factor
n = number of periodic rentals in lease term
i = interest rate per period payable by lessee
x = number of rentals payable in advance
C = cost of equipment
P = payment of rental

Based upon these formulae,

$$a = \frac{1 - \left[\dfrac{1}{(1 + .025)^{20 - 1}}\right] + 1}{.025}$$

$$= 15.97889$$

therefore

$$= P = \frac{C}{a} = \frac{£1,000,000}{15.97889}$$

$$= £62,582.57/\text{quarter}$$

It is true to say that the key element of a lease transaction is the rental. Other factors, however, may be important depending upon the individual circumstances of the lessee. Some will seek a long lease, others a short; some will require fixed rentals, other variable; and some will look for a structured rental profile. It is only by optimising the various components of a lease that one may be able to achieve the most attractive package for the lessee.

9.03 ADVANTAGES OF LEASING

Companies lease (are lessees) for many reasons and only certain of these reasons apply in any specific case. They should all be considered, however, when deciding whether or not leasing is the most appropriate form of finance for a particular project.

1 100% financing

Most lease facilities provide 100% finance for the project under consideration. This is not usually available with other forms of finance.

2 Leasing conserves lines of credit

A leasing facility provides an alternative source of finance to more traditional sources, such as lines of credit.

3 Cash flow — matching of income and expenditure

It is possible to structure a lease to match the debt payments with the cash flow and profits generated from the use of the equipment. Under a standard loan it is likely that the debt and interest payments would be highest in the early years, which would have the effect of dispersing a company's earnings.

4 Amortisation of cost of acquisition

Most costs, such as arrangement fees and legal expenses, incurred in connection with acquisition of equipment can be structured into the lease and amortised over the life of the lease as rent payments. Leases may also be structured to include interest capitalised during the construction or installation period of a project.

5 Leasing may be tax efficient

Lease rentals are generally fully tax deductible for corporation tax, but a lessee will lose capital allowances. Expenditure may be incurred closer to a lessor's tax year-end which reduces the time between a claim for depreciation allowances and the receipt of such payments.

6 Convenience

Leasing may be more convenient and more readily available than other sources of finance. Documentation of a lease is generally simple and flexible.

7 Fixed cost

Most leases with a primary period of up to seven or eight years are fixed rate which means that the rentals are pre-determined and fixed. This could prove valuable in the use of a leased asset for a specific project with a constant rental stream.

8 Tax considerations

A lease is usually the cheapest financing available to a company which cannot immediately utilise the first-year allowance (FYA) and writing down allowance (WDA). The lessor is able to absorb the FYA and WDA and pass on a benefit to the lessee by way of reduced lease rental. Expenditure can be incurred close to a lessor's tax year-end to minimise the period between claiming and obtaining the benefit from tax allowances. For tax-paying lessees, lease rentals are generally fully tax-deductible for corporation tax, although in these circumstances lessees will lose capital allowances.

9 Loan covenants

A lease may provide financing not otherwise permitted under borrowing covenants in existing loan agreements, although following SSAP 21, borrowing covenants may now require leasing to be taken into account.

9.04 THE LEASE v BORROW DECISION

1 The investment and financing decision

In considering the acquisition of a capital asset method of finance, a user will first make an assessment of the return on the investment which such asset may be expected to yield having regard to its marginal contribution. An assessment using the concept of net present value (NPV) enables an evaluation to be made of the viability of acquiring the use of the asset. This method of evaluation effectively takes account of the time value of money in equating the receipt of sums of money in the future to its receipt today, by discounting those sums at the after-tax cost of borrowing. In the case of a non-tax paying lessee, pre-tax cost equals after-tax cost.

Under a finance lease with a secondary period rental at a nominal rate, one is effectively acquiring the use of an asset for the whole of its useful economic life by means of a deferred payment. Given the company's marginal cost of borrowing, it is possible to establish the NPV of leasing rather than buying.

Based upon the following assumptions, we consider the NPV approach in respect of:

(a)   a non-tax-paying lessee; and
(b)   a tax-paying lessee.

Table 9.1   (a) Non-tax-paying lessee

Date	Rental £	Discount factor (10% pa)	Present value 31.12.86
31.12.87	300	0.909	272.73
31.12.88	300	0.826	247.93
31.12.89	300	0.751	225.39
31.12.90	300	0.683	204.90
Sum of present value of rentals			950:96
Present value cost of asset at 31.12.86			1000.00
NPV benefit from leasing instead of borrowing			49.04

Since the asset cost of £1,000 is greater than the present value of the rentals at the assumed borrowing cost of 10% per annum, leasing is shown to be more attractive than borrowing. An alternative way to consider this is to say that if the lessee placed £950.96 on deposit at 10% pa over four years, it would be able to fund the payment of the rentals due under the lease.

(b) A tax-paying lessee

Because of the delay between the payment of interest and the cash benefit of tax relief thereon, the derivation of a net of tax discount rate from a pre-tax rate is not simply a matter of deducting the standard rate of tax from the latter. Instead the following formula has to be used which is itself an approximation satisfactory for small values of n:

$$I2 = I1 - \frac{I1 \times T}{[1 + (I1 \times T)]^n}$$

where:

I1 = the lessee's pre-tax borrowing rate from which the net rate is to be derived

I2 = the net rate

T = the rate of corporation tax (0% in the case of a non-tax payer)

n = the delay in tax payment in years

Thus in a case where the average tax delay is nine months from the mid point of the year:

$$I2 = 0.10 - \frac{0.10 \times 0.35}{[1 + (0.10 \times 0.35)]^{0.75}}$$

$$= 0.10 - \frac{0.035}{1.0261}$$

$$= \underline{6.59\% \text{ per annum}}$$

Table 9.2 below shows the calculation of the NPV to the tax-paying lessee using this discount rate.

Table 9.2

Date	Cost/ (rental) (£)	Tax (35%) (£)	Total (£)	Discount factor (6.59%)	Present value (31.12.86) (£)
31.12.86	1,000	—	1,000	1,000	1,000
31.12.87	(300)	(350)	(650)	0.938	(610)
31.12.88	(300)	105	(195)	0.880	(172)
31.12.89	(300)	105	(195)	0.826	(161)
31.12.90	(300)	105	(195)	0.775	(151)
31.12.91	—	105	105	0.727	76
					(18)

The NPV is negative which means that leasing on the terms offered costs more than purchase using a source of funds costing 10% per annum. In this case the lessee would have had to borrow £1,018 at 10% per annum to discharge the rentals taking into account the related tax effects. Clearly he would be better off borrowing £1,000 to buy the asset.

It is possible to assess the present value benefit under a number of different scenarios depending on the tax position of the lessee. These need to be considered on a case basis to ascertain the net benefit from leasing if the lessee's tax position changes a number of times.

9.05 IMPORTANT ASPECTS OF DOCUMENTATION

There is a clear legal distinction between a lease contract and a hire-purchase or instalment sale contract. The permanent separation of ownership and use is central to the whole concept of equipment leasing and this does distinguish it from other payment-by-instalment types of transaction, where ownership and use are not separated. The lessor in a finance lease has the legal role of purchaser, owner and eventual seller of the leased asset but, with the exception of making payment for the asset, the practical consequences of this role are delegated to the lessee. The lessee will normally negotiate the specification, price and delivery terms of the asset (usually as agent of the lessor) and will be responsible for maintaining and insuring it during the lease period. The lessee will indemnify the lessor against any expenses or claims arising from ownership or use of the leased asset and, on termination of the lease, will normally find a buyer and negotiate the sale of the asset as agent of the lessor. In the case of an instalment sale or hire-purchase contract, on the other hand; legal ownership will pass to the lessee, either immediately or on the completion of the contract. Lease and purchase contracts are governed by the Consumer Credit Act in the UK. This Act is used as a means of controlling consumer credit generally.

The hiring of a chattel for use is a form of bailment and is, therefore, subject to the rules of common law. There has been virtually no commercial case law in the UK concerned with equipment leasing, and provisions which regularly appear in leasing agreements largely remain uninterpreted in the English courts. The distinction between hire-purchase and finance leasing has been examined by the courts and if it is found that ownership by the lessor is false, the arrangement may be considered, in law, as being a hire-purchase or a conditional sale.

The UK leasing market is becoming increasingly competitive. The level of competition has been increasing steadily since the 1984 Finance Act, since with buoyant earnings but a lower level of capital allowance, lessors have had to complete more leasing transactions of a given value to defer the same amount of tax. This may be illustrated as follows using the rates of capital allowance and corporation tax rates introduced by the 1984 Finance Act.

Table 9.3

	Capital allowance	Corporation tax rate	Volume of new leases to shelter £1m of taxable income
1983/84	100% FYA	50%	£1m
1984/85	75% FYA	45%	£1.33m
1985/86	50% FYA	40%	£2m
1986/87	25% WDA	35%	£4m

These exists a finite demand to finance assets by way of leasing but an increasing appetite for assets. In such a competitive market, it is essential for lessees to obtain quotes from a wide range of lessors. A lessee's name, however, should not be too widely spread around the market as lessors put more time and effort into tenders for transactions if they believe that they have a good chance of being successful, assuming the credit is acceptable.

The lessor would either appoint the lessee as its agent to acquire the equipment or would acquire the equipment itself from the manufacturer at the direction of the lessee. In return for payment of the rental, the lessee enjoys economic ownership and quiet enjoyment of the equipment and derives income itself from the use of the equipment. On a finance lease, the lessor is essentially a source of finance, earning a financial return on its investment. The responsibilities in respect of insurance, maintenance and operating costs, etc are met by the lessee. It is therefore only reasonable that supplier benefits such as discount, warranties and service agreements are passed through the lease agreement to the lessee.

It is usual for the lease of an asset to contain what is known as a 'tax variation' or tax indemnity clause. This will provide for the lease rentals to be adjusted in the event of legislative changes affecting, inter alia, the availability or rate of capital allowances, the rate and method of charging corporation tax and the system of group relief. The clause will generally provide for the rentals to be adjusted to a level sufficient to maintain the lessor's originally anticipated after-tax rate of return from the transaction. Similarly, there would usually be a tax indemnity from the lessee to cover any adverse tax consequences arising from the arrangement whereby the lessee disposes of the leased asset and retains the majority of the proceeds, either by way of a rebate of rentals or as a selling commision.

Whatever convenants, indemnities, etc are written into the lease, the degree to which a lessee complies with this or not will depend on its position and to some extent upon the degree of flexibility inherent in the default provisions. The default provisions provide an opportunity to protect the lessor's position so that it may be possible to end the relationship before the lessee goes into liquidation. Default provisions should, however, not be too onerous and should be such as to enable the lessee to carry on the normal course of its business without undue interference.

The leasing industry in the UK is fairly unregulated at the present time. The Equipment Leasing Association, which has been established by major UK lessors, has a code of conduct and certain ethical guidelines. Apart from this, there are no special permissions required for entering into these contracts, no general governmental reporting requirements or supervision of lease contracts, and no form of registration is required.

9.06 SOURCES OF LEASING

1 Clearing banks

In the UK the clearing banks have established their own leasing companies to provide lease finance to their clients as well as to reduce their own level of taxation. Because such leasing companies have a very large tax base, they are often able to offer leases at particularly favourable rates.

2 Merchant banks

Such organisations are sometimes able to provide a source of leasing in the same way as the clearing bank subsidiaries. Usually, however, their role would be that of a financial intermediary, structuring an overall financing as an arranger. This distinguishes them from the clearing banks' subsidiaries, which are usually just sources of tax shelter.

3 Lease packagers

Particularly since the 1984 Finance Act, there has been an increasing need for the specialist packager capable of structuring complex financings. This would be for equipment such as aircraft, property, etc. often using tax benefits in various countries to enhance the attractiveness of the overall transaction. In this category would be such companies as AML Babcock and Brown and Sheldon and Partners, who have built up their reputation on large aircraft financings.

4 Brokers

On small transactions lease brokers often have a role to play. They act as a go-between, bringing together the lessee and the lessor. Their brokerage can be justified by their knowledge of available lease rates and their ability to play one lessor off against another. A broker should be able to obtain lease quotes, advise on the credit of the lessee and advise on taxation, accounting and legal issues.

9.07 A CHANGING MARKET

The UK has seen a fundamental restructuring of its system of corporate taxation due to the changes introduced by the 1984 Finance Act (FA 1984). A gradual withdrawal of first-year capital allowances (FYAs), combined with simultaneous reductions in the rate of corporation tax, made leasing particularly attractive until March 1986. After March 1986 first-year allowances were replaced by writing down allowances which will have the effect of reducing substantially the benefits available from leasing.

The leasing market in the UK is very diverse: transactions range from small-ticket leasing of typewriters, etc, to big-ticket leasing involving large-scale plant such as aircraft, ships and oil-related projects. The driving force for each type of lease varies but with such variety the growth and attractiveness of leasing cannot be explained in terms of tax benefits alone.

The small-ticket, sales-aid sector has grown significantly, and yet this growth has been largely independent of tax benefits: lessees have been driven by fixed rate finance, known cash flow, service and convenience. Tax-based leasing has been most important in medium to big-ticket finance, where cost reductions are most important.

At the time of writing, the tax allowances available to a lessor have been reduced significantly. The effect of these reduced allowances may be as follows:

(a) leasing rates to lessees will increase and lessor returns will decline. It is likely that operating leases will become more attractive, with lessors taking a residual risk in the equipment;

(b) small-ticket leasing will continue to grow since tax benefits are not the main driving force;

(c) medium-ticket leasing will be seriously affected and this market may become more orientated to hire-purchase; and

(d) the big-ticket market does not rely solely on tax benefits and the participants in the market will rely increasingly on innovation to develop new, attractive financings. There may be a tendency to longer-term leases, for which writing down allowances still give an advantage.

Overall, leasing is likely to decline initially but subsequent recovery and re-alignment of the market is likely to occur with the non-fiscal benefits of leasing being emphasised.

9.08 FUTURE OPPORTUNITIES FOR LEASING

Even though reducing allowances and the lower rate of corporation tax will affect the UK market, leasing has not changed fundamentally. Transactions will be more difficult to structure but there are still opportunities to make leasing attractive.

One of the biggest advantages of leasing is 100% financing at fixed rates, a facility rarely available in traditional loan markets. The costs are locked in, with the exception, in the current market, of a variation in rental due to changes in the rate of corporation tax. Due to the low levels of corporation tax and capital allowances, the discount from debt which is capable of being passed through to the lessee is low and if there were to be an adverse tax change it would be wiped out completely.

Returns to lessors are currently down to as low a margin as 1.0% pre-tax over a ten-year period. It is not realistic to expect the level of acceptable return to fall much lower and hence it is appropriate to try to reduce a lessor's cost of funds much more by conventional means.

Methods of doing this are now considered:

1 Double dip leases

Such leases take advantage of asymmetry between the tax regimes in different countries. In certain countries, a lessor entering into a conditional sale (hire-purchase) agreement may be able to claim depreciation deductions even when the asset is used outside its own jurisdiction. Under such a structure the offshore lessee is considered to be the economic and legal owner in its own jurisdiction thus enabling that party to claim depreciation in its own country. If a UK lessor were to be the 'lessee' in such a structure it could reduce its own cost of funds so that it in turn may pass benefits on to the UK lessee, given that it has been able to achieve a lower cost of debt itself (see Fig 9.1 below).

Fig 9.1 Cross border lease

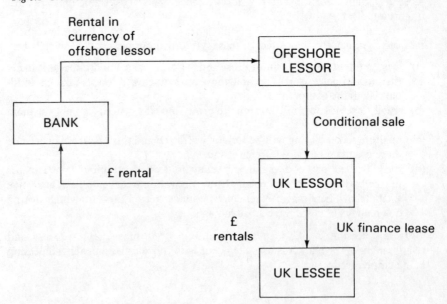

2 Swaps

As the capital allowances that are available on equipment purchases reduce, a lessor's period of investment in a lease increases; hence the average life of its investment also increases since it is obtaining lower deductions. This means that fixed-rate funding is more difficult to achieve and most lessors would prefer to fund on a floating-rate basis. When first-year allowances were at the 100% level, a lessor's investment reduced quite rapidly and a lessor might take a view on rates without actually locking in its funding cost. This would maximise its profits if rates moved in its favour and there was only a relatively small downside. Now, however, the funding period is much longer and the lessor is far more exposed than previously.

Most lessors prefer a floating-rate lease but to lock in the costs of a transaction, lessees may well prefer a fixed-rate lease. It is difficult to fulfil each party's objectives, although this may be achieved by entering into an intermediate swap with a financial institution. This is now relatively common on leasing transactions and provides attractions to all parties in the chain: the lessor receives floating-rate income; the lessee pays fixed rate; the bank arranging the swap receives an attractive fee.

(a) Head lease (£ — floating): sub-lease (£ — fixed)

When a lessor provides a fixed-rate facility the required return over cost of funds is usually in excess of that required for a floating-rate lease and does not provide such an attractive facility to the lessee. By incorporating a bank in the lease chain, however, it is possible to arrange that the lessor leases into a bank on a floating-rate basis. This is facilitated by means of a swap and often enables a lessee to achieve a much more attractive financing than would have been the case if the lessor had provided a fixed-rate lease.

The downside of this is that there would be a cost to breaking a fixed-rate lease since funds would have been locked in for the full period of the lease. Thus, in the event of a termination, an amount would be included in the termination sum to compensate the intermediary bank for taking the risk position. The exact amount would be calculated at the date of termination.

(b) Head lease (£ — floating): sub-lease (either $ — fixed or $ — floating)

The structure for the facility again involves the bank standing between the lessor and the lessee and enabling the lessee to have either a fixed- or floating-rate dollar obligation. Although the dollar is used here as an example, it should be possible to arrange a lease in certain other main currencies with the lessor leasing in floating-rate sterling to the bank.

3 Residual guarantees

There may be significant cash flow benefits from incorporating a residual value into the transaction. The advantage of this is that an asset is then amortised from its initial cost of 100% to an assumed residual of say, 30%, rather than to zero, as in a full-payout lease. This means that a lessee has to pay a lower rental with the lessor amortising a lesser amount, as may be seen in Figs 9.2 and 9.3 below.

Fig 9.2 Full payout lease

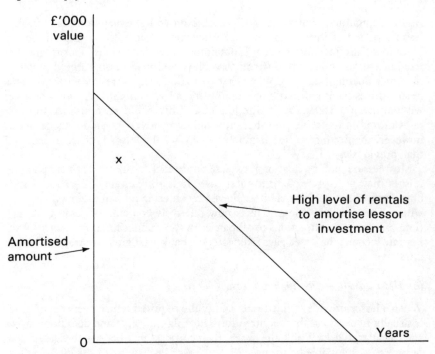

Fig 9.3 Residual value assumed

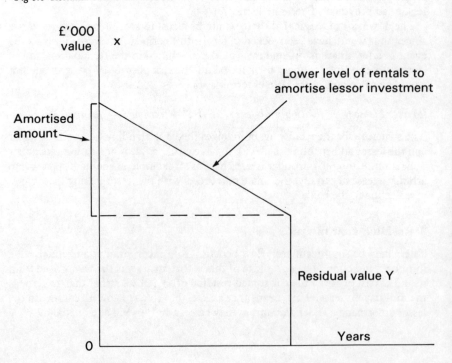

The benefit of building in a residual value is that it may be easier to match income to outgoings if the latter are at this lower level.

To give an indication of the level of benefit when a residual is built in, if a lease without a residual has an IRR of 8.25%, one with a residual of 30% would have an IRR of 4.4% (ignoring the last residual value). What has actually happened is that the lessee has incurred an opportunity cost. The lessee is giving away its interest in the residual to the lessor which effectively removes its economic interest in the asset.

The parties who may be prepared to take a risk in the asset value include:

(a) the vendor;
(b) the lessee;
(c) a specialist guarantor; and
(d) a tradeable asset guarantor.

It is really the responsibility of packagers of leasing transactions to find new opportunities, to test these products and to determine their commercial viability. It is only through this process that an idea may be turned into the reality of a new financial tool.

PART II FACTORING

9.09 INTRODUCTION

The use of factoring to finance extra working capital from debtor assets has become widely recognised by companies of all sizes as a way of meeting cash flow needs brought about by successful sales growth.

Britain's nine leading factoring companies, which make up The Association of British Factors and which account for around 90% of UK factoring business, in 1986 handled over £5.76 of business from around 5,000 clients.

The difficult trading conditions of recent years have undoubtedly accelerated the use of factoring because they have helped to focus attention on the need for businesses of all sizes to manage their working capital more effectively. Factoring is very much a part of this management process, concerned with an asset — trade debtors — that all businesses have and yet many often overlook as a source of finance.

An average collection period of 70 days, quite common in industry and commerce today, means that a business will have approximately one-fifth of its turnover outstanding in trade debts at anytime: for example £50,000 on a £250,000 turnover and £100,000 on £½m.

These are large sums for the businesses concerned, and with customers taking so long to pay while suppliers press for prompt payment, otherwise healthy and growing companies become squeezed into cash difficulties with little hope of escape without the kind of professional help that factoring can provide.

One of the main purposes of factoring is the release for use in the client's business of funds tied up in financing trade credit. These funds can be used in a variety of ways, including the support of extra stocks and work in progress, to obtain cash and quantity discounts from suppliers, to enable costly discounts to customers for prompt payment to be eliminated, or to support higher levels of profitable trading.

9.10 ELEMENTS OF FACTORING

The three closely integrated elements of factoring are: sales accounting and collection; a credit control service, including in the case of non-recourse factoring 100% protection against bad debts on all approved sales; and the availability of finance against sales.

1 Accounting and collection

Clients are paid by the factor either as individual invoices are settled by customers ('pay as paid') or after an agreed average settlement period ('maturity'). The latter, perhaps, offers some advantage in that it facilitates very precise cash flow control and forecasting. Clients may also obtain advances of funds based on the invoices factored, although an interest charge is made for this facility.

2 Credit control

The method of controlling the credit risk through factoring is very different from credit insurance and provides a greater measure of cover. Factors offering a non-recourse service provide 100% cover on all sales that they have approved. In addition they often operate discretionary arrangements within which clients sell to the majority of their customers without having continually to seek credit approval.

Factors provide this credit protection by applying their expertise to actual customer payment performance and to the active ledgers maintained on behalf of clients. This vast, growing and accurate information base enables them to assess the changing position with regard to payment performance on individual customers of each client, as well as the aggregate trading position of any customer with all clients serviced by the particular factoring company.

Their credit and collection expertise enables the factor to improve generally the speed with which customer payments are received by up to 10% or more, and is usually able to make payments on account of up to 80% of the value of sales at the time of invoicing, providing an ideal way of financing growth, with the amount of money made available being always linked to sales expansion.

3 Finance for sales growth

Companies contemplating factoring should bear in mind that actual size is less important than growth potential. Most factors,including ABF members, will be happy to consider any company with turnover of between, say, £100,000 and many millions of pounds. In its negotiations with prospective clients, the factor will be looking for sound management committed to growth, profitable trading and evidence that any need for extra working capital is created by sales growth; in other words, to finance additional stocks, raw materials, work in progress and credit to customers, and not just to bale the company out of financial difficulties.

9.11 INVOICE DISCOUNTING

Invoice discounting is a variation on full factoring used by many large companies with strong accounts administration and low bad debt risk seeking off balance sheet finance.

This service is normally undertaken for clients on a confidential basis and provides cash through the sale to the factor of either all sales invoices or those on selected accounts. The service is normally recourse, ie without credit cover, although non-recourse invoice discounting can be arranged in certain circumstances. Naturally, to preserve the confidential nature of the service, clients must remain responsible for their own accounts collection and credit administration.

9.12 EXPORT SERVICES

The description export *services* is used advisedly here because, whilst the basic sales accounting, collection and credit management elements of factoring apply as for domestic sales, the services provided by those factors with export expertise extend well beyond these parameters.

Using their own or associated factoring companies, staffed by nationals in overseas markets, these factors have put together packages of services which fulfil from one source many of the needs of companies selling to customers thousands of miles away. Many of these services the exporter would otherwise need to coordinate from a variety of outside sources.

Factors can help exporters to overcome difficulties when trading abroad on open account caused by differences in language, currency, trading terms and other aspects, to the extent that selling in export markets can become as straightforward, secure and profitable as selling at home.

By providing credit protection on export sales on open account and protection against fluctuations in foreign exchange rates, factors make it easier for their exporting clients to compete on equal terms with local competition. Taking advantage of the local knowledge and expertise of his overseas offices, the factor will research customers' financial standing and present statements and any necessary reminder letters in the form, language and currency of the country concerned. If there is a dispute with a customer on payment, the factor has his associates in the market concerned who know the local legal situation and trading terms and conditions.

By using a factor with an overseas operation, therefore, the exporter is established on equal terms with local suppliers, not only in the way he markets his products, but also in the way he manages the credit offered to his customers.

9.13 CHARGES AND BENEFITS

Factoring is paid for in two ways. A fee is charged for the service elements, expressed as a percentage of the client's sales turnover and usually falling between 0.5% and 2.5%.

The charge for finance, as and when it is taken, is geared to current base rates and will be very close to the cost of bank overdraft finance.

Most users of factoring find that the charges for the service and finance are more than outweighed by the value of the benefits derived in terms of savings in accountancy and collection administration, elimination of bad debts where non-recourse factoring is obtained, greater availability of funds for use in the business, and the freeing of management time for more constructive purposes.

International finance

CHAPTER 10

Sources of international finance

Alasdair J. W. Watson

10.01 INTRODUCTION

Sources of UK short- and long-term debt are covered in Part B above, as indeed are the specialised forms of finance, such as project finance and leasing. There is a distinct overlap between national and international finance, since residents of one country may, subject to permissive exchange control, freely gain access to available forms of finance in various foreign countries in local financial markets. Accordingly, UK companies may tap the US, Canadian, Japanese and many West European domestic markets for funding, in the same way as non-resident companies of the UK may benefit from using the UK domestic markets.

A publication of this size will not be able to include a fully comprehensive description of all the overseas domestic markets and therefore only some of the more important ones have been included. The truly international markets are also to be found in other parts of the world, such as Singapore, where the market is referred to as the Asia Dollar Market. This chapter also tends to concentrate on the cash markets as opposed to futures markets, which are covered in ch 12 below.

It has been said recently by many banks that a straightforward international loan is indeed a rarity. Complex financial and balance sheet engineering arrangements are now being packaged by bankers in order to meet the specific and specialised needs of the corporate treasurer. Driven by a fiercely competitive environment, there has been a new products explosion, bringing with it a regular flow of innovative schemes and an endless variety of themes on known ideas. Buzz words abound, and the technical terminology often used in connection with these new financial arrangements, much of it being invented overseas, particularly in North America, tends to be unnecessarily confusing to the layman. One of the objectives of this chapter is to describe some of the principal schemes in simple language.

10.02 INTER-GROUP RESOURCES

Companies with multi-national operations generally have subsidiary and affiliate companies located overseas or, if not, other forms of representation such as branches of the parent or even trade investments. Cohesive treasury management for such an organisation is essential in order to achieve maximum benefits from internal resources. So far as finance is concerned, the first consideration for the effective cash management of a multi-national group must be to achieve minimal float time for inward funds in transmission, and to maximise 'value dating' on payments abroad. The various group bank accounts should be carefully controlled to take advantage of pooling of resources, automatic set-off arrangements between accounts maintained with the same banking group, and to make arrangements to target for zero balancing or minimum target balances to be maintained in the banking system. All this, of course, requires up-to-date balance reporting information and carefully negotiated arrangements with the group's bankers. Within the treasury mix the co-ordinated groups funds management may control interest rate exposure of both finance and investments, eg assets and liabilities, and, therefore, should any exposures require hedging either at company or group level, the overall position can be closely monitored and controlled so that options, swap agreements, FRAs or futures contracts can be entered into for this purpose to provide the most effective cover in the context of the group as a whole, and probably on the finest terms. Major funding decisions can be taken by group treasury for both strategic/structural reasons and for operational requirements.

Other forms of inter-group co-operation include inventory items such as trade credit between associated companies which is mentioned again in the next chapter. A variety of piggy-back and other co-operative agreements can sometimes be entered into with non-associated companies whose products are complementary rather than competing.

Some companies which have natural liquidity may prefer to place some of these funds with other companies, perhaps for a better yield, rather than leave them in bank deposits or place them in other forms of investment. There are occasions where general purpose facilities including overdrafts, can be, and have been, used by major corporates to provide facilities for other companies on terms which are competitive with those offered by the banks. This is sometimes referred to as the inter-company market and a natural development of this market is the commercial paper market.

10.03 BANKERS ACCEPTANCES

Bankers acceptances are widely used in trade financing which is described in some detail in the next chapter. Various local markets exist for bankers acceptances, probably the most important being the UK, US and leading West European countries such as Germany, France and Italy. It is possible for non-residents of the UK to source the US bankers acceptance market when rates are propitious. There are two important points to consider in this connection, the first is price and the second flexibility of procedure to enable funding to be arranged without delay before the price changes. On the subject of price, the bankers acceptance market in some countries, notably the US, is tiered with some banks being able to re-discount paper with their name as acceptors at better rates than others. In the UK there is a distinction between eligible and ineligible paper which is described in the next chapter, and this too involves a price differential. Companies which wish to have access to an overseas bankers acceptance market should normally be prepared to issue financial paper (usually bills of exchange) to be held in safe custody by the banker in the local centre abroad which is managing the facility. UK corporates can tap the US bankers acceptance market for same day funding provided suitable authenticated instructions are received by the bank in America before close of their business.

In certain countries single name paper can be financed on the bankers acceptance market. This includes bills of exchange drawn by a bank in, say, the UK, on its branch, say, in the US. It also includes promissory notes which may be financed in the West German bill market. In the UK term bills of exchange drawn in foreign currency may be re-financed by access to the US bankers acceptance market. Alternatively, they may be discounted locally on terms equating to the euro currency rates for the applicable financing period.

10.04 EURO CURRENCY LOANS

Loans provided by banks in currencies other than the indigenous currency of the borrower may be described as euro currency finance. Euro currency finance is an established practice, which has its origins in the 1950s, and the volume of transactions continued to grow at a dramatic rate through the 1960s and 1970s. Substantial sums were made available to corporate, sovereign and supranational borrowers in the form of euro credits. Coincident with this development was the growth of the inter-bank market in deposits and placings, and it is estimated that inter-bank deals now account for some 90% of total euro currency transactions.

With the world debt crisis of the 1980s the growth of new loans to sovereign borrowers slowed dramatically and, at the same time, the development of securitisation fanned by investment and merchant banking houses operating internationally, provided alternative and price competitive sources of finance for the corporate treasurer. High interest rates will discourage the corporate treasurer from seeking long- or medium-term fixed interest funding, as indeed does falling rates of interest. In most currencies during the early part of the 1980s, interest rates have either been at historically high levels or tended to fall, thereby creating a further disincentive to the corporate treasurer from acquiring medium- or long-term funds at fixed rates of interest.

Floating rate facilities are relatively common and these have been used significantly when interest rates are high or falling. When a rising interest rate trend is perceived, the demand for longer-term fixed-rate monies in a variety of currencies tends to build up. Euro currency finance tends to be provided for fixed periods of time. For longer-term requirements, however, where fixed interest funds are either not available in the market, or too expensive for the corporate borrower, lending banks will provide their commitment to lend for, say, five years on a rollover basis where the rates are adjusted at agreed intervals, monthly, quarterly, or perhaps semi-annually, in line with the then current market rates.

The interest rate will normally be determined two business days prior to the draw-down for the initial period, say, six months. Thereafter at each six-monthly interval the interest determination date for the next interest period will once again be two business days prior to the new interest period. The lending bank will advise the borrower of the interest applicable to the next period.

Euro currency loans vary considerably in their structure and features such as splintered draw-down and staged repayments can sometimes be accommodated to meet the corporate treasurer's needs. Additionally arrangements may be made for the corporate treasurer to have option over the rollover period. This means that if interest rates have fallen to an acceptably low level by the time the next interest period arrives, the treasurer may opt for, say, six months or one year for the proximate rollover period. On the other hand, should interest rates look as though they are going to fall still further, then the treasurer would be likely to choose a one-month or shorter-term rollover period so as not to lock in a relatively high rate.

When the corporate requirement for euro currency finance is substantial, a syndicate of banks may be required to participate in the financing. The interest rate for a syndicated euro currency loan will be determined by an agreed formula, which would probably involve several reference banks quoting their price for lending the currency at a given time, usually 11.00 am on the morning of the interest determination day. As the market has developed, the pricing of euro currency loans has become more competitive and the lending banks' margins have been substantially reduced. The formulae used to determine euro credit interest rates have also become more sophisticated. Whilst most loans are priced on the basis of LIBOR +, this is by no means always the case and prices based on the arithmetic mean of LIBID and LIBOR are sometimes seen, and very occasionally prices have been based on LIBID, although it is true to say that such a pricing concept is not popular with the majority of banks.

Another feature of euro currency finance is the multi-currency credit facility. This enables the corporate treasurer to draw down in any currency of his choice, although invariably the loan agreement will contain a covenant saying that the option will be limited to the availability of the funds in the market at the material time.

As euro currency loans are provided by banks, the nature of the finance available must depend on the ability of the bank to obtain the funds for the periods and in amounts required by the corporate borrower. Traditionally, the euro currency deposits which a bank takes in the market-place are short term, eg for major currencies up to one year, and in the case of US dollars, sterling and Deutschemarks perhaps up to five years, depending on amount. The degree to which a bank will mismatch its book, eg borrow short and lend longer, will be strictly controlled by commercial prudence of the management of the bank, as well as by the banking supervisory authorities. It follows, therefore, that the degree to which banks may provide longer-term funds when they are only able to attract shorter-term funds in a particular currency, is strictly limited. The vast majority of euro currency finance, therefore, is provided by banks on a matched basis. If a currency is freely convertible and there exists a forward exchange market in that currency, finance may be available through the US dollar for funds created out of swaps. This is of particular importance with the minor currencies where there exists no ready market in deposits.

Although London is undeniably the principal source of euro currency finance, important markets exist in other financial centres around the world. The extent of the development of other centres has been limited on occasions by the imposition of reserve costs on euro currency business by the monetary authorities of the centres concerned. In other centres exchange control regulations may make it equally uneconomic for borrowers to raise funds in a local euro currency market and in a number of countries exchange control regulations are prohibitive in this connection. Important euro currency centres exist in Frankfurt, Brussels, Paris, Nassau, New York, Singapore, Hong Kong and Tokyo. In the Far East the market is often referred to as the Asian dollar market. Facilities provided from other centres will normally be on the basis of the local lending rate for dollars or other euro currencies, such as HIBOR, the Hong Kong inter-bank offered rate. Whilst the rates in the markets are relatively close, particularly with the excellent communication system existing between the banks within the market, nevertheless because of time differences around the world, and the continual movements in rates, a HIBOR closing rate of one day would probably be quite different from a LIBOR closing rate on the same day.

10.05 CERTIFICATES OF DEPOSIT AND BEARER DEPOSIT NOTES

Certificates of Deposit (CDs) and Bearer Deposit Notes (BDNs) constitute 'deposits' with the bank issuing the instrument. There exists for prime bank CDs and BDNs an active secondary market made by bankers and brokers in London which helps to maintain a high degree of liquidity for such investments. CDs and BDNs are, therefore, primarily a source of funds to financial institutions rather than otherwise. They are, of course, frequently held by companies with liquidity resources and have the advantage of being readily sold for cash in the secondary market as opposed to tying up funds on fixed-term deposit accounts with a bank. CDs are now issued in sterling, US dollars, Canadian dollars, Australian dollars, Deutschemarks, French francs, Japanese yen, ECUs and SDRs, inter alia.

CDs are issued on a tap or on a tranche (managed) basis for maturities of up to five years and may be priced on a fixed interest or floating rate interest formula broadly in line with euro currency inter-bank yields. The corporate treasurer may benefit from the greater degree of liquidity of the instrument compared with a euro currency bank deposit, since the latter may normally be broken on payment of a penalty whereas the CD may be sold in the secondary market at current yields. Furthermore, the treasurer will also benefit from the sale of a CD if interest rates have fallen during the time he has held the paper if the yield on the remaining period to maturity at the time of sale is greater than when the instrument was purchased. He will receive interest for the period the CD was held by him at the predetermined rate, together with a par plus value on the original deposit. This does, of course, work to his disadvantage if current market rates should rise in the meantime, although he will be assured of par redemption from the issuer at maturity.

Following developments in managing corporate and bank interest rate exposures, interest rate CD caps were introduced in 1983 to enable borrowers to put a ceiling on floating-rate costs.

10.06 COMMERCIAL PAPER

Commercial paper is short-term unsecured promissory notes, normally sold on a discount basis, issued by high quality financial corporate and sovereign borrowers. The leading commercial paper market is in US domestic commercial paper for both domestic and foreign issuers. Markets are also developed in euro commercial paper and sterling paper.

The US commercial paper market is an important source of funds for the US corporate treasurer. Notes which are payable to bearer are issued in denominations usually of US$1m for periods up to 270 days, but typically for periods of between two and four weeks. US commercial paper programmes do not require registration with the US Securities and Exchange Commission, and the funds do not have to be allocated to any specific asset but may be used for general purposes. The promissory notes may be placed directly with institutional investors by the issuer or more commonly may be placed through US investment houses in the form of a commercial paper programme.

The pricing of commercial paper depends initially on its quality. The highest quality borrowers are naturally able to attract finest terms, but this does not necessarily exclude firms of lesser standing issuing their paper in the market on competitive terms. In order to give support to commercial paper, they may be backed by letters of credit (LOCs). These are issued by leading banks to provide a 'standby guarantee' for the paper. In order to obtain the widest possible market for commercial paper, the issuer may be well advised to seek a commercial paper rating. The principal US rating agencies are Standard & Poor's Corp, Moody's Investors Service Inc, and Fitch Investors Service Inc. These agencies make a detailed appraisal of the issuers' affairs and with the issuer's permission will make public the rating they feel applies to the investment quality of the issue. The highest ratings for Standard & Poor's and Moody's respectively would be designated A-1/P-1.

After establishing a commercial paper programme, but before any paper is issued, the corporate treasurer will assess the alternative costs of funds available on other markets. In assessing the costs the following should be borne in mind: legal fees in establishing the programme and note printing costs as an initial outlay, and for running costs the issuing and paying agent's fee, rating agencies' fees and the bank's fee for LOC support if required.

Euro commercial paper, or 'Euro notes', may be denominated in US dollars or ECUs. This facility is available from merchant banks and investment houses in the UK under a Euro commercial paper (ECP) programme. This market, which started in 1984, is a logical development of the note issuance facilities which emerged over the previous three years. ECPs are dealt in the same way as money market instruments, unlike the US domestic commercial paper which is more effectively placed with institutional investors. To comply with the UK Companies Act 1985, a prospectus must be produced if the issuer is a UK company, and an offer made to the public. In order to reduce costs and accelerate issuing procedures some UK borrowers have arranged for their ECP funding to be raised through an offshore borrower.

Whichever route is adopted, the tax implications should be examined carefully. The UK treasurer has the option of selecting one or more dealers to buy/place the paper, or he can arrange for a number of dealers to tender for the paper. If he chooses the latter route, which is the most common arrangement, then he is effectively issuing his own paper and is reliant on the notes being taken up at the auction price. It is probable that as the market develops, corporate treasurers will seek to have their paper placed with a wider spread of investors than can normally be achieved following a tender panel auction approach to the market. More dealers are likely to be appointed with this in mind to achieve a more formalised placing of the paper as is practised in the US domestic commercial paper market.

By way of illustration, a specimen Euro note is shown below, and the summary of the terms of this note issue are as follows:

Issuer:	AB Volvo, Sweden.
Amount:	Up to US dollars 150,000,000 at any one time outstanding.
Form of the notes:	The notes will be issued in bearer form on an interest-bearing basis as shown.
Interest rate on the notes:	The notes will bear interest at a rate per annum 0.25% below the lowest yield (converted by the tender agent into a fixed annual percentage yield in the manner specified in determination of subscription price below) at which any offer for notes to be subscribed on the issue date therefor was accepted by Volvo.
Determination of subscription price:	The subscription price payable for any note shall be determined by the tender agent and shall equal:

Fig 10.1 Specimen Euro note

Serial Number
000000

VOLVO

AKTIEBOLAGET VOLVO

(Incorporated with limited liability in Sweden)
S-40 508 Göteborg, Sweden

Amount: US$500,000

Issued in: London   Maturity Date: ....

Issued on: ....

FOR VALUE RECEIVED, **AKTIEBOLAGET VOLVO** (the "Issuer") promises to pay to the bearer (the "Holder") on the Maturity Date hereof the principal sum of FIVE HUNDRED THOUSAND UNITED STATES DOLLARS ("dollars") upon presentation and surrender of this Note at the offices of Manufacturers Hanover Limited in London as principal paying agent, being at the date hereof at 7 Princes Street, London EC2P 2EN, or at the offices of Manufacturers Hanover Bank, Luxembourg, S.A. in Luxembourg as sub-paying agent, being at the date hereof at 39 Boulevard du Prince Henri, 1724 Luxembourg, during the office hours of such person by cheque or draft drawn on a bank in New York City and delivered or mailed to an address outside the United States, or by transfer to a dollar account maintained by the payee with a bank outside the United States.

All sums payable by the Issuer under this Note shall be paid free and clear of and without deduction or withholding for or on account of any tax now or hereafter imposed, levied, collected, withheld or assessed by or within the Kingdom of Sweden or the United Kingdom or any political sub-division or authority thereof or therein or any federation or organisation of which the Kingdom of Sweden or the United Kingdom may now or hereafter be a member (herein "Applicable Tax") except to the extent (if any) required by law, and shall be paid free and clear of and without any deduction for or on account of any set-off or counterclaim. If the Issuer or any other person is required by law to make any deduction or withholding on account of any Applicable Tax from any sum paid or payable by the Issuer under this Note, then (except to the extent that the requirement to make such deduction or withholding arises by reason only of some connection which the Holder has with the Kingdom of Sweden or the United Kingdom other than the mere holding of this Note) the sum payable by the Issuer in respect of which such deduction or withholding is required to be made shall be increased to the extent necessary to ensure that, after the making of such deduction or withholding, the Holder receives and retains (free from any liability in respect of such deduction or withholding) a net sum in dollars equal to the sum it would have received and so retained had such deduction or withholding not been required or made Provided that the sum so payable by the Issuer shall not be so increased in respect of any deduction or withholding for or on account of United Kingdom tax which would not have been required to be deducted or withheld if the Holder had been either:

(i) a bank carrying on a bona fide banking business in the United Kingdom (and recognised as such by the Inland Revenue) which certified to the said principal paying agent or, as the case may be, sub-paying agent that such bank was beneficially entitled to such payment; or

(ii) not resident in the United Kingdom for the purposes of United Kingdom tax and gave to the said principal paying agent or, as the case may be, sub-paying agent an appropriate affidavit as to such fact.

This Note is negotiable and, accordingly, title hereto shall pass by delivery and the Holder shall be treated as being absolutely entitled to receive payment upon due presentation hereof free and clear of any equity, set-off or counter-claim on the part of the Issuer against any previous Holder hereof.

By presenting this Note for payment the Holder represents to the Issuer that the beneficial owner of this Note (a) is not a US person or (b) is a branch located outside the United States of a bank organised under the laws of the United States which has acquired this Note in accordance with the selling restrictions applicable hereto.

This Note shall be governed by, and construed in accordance with, English law.

Signed in facsimile for and on behalf of
AKTIEBOLAGET VOLVO

By: ....
Authorised Signatory

This Note shall not be validly issued until completed and authenticated by Manufacturers Hanover Limited as issuing agent.

Signed for and on behalf of
MANUFACTURERS HANOVER LIMITED
as issuing agent without recourse, warranty or liability

By: ....
Authorised Signatory

By: ....
Authorised Signatory

This Note has not been registered under the Securities Act of 1933 of the United States of America. This Note may not be offered or sold directly or indirectly in the United States of America, its territories, its possessions (including the Commonwealth of Puerto Rico) or any areas subject to its jurisdiction (the "United States"), or to any national or resident thereof (including the estate of any such person or any estate or trust other than a foreign estate or trust as to the United States and any corporation, partnership or other entity created or organised in or under the laws of the United States or any political subdivision thereof) (a "US person") Provided that this Note may be offered or sold, in accordance with the restrictions agreed to by the Holder in connection with its acquisition of this Note, to (a) a branch located outside the United States of a bank organised under the laws of the United States which has had access to such financial and other information concerning the Issuer as it has deemed necessary in connection with its decision to purchase this Note and which is acquiring this Note for its own account without any view to the distribution or any other disposition hereof or (b) an agent, custodian or fiduciary located outside the United States and (not being an individual) who is a US person acting on behalf of a person who is not a US person pursuant to specific instructions and without discretionary authority to purchase or hold this Note

Any US person who holds this Note will be subject to limitations under United States income tax laws, including the limitations provided in Sections 165(j) and 1287(a) of the United States Internal Revenue Code

SPECIMEN NO VALUE

* Reproduced with kind permission of AB Volvo, Sweden

$$1 + \frac{(R \times D)}{360}$$

$$P \times 1 \times \frac{(Y \times D)}{360}$$

P = the principal amount of such note.

R = the rate at which interest is payable on such note, determined as above and expressed as a decimal fraction.

Y = the yield specified in the offer for such note, converted by the tender agent into a fixed annual percentage rate by reference to the applicable basis rate (as determined by the agent at the request of the tender agent) on the second business day prior to the proposed issue date for such note and expressed as a decimal fraction.

D = the number of days in the tenor of such note.

Maturity: The notes will have a tenor, at the option of Volvo, of one, three or six months. At maturity of the notes, Volvo will repay the principal amount of the notes and will pay the total amount of interest calculated as set out above.

Denomination: Minimum denominations of US dollars 500,000.

Withholding taxes: All payments under the notes will be made free and clear of all withholding taxes and after deductions in Sweden, except as stated in the notes.

Tender agent: Bank of America International Limited.

Principal paying agent: Bank of America NT & SA, 25 Cannon Street, London, EC4P 4HN, England. Bank of America NT & SA, 34 Van Eycklei, B-2018, Antwerp, Belgium.

Reference banks: Bank of America NT & SA, Amsterdam-Rotterdam Bank NV, International Westminster Bank PLC and Société Générale.

Governing law: The notes will be governed by and construed in accordance with English law.

10.07 REVOLVING UNDERWRITING (RUFs) AND NOTE ISSUANCE FACILITIES (NIFs)

A RUF is a revolving facility which allows the corporate borrower to issue short-term paper under a medium-term underwriting commitment. It has some of the characteristics of capital market paper and some of bank credits. Because of the capital market nature of these facilities, the issuers' creditworthiness is of considerable importance so far as market placing is concerned, and whilst no formal rating is required, an equivalent of Standard & Poor's BBB + or higher quality would be a necessary attribute of a potential borrower using these instruments. An essential feature of a RUF is that it is an underwritten facility, and notes may be drawn at the borrower's option under the facility, with the institution or institutions providing the facility being committed to take up the paper required by the borrower from time to time under the medium-term arrangement. An undrawn RUF is virtually a standby arrangement, and a RUF which has been drawn down is indeed an underwritten NIF.

RUFs and NIFs started in the early 1980s and Euro commercial paper facilities are a further logical development being note issuance facilities usually called 'Euro notes', which unlike RUFs, are not issued on a fully underwritten basis. The normal terms for RUFs range from two to ten years, although maturities of up to 15 years have been known. The period for paper drawn under RUFs is generally for one, two, three, six or 12 months at the borrower's option.

In keeping with the growth of capital market terminology and buzz words, there are a number of other variations of NIFs and RUFs, such as MOFFs (multiple option funding facilities) and BONUSs (borrower's option for funds and underwritten standbys). MOFFs provide the borrower with the opportunity of drawing on a variety of short-term paper markets, including perhaps Euro note, the US commercial paper market, committed bank lines, bankers acceptances and floating-rate notes. These facilities may also be in one or more currencies and markets. A variety of the MOFF is the BONUS, which is a global note facility enabling the borrower to have the option of drawing commercial paper or Euro notes, and being able to arbitrage between the two markets to obtain the cheapest funding currently available.

The pricing mechanism of NIFs and RUFs depends on the precise structure of the facility. The borrower may decide to use one or more banks or investment houses as placing agencies. Where a sole placing agent is involved, the note will be priced at a fixed rate, usually based on LIBOR, and that agent will be solely responsible for the distribution of the paper at the price quoted. Where more than one agent is used, the pricing is usually done between the agents, who are jointly responsible for the distribution during the selling period, and agreed with the borrower in the initial documentation. Tender panels consisting of a consortium of investment houses and banks may be asked to bid for short-term notes to be issued. The development of the tender panel concept for a revolving facility is the continuous tender panel, which enables underwriters to bid competitively against the strike offered yield which is normally determined by the institution(s) responsible for the RUF.

10.08 FORWARD RATE AGREEMENTS (FRAs)

A forward rate agreement is sometimes referred to as a future rate agreement and is an arrangement generally between two banks, although it may be between a bank and a commercial counterparty, to require a cash settlement of the difference between the contract rate and a pre-defined reference rate, normally referred to as the settlement rate, on an agreed date in the future. The facility is used to protect the parties from an adverse future interest rate movement in the currency of the contract, without the need for either party to actually borrow or lend the contract amount. The buyer of an FRA will agree to pay the seller on the settlement day, if the nominal contract rate exceeds the settlement rate. The seller will agree to pay to the buyer, again on the settlement date, the difference between the settlement rate and the contract rate should the settlement rate be the higher.

Whilst there exists a developed inter-bank market for FRAs, there has so far been limited development in the application of this facility for non-bank users. An advantage of FRAs over futures contracts as a hedge mechanism for a corporate treasurer is that there are no margin requirement for FRAs. Unlike futures or forward exchange contracts, which may be closed out (and, in the case of the former, usually are closed out), an FRA agreement demands that settlement is effected at maturity on the settlement day. Any exposure received as a result of an FRA can therefore only be reduced or negated by entering into another FRA in the opposite direction, should this be possible to do at the time.

Strictly speaking, FRAs do not constitute a 'source' of finance. However, they do provide an important management tool for the corporate treasurer to use to hedge his interest rate exposure and protect his pre-tax profit position. The FRA may be arranged for the fixed LIBOR rate to run from any time between one day and one year ahead of the spot period and for the tenor of between three and 12 months. It is essentially a forward forward transaction in interest rates and is available in US dollars, sterling, ECUs, Deutschemarks, Swiss francs, French francs, Canadian dollars, guilders and yen. Perhaps the reason for the relatively slow development of the direct use of the FRA by the corporate treasurer is that banks will generally be prepared to meet his needs by quoting for deposits and loans on a forward forward basis and hedge their own positions with inter-bank FRAs. This method of using the FRA market reduces the use of credit lines by reducing the number of deals required.

A simple illustration of an FRA transaction for a corporate user may be helpful. On 6 January the treasurer learns of a need to fund a new acquisition in the US. Funds will not be required until early April and the intention is to employ existing euro currency bank lines for six month funds in due course (April). He is concerned in case interest rates rise over the period between now (January) and April, so he buys a six-month FRA from his bank, with a settlement day on 8 April. If on 6 January the six month Euro dollar interest rate was 8 1/4% the bank and treasurer may agree a nominal FRA price of, say, 8 5/8% pa for the six-month period from 8 April. On 6 April (weekends permitting, two business days before the settlement date) the nominal interest rate is compared with the current market rate for six-month Euro dollars and if rates had risen to, say, 9 1/4% then the bank would make a cash settlement of the net difference of 5/8% on the principal sum for six months. Since the treasurer intended to borrow six-month Euro dollars from 8 April, the cash adjustment and the current market rate would equate to the original level acceptable to him (8 5/8%). Clearly, if the market rate were to fall, the treasurer would have to pay the cash difference to the bank, value 8 April, but the cost would be the same for borrowing six-month dollars thereafter.

A further development in FRAs has taken place with the interest rate guarantee (IRG). This is an over-the-counter interest rate option and provides the corporate treasurer with a degree of flexibility not inherent in the FRA, namely the right to take up the option on settlement day or not. Clearly, if the option is in the money at the time, it will be exercised or otherwise it will be allowed to lapse. However the IRG (as with all options) will require the treasurer to pay a premium for the facility when it is written.

10.09 SWAPS

Swap transactions do not in themselves generate new or additional funding and so cannot strictly be described as a source of funds. In a typical swap transaction, a treasurer who has previously raised floating-rate money swaps this debt with another corporate or perhaps a bank intermediary which has a long position in fixed-rate funds. Sometimes the currency of the two underlying borrowings is the same and the transaction is then just known as 'an interest rate swap'. If the currencies differ it will be termed 'a currency swap'. An interest rate swap at its simplest is an agreement for two counter-parties to pay each others' interest flow commitments on a nominal principal sum. The effect of this will be to convert a floating rate liability to one of a fixed interest for one treasurer whilst the other treasurer's position is the reverse. Normally what happens is that a net difference is paid by the party who is committed to pay the higher rate. A simple illustration will probably help:

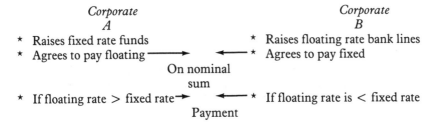

| | *Corporate* | | *Corporate* |
| | *A* | | *B* |

* Raises fixed rate funds   * Raises floating rate bank lines
* Agrees to pay floating ⟶   ⟵ * Agrees to pay fixed
           On nominal
           sum
* If floating rate > fixed rate ⟶   ⟵ * If floating rate is < fixed rate
           Payment

How can both parties benefit from such an arrangement? Many large, highly-rated banks have raised fixed interest debt expressly to swap at a price to cover all costs of the issue and create sub-LIBOR funding which can then be used to source some of its commercial lending portfolio. The other counterparty to such a swap would probably be a lower-rated corporate borrower, with an appetite for, but not necessarily the ability to attract, fixed rate funds at the all in cost being offered by the bank.

Banks often act as intermediaries in a swap in cases where the credit standing or existing level of exposure to one counterparty is an unsatisfactory risk to the other. The market in early 1986 was estimated to be in excess of US$250b, with a thriving inter-bank market and standardised documentation and conditions.

Currency swaps are those in which either of the two parties exchange payments determined by reference to fixed rates of interest in two currencies, or one makes payments at a fixed rate of interest in one currency and the other in US dollars by reference to market deposit rates. Normally the principal sums are agreed at the outset with an agreed exchange rate for calculation of the equivalent amount in the other currency. Whilst the parties have the option to agree an exchange of principal at the outset, they must undertake to exchange principal sums in the reverse direction at maturity whether or not an initial exchange was made at the commencement of the swap agreement.

Swaps were designed initially as a liability management facility. With the development of this market, asset-based swaps are now commonplace. Assume one fund manager has fixed interest income exposure and another has FRN income exposure. It may be possible for each to negate their unhedged positions and lock in an acceptable level of return on their investment portfolios by a swap agreement.

10.10 EUROBONDS — FLOATING-RATE NOTES

A steady growth of investor demand for floating-rate capital market instruments in the early to mid 1980s for floating-rate notes mirrors the preference for short-term deposits in the Euro currency markets over medium-/longer-term fixed-rate interest investments; indeed the volume of US dollar floating-rate eurobonds in

1985 exceeded the volume of straight Eurobonds (fixed rate issues), when a record US$158b was raised through international bond issues that year. Whilst it is true to say that several US$b FRNs were raised by banks and sovereign borrowers over this period, the majority of FRN issues were for corporate borrowers. The FRN market over the last nine years has not only seen an increase in volumes, but also the average size has grown from about US$50m in 1977 to over US$200m in 1985. Some of the major borrowers in the market have raised funds of US$1b at a time. Over the same period there has been a trend of lengthening maturities. 12, 15, 25 and even 100 years' final maturities were used by various borrowers during 1985, and some banks issued undated floating-rate notes with attributes similar to irredeemable debentures.

A third major important trend has been the narrowing of margins over the cost of funds from some 40 basis points over LIBOR in 1977 to approximately 10 basis points over LIBOR in 1985. Regular borrowers in this market have taken advantage of the trend of diminishing margins to refinance the more expensive earlier debt with new issues, generally with longer maturities and, of course, on finer margins.

It is estimated that in 1985 some US$13b worth of old issues were called. By far the largest market for floating-rate capital notes is that in the international US dollar FRN. Only in 1985 did the Deutschemark FRN market open, and apart from this there exists a market for floating-rate ECUs and, of course, sterling FRNs but no other currency as at January 1986.

The development in securitisation of corporate finance gained momentum from 1983 coincident with the decline in demand for syndicated credits. There has been a blurring of the distinction between the FRN and the syndicated loan as the participant providers (investment houses and commercial banks) have been basically the same institutions. The reason is quite simple: the FRN market has provided sovereign and commercial borrowers with longer-term funding at lower costs than they previously enjoyed with syndicated loans. Banks as providers have been prepared to take lower returns in exchange for the liquidity inherent in quality paper which is highly marketable; furthermore they required high-quality assets to replace the reduced demand for syndicated borrowing. The difference between the syndicated loan and FRN narrowed still further in 1985 when an FRN issue for CNT had a borrower's option to drawdown one-, three- or six-month funds for the next interest period at specified margins over LIBOR. Tranche issues can also be made so that the borrower does not have to draw the entire facility at one go.

FRN issues are generally not highly sensitive to interest rate movements, partly since the rates are brought into line with current market levels on a regular short-term basis and partly because they often carry a minimum coupon (collar) insuring holders against a substantial decline in interest rates over the life of the FRN.

Most FRNs are listed on a stock exchange, usually London or Luxembourg. However, the market in them is almost entirely an over-the-counter market with business conducted by telephone and electronic communication systems.

10.11 EUROBONDS – FIXED INTEREST (STRAIGHT)

The range of currencies for issues of longer-term capital debt with fixed interest coupons is much greater than that for floating-rate issues. For local reasons, some markets are strictly limited and demand for certain currencies may not be high, particularly if the cost of borrowing the currency is considered too high. For various reasons, many of the national capital markets are only open for relatively short periods and sometimes for locally resident borrowers as opposed to non-residents of that country. Straight issues have been made in the 1980s in the following currencies: Australian dollars; Austrian schillings; Bahraini dinars; Canadian dollars; Dutch guilders; ECUs; French francs; Hong Kong dollars; Japanese yen; Danish kroner; Norwegian kroner; Kuwaiti dinars; Luxembourg francs; New Zealand dollars; Saudi riyals; sterling; and SDRs. Additionally, dual currency issues have been made in: yen and sterling; US dollars and sterling; US dollars and Australian dollars; Australian dollars and Deutschemarks; and no doubt other mixes will take place as and when borrowers' requirements can be matched with potential investor demand. Readers may be conscious of the absence of two major currencies from the foregoing list, namely Swiss francs and Deutschemarks. There is no effective Euro market in either currency and the national debt markets cater adequately for the needs of non-resident borrowers and resident borrowers alike. A substantial market exists for US dollars and sterling paper. As from January 1986 there has been a liberalisation of the Dutch guilder market as well.

Issues of Eurobonds are normally made in bearer form and are sold internationally usually through a consortium of banks and brokers called 'the selling group'. The managing bank(s) of the issue form the core of the selling group and take the largest share of the securities being issued. Both Eurobonds and foreign bonds (the latter being issued by non-residents in a domestic capital market) are inevitably structured so that the coupon income is received by investors free from withholding tax. The regulatory and fiscal authorities in certain countries are keen to encourage issuers to opt for registered issues rather than in bearer form. However, the Euro issues which are made outside the jurisdiction of such authorities have tended to cater for offshore investors' preference for bearer securities.

Zero coupon bonds may be classified as a form of fixed interest security, the rate being 0%. Such issues are sold on a deep-discount basis and have attraction for investors whose tax domicile provides for a lower incidence of capital gains tax compared with tax on coupon income. The borrower, whilst not paying any interest on the funds received, nevertheless must make some provision for repayment at maturity for the equivalent of principal and rolled up interest.

The majority of Eurobonds and foreign bonds issued are public issues and indeed quoted on a stock exchange. For names which may be less well known to national or international investors in general, new securities may be offered to a limited number of institutional investors who are known or thought to have an appetite for such an offering. When issues are so privately placed the cost to the borrower may well be higher than an equivalent public debt issue to compensate the investor for lack of liquidity as no secondary market (or a very limited one) is likely to exist.

10.12 EUROBOND — CONVERTIBLE AND WARRANT ISSUES

Convertible Eurobonds fall into two categories. Those which are convertible into equity and those FRNs which are convertible into fixed-rate debt instruments. For the latter, there exists a halfway house instrument in the form of a drop-lock bond which automatically converts when market rates reach the strike price previously determined which triggers the conversion. An important feature of the convertible bond is that conversion is at the investor's option, and potential

issuers should be alert to the following factors when considering granting investors such an option:

(a) the option/conversion period when the investor may exercise his conversion
    rights. What call features should be included and when should they
    commence?;

(b) the conversion terms and premium. Whether conversion is into debt or
    equity. In what currency is the new instrument denominated, and if other
    than that of the original bond, what fixed rate of exchange should be used?;
    and

(c) what coupon is set on the bond and does it properly reflect the conversion
    premium set in terms of potential benefits to be given to the investor?

Whereas one of the benefits to the issuer of an equity convertible bond is a lower
coupon, the lower the coupon the more likely that early conversion will take
place, thereby limiting the duration of the benefit to the borrower. Warrant issues
tend to overcome this constraint. A warrant may be described as the right to buy
(a call option) a given security (which may be further debt of a similar or different
type, eg fixed/FRN, or equity) at a given price (known as the exercise price),
during a given period of time (known as the exercise period).

Borrowers usually issue warrants for a cash premium and/or an adjustment by
lowering the coupon on any bond attached. Warrants have been issued by themselves without any debt instrument and those more common issues (bonds with
warrants attached) may have the warrants traded with or without the original
bond — the market quotes separate prices for such issues. As warrants normally
have greater volatility than the underlying equity, they have significant attraction
to the investor. It follows therefore that the valuation of the warrant requires to be
set critically and needs to take into account the following criteria:

(a) the current share price;
(b) the subscription price;
(c) the current dividend per share;
(d) the perceived growth of dividends;
(e) the timing when subscription can be made; and
(f) the alternative rate of return an investor might otherwise obtain.

10.13 SUPRANATIONAL FINANCE

This section concentrates on the two most important supranational providers of
finance: the International Finance Corpn (IFC); and the European Investment
Bank (EIB).

IFC is an affiliate of the World Bank (International Bank for Reconstruction
and Development — IBRD) which, inter alia, makes both loans and equity
investments without requiring government guarantees to privately-owned enterprises, as well as those containing an element of government ownership. Its stated
basic objectives are:

(a) direct investments in individual productive private enterprises;
(b) project identification and promotion;
(c) helping to establish, finance and improve privately-owned development
    finance companies and other institutions which assist development of the
    private sector;
(d) encouraging the growth of capital markets in the developing countries;

(e) creating in the capital exporting countries interest in portfolio investments in enterprises located in the developing countries;

(f) giving advice and counsel to less developed member countries on measures that will create a climate conducive to the growth of private investment.

Provided the project being financed is potentially profitable and likely to provide a direct benefit for the economy of the country in which it is being carried out, IFC may provide some, but not all, the financial support sought. Indeed, it tends to limit the amount of the investment to 25% of the project cost and the size to between US$1m and US$30m. Investments are, however, made of smaller and, indeed, larger amounts in exceptional projects. A common feature of IFC financing is an equity stake accompanied by a longer-term debt arrangement. Finance is usually provided in US dollars, although loans may be provided in other major convertible currencies. Longer-term debt is normally between seven-and twelve-year periods, with a sinking fund amortising the loan on a semi-annual or quarterly basis after initial grace period of, say, two years. Commitment fees are usual on undrawn portions of agreed facilities and the interest rate charged can be arranged on a fixed or floating basis, at rates applicable to market and local conditions at the time of the arrangement. Back-up standby facilities are also provided from time to time by IFC to support new issues both of shares and loan stocks raised by corporate borrowers on a variety of capital markets. This support usually takes the form of an underwriting commitment.

EIB is an independent public institution within the European Economic Community with a mandate to make available loans on behalf of the Community in support of capital investment projects within the Community and associated territories. Private or public institutions can obtain loans from the EIB provided their projects conform to the stated criteria, such as for developing lesser-developed regions and modernising, converting or developing new activities which cannot be completely financed by other available means within the Community. EIB finance does not normally exceed 50% of the cost of the asset being funded, and whilst there is no laid down maximum or minimum figure, it is normal for individual loans to be for at least ECU 2m per project. Loan terms vary between seven and twelve years, although for major industrial projects finance for up to 20 years may be provided in exceptional circumstances, subject to market conditions.

So far as currencies are concerned, EIB have indicated that principal loan formats are as follows:

(a) loans disbursed in several currencies, consisting of standard mixes, with make-up, term and interest rate all fixed in advance;

(b) loans disbursed in several currencies, but in varying mixes tailored to the borrower's preferences and the EIB's holdings;

(c) loans disbursed in a single non-Community currency, mainly the US dollar, Swiss franc and yen, or, for certain major financing operations, matched maturity arrangements in Community or other currencies; and

(d) the ECU may be used for disbursement of loans, treated either as a single currency or as one component of a mixed-currency loan.

As with the World Bank, EIB finances its loans from borrowing on the various international and national capital markets and operates on a non-profit-making basis. Interest rates charged, therefore, are relatively close to funding costs.

CHAPTER 11

International trade finance

Alasdair J. W. Watson

11.01 INTRODUCTION

The credit department usually controls the risks associated with the settlement of international trade so far as a firm's corporate exposure is concerned. In respect of export sales, these risks will include non-payment for goods as a result of a buyer's default or transfer risks as a result of a country default or moratorium. So far as import transactions are concerned, risks of delays in receipt of goods ordered, or payment made in advance for goods which do not conform to contractual requirements, may well give rise to losses. The section of a settlement system which provides adequate security in the transaction is of paramount importance to the credit controller. This must be a matter of commercial judgment backed up by up-to-date relevant information. The more secure the settlement system, the more expensive it is likely to be as banks or other third parties act as stakeholders/guarantors in the payment/underwriting mechanisms. There are four principal methods of settlement which are, in order of decreasing safety to the exporter, as follows:

(a) payment in advance from the buyer;
(b) documentary credit;
(c) collection of payment through the banking system; and
(d) settlement by open account

In addition, there are a variety of compensation and barter transactions which often involve settlement, either in whole or in part, in goods rather than money.

Having determined an appropriate method of settlement, which meets the criteria for security in the transaction so far as the corporate credit controller is concerned, the next risk exposure to be addressed is usually liquidity. Liquidity management and adequacy of cash flow are matters normally addressed by the corporate treasurer or finance director. International trade transactions invariably involve a longer funding period as a result of the geographical locations of the two trading counterparties, particularly if the importer requires credit and is not prepared to pay until some time after the goods are received in his own country. Banks and other financial institutions provide a range of financial techniques for accelerating payment for both the buyer and for the seller. Some of these techniques involve outright payments and are made without recourse to the beneficiary and have the effect of converting 'debtors' into 'cash', without increasing the size of the balance sheet. A substantial number of techniques, however, involve the creation of current liabilities in the form, for example, of bank loans or overdrafts in order to generate new cash. Such facilities will naturally increase the size of the corporate balance sheet. Most financial facilities form an integral part of the settlement method.

11.02 TRADE CREDIT

Finance may be provided by the trading counterparty. If an exporter, for example, is prepared to grant deferred payment terms to his overseas buyers, and has sufficient liquidity without recourse to external funding, then he, the exporter, is providing trade credit for his overseas buyers. The cost of providing such credit will be passed on to the buyer in the invoice price. This form of trade credit can be provided for the buyer's benefit under an open account settlement arrangement or under a clean or documentary collection arrangement through a bank, accompanied by term bills of exchange with documents, if any, being released to the buyer against his acceptance.

Trade credit can also be provided by the buyer for the benefit of the exporter. In circumstances where the buyer is required to make payment at the time an order is placed, or prior to or on shipment, the seller receives an accelerated cash flow direct from the buyer as a result of this advance payment. In respect of the sale of capital goods abroad, it is quite common practice for payments to be made in stages, typically 10% in advance with order, 10% on shipment, and 80% spread over, say, five years from shipment date with payment in six-monthly instalments. So far as the advance payments are concerned, an exporter with sufficient liquidity would not need supporting funding from a bank or other source and, therefore, would be able to provide from his own resources the required 'trade credit'. In a number of countries exchange control restrictions either prohibit or inhibit advance payments as a method of settlement/finance.

1 Negotiation of collections

Negotiation facilities are generally used by exporters who use their bank to remit outward collections to various overseas buyers and obtain settlement through correspondent banks in the buyers' countries. The negotiating bank will credit the exporter's account at the time it despatches documents to its correspondent overseas. In due course, if all goes well, the funds will be received from the overseas buyer to reimburse the negotiating bank. Negotiations of this nature are made with recourse to the exporter so that if the funds do not materialise within what the negotiating bank deems to be a 'reasonable period of time', the exporter will have to repay the money credited earlier, with interest. Negotiation facilities are available in London in sterling and all freely-convertible currencies, so the exporter has the opportunity to 'borrow' in the currency of his choice and for the exact period of the outstanding collection by this method.

2 Loans against collections

Where a company's cash flow requirements do not merit a full negotiation facility but where some support would be helpful, bank loans of, say, 50%–80% of outstanding collections may be arranged. These facilities have some similarity to negotiations in their structure differing only in the amount *originally credited* to the exporter by his bank, the balance being credited on *receipt* of funds from the overseas buyer.

3 Discount facilities — trade bills

Banks and discount houses are prepared to buy trade bills of exchange accepted by importers and payable locally. These term bills will be purchased by way of discount for less than their face value, and on their due date will be presented to the importer for payment of the full face amount of the bill. Rates applicable to trade bills discounted are invariably higher than those applicable to prime bank bills.

4 Discount facilities — bank bills drawn under clean acceptance credits

Bank bills of exchange are those which have been accepted by a bank rather than an individual or corporate entity which is not a bank. A bank bill will normally attract a finer discount rate than a trade bill (one which is not accepted by a bank). In London the market does not differentiate between one bank bill and another drawn in a foreign currency, but does make a difference, so far as prices are concerned, for sterling trade related paper with an original tenor not in excess of 187 days. The Bank of England has issued a list of banks whose paper may be eligible for rediscount by the Bank of England and such banks are described as eligible banks. Finer terms (lower rates) are available for eligible paper (paper accepted by eligible banks) than for paper accepted by recognised banks which do not have 'eligible status'. In order to qualify as eligible paper, the bill of exchange must be drawn in sterling and contain two good names, the drawer and the acceptor. It must be accepted by one of the 120 odd recognised banks whose bills are eligible for rediscount by the Bank of England. The bill must be a properly executed bill of exchange and payable in the UK, bearing a clause which clearly identifies the underlying transaction for which the bill was drawn. The nature of the transaction must be self-liquidating and is normally trade-related, with evidence of a movement of goods across frontiers, not necessarily involving the UK. In certain circumstances, where an unconditional obligation to pay has been previously established, bills of exchange related to settlement of services or those relating to stocks of goods warehoused may be deemed eligible. Under no circumstances may an eligible bill have an original tenor in excess of 187 days.

There are two prime elements to the cost of bank bill finance:

(a)   the acceptance commission charged by the Bank for adding its name to the bill of exchange, thereby turning it into a negotiable bank note; and

(b)   the discount price. It is important to recognise that the effective yield on a discount is greater than the rate appears to imply as the discounter is receiving his return at the commencement of the transaction, rather than at the end of the transaction as is the case with an interest rate.

Finance by way of clean acceptance credits may be made available to importers, exporters and others. An agreement between the corporate client and the Bank providing the facility contains provisions for the client to draw term bills of exchange on the Bank. Such paper is then discounted. At maturity the facility may be continued by drawing fresh bills again on the Bank and the proceeds of these bills being applied to repay those which have now matured. The acceptance commission and discount price as described above being the charges levied on each rollover. Alternatively, the bill(s) may be redeemed from sale proceeds received prior to the maturity of the financing bill.

Many acceptance facilities are arranged for exporters selling goods on open account or on a collection basis. Calculations are made of the corporate liquidity requirements with regard to the aggregate of the collection period and credit period which is likely to elapse from shipment to receipt of cleared funds, and with regard to the volume of outstanding collections over any such given period. The underlying acceptance facility will then be arranged so as to provide a margin for possible late payments and non-payments, yet ensure that there is likely to be a sufficient cash flow from the outstanding trade bills to meet the financing bill when it matures. The finance bill(s) which may be drawn might cover, say, 70%–90% of the calculated outstanding bills over a given period, and the financing bill will normally be drawn to maturity at a tenor slightly longer than the aggregate for collection and credit periods of the underlying trade bills. For such trade-related acceptance facilities as described in this paragraph, it is quite normal for bankers to take an assignment over an ECGD Comprehensive Guarantee if the exporter has one.

Import finance can be arranged in a similar manner as described above, with the cash flow coming from the ultimate buyer in due course, but enabling the importer to settle sight collections and sight documentary credit payments, obtain the shipping documents and thereafter goods, prior to manufacture/processing and re-sale.

Bankers acceptance facilities require that bills of exchange which have been executed in accordance with the requirements of the local bill market are available to the discounter and to the rediscount secondary market during market hours on the day of discounting. This can create logistics problems where companies wishing to use such facilities are not resident in the local centre, e g not in London for paper to be discounted in the London bill market. In order to overcome this constraint and to enable companies to take advantage of immediately current discount rates, inchoate paper may be held by the accepting bank pending its client's instructions to complete the bill(s) with the amounts required and date them, and thereafter to accept and discount them.

5 Discount facilities — bank bills drawn under documentary credits

A UK importer of goods or services may request his bank to issue a credit requiring the overseas beneficiary to draw term bills on the UK issuing bank. Such term bills as eventually presented under the credit would be accepted by the issuing bank when received, always assuming the documents are in order or are acceptable to the applicant, and the local UK issuing bank would then discount the bill in the London market. The credit when issued would normally instruct the advising bank to pay the beneficiary on a sight basis, thereby providing the exporter with finance as described under 'Sight documentary credits' below.

The alternative structure for documentary acceptance credits can arise whereby, for example, a UK beneficiary is required under an export credit to draw term bills on the local London advising/confirming bank. Subject to correctly presented documents the advising bank would accept the bill and discount it. This would provide the exporter with liquidity should he require it and, of course, he has the option to retain the accepted bill without having it rediscounted if it does not require finance. It will also give the importer time in which to pay since his account will not be debited until the bill matures and the respective banks seek reimbursement.

Discount charges under documentary acceptance credits may be for the applicant's account or for the beneficiary's and the credit will normally indicate which. If discount charges are for the applicant's account, then the beneficiary will receive the face amount of the bill drawn without deduction. In the absence of specific instructions, discount charges will be for the beneficiary's account.

6 Sight documentary credits

Documentary credits have been described as 'conditional payment orders'. They take the form of an inter-bank payment instruction to be applied only provided that the accompanying terms and conditions have been complied with by the beneficiary. If the mandate has been fulfilled, and adequate reimbursement instructions have been received by the paying bank, the beneficiary, frequently an exporter of goods or provider of services, will receive his money from the local bank advising the credit. To be able to draw cash against correctly presented documents immediately after shipment of goods is, in effect, providing the exporter with finance since he will not experience the normal delays in collecting proceeds of his overseas sales.

Whether a payment to an exporter's account under a sight documentary credit will constitute an outright settlement or be conditional upon the paying bank obtaining reimbursement, depends upon the nature of the documentary credit and the instructions given to the advising bank in the exporter's country. If the exporter receives a confirmed credit and can comply with the terms and conditions, then any payment made by the confirming bank will be an outright payment and not subject to any recourse or reserve. If the credit is not confirmed, the advising bank is under no obligation to make an outright payment even against correct documents if they consider that reimbursement from the issuing bank may not be forthcoming when establishing a credit. The issuing bank, who is normally the importer's bank, will authorise the advising bank in the exporter's country to pay against correct documents presented or negotiate against correct documents presented. Payments under credits which are expressed to be 'negotiable' are made with recourse to the beneficiary unless they have been confirmed by the advising bank.

On the other hand, payments made to beneficiaries under credits which are 'payable' rather than 'negotiable' are made as outright payments without recourse to the beneficiary in the event that the advising bank is unable subsequently to obtain reimbursement.

So far as the importer's/applicant's position is concerned under sight documentary credits, there is no question of the credit itself in this form providing finance. Indeed, the importer/applicant would probably have to make payment possibly before the goods arrive and immediately after correct documents have been tendered to his bank, the issuing bank.

7 Red clause credits

Sight documentary credits may contain an advance payment instruction to the advising bank, traditionally typewritten in red so that it stands out from other terms and conditions. These so called red clause credits authorise the advising/confirming bank to exercise their own judgment on lending up to 100% of the credit amount to the beneficiary against the issuing bank's undertaking to reimburse them in the event that no documents were subsequently presented or the beneficiary defaults on the loan. If all goes well, the beneficiary can use the funds in order to obtain the goods and thereafter the shipping documents for presentation under the credit established in his favour. It is normal for the beneficiary to be able to draw any balance due under the terms of the credit on presentation of correct documents thereunder. Normal local loan conditions and rates usually apply to red clause loans made by the advising bank. As this is a form of advance payment, exchange control regulations which prohibit advance payments tend to restrict the range of countries which permit such transactions.

8 Deferred payment credits

A company which draws a term bill of exchange which is subsequently used for financing purposes will retain ultimate liability as drawer of the bill until it is paid, albeit on a contingent liability basis. In order to avoid increasing the company's contingent liabilities, yet still provide finance for the importer, the beneficiary may arrange with the applicant for a deferred payment credit to be established in his favour. The credit will then stipulate the future date on which payment(s) will be made; no bill of exchange will be required from the beneficiary; and should the beneficiary need funds in the meantime, he will have to resort to finance from other resources such as bank borrowing.

9 Refinance documentary credits

A sight documentary credit may be established in favour of the beneficiary, and the advising bank receives in addition, inchoate term bills drawn by the applicant on the advising bank, accompanied by instructions to hold them pending presentation of documents in due course. When the beneficiary presents his documents he will be paid straightaway provided they are in order, and he will be unaware of any financial support being provided to the buyer by the advising bank. The buyer will only have to pay the discount charges when documents are presented and will settle the face amount of the term bills at maturity.

10 Transferable documentary credits

Finance under a transferable credit may be provided for the buyer or for the seller or for the ultimate supplier(s) in the manner described under the various headings on documentary credits above. If the first beneficiary chooses to transfer the credit to an ultimate supplier(s) for a smaller figure than the original credit in his favour, he has the right to draw the balance of the credit when correct documents are presented by the second beneficiary. Transferable credits, therefore, can be used to provide traders and agents, inter alia, with a secure method of settlement which may be accompanied by the aforementioned documentary credit finance techniques.

11.03 BANK LOANS AND OVERDRAFT FACILITIES

1 Overdraft

General purpose overdraft facilities may be used for trade finance as well as for other commercial reasons. They provide companies with the most flexible form of borrowing, and undrawn facilities provide the corporate treasurer with a useful standby arrangement in case of need. Overdrafts are available from London banks in sterling and all convertible currencies and may be drawn down or repaid at the option of the corporate treasurer.

This maximises the use of funds and minimises the outstanding amount borrowed. Because of the increased flexibility, overdraft costs tend to be higher than fixed-interest bank loans. The methods that banks use to calculate overdraft charges vary. One of the most common is a margin over a base or prime rate which is changed from time to time in accordance with the general level of short-term interest rates. Most sterling overdraft facilities in London are arranged at a margin over a lending bank's base rate. In the US and Canada some short-term lending (but not specifically overdrafts) are geared to the current New York prime loan rate (NYPLR) or the Canadian prime loan rate (CPLR). Canadian dollar and US dollar overdrafts in London are sometimes linked to such base rates, although most foreign currency facilities, including in particular US dollars, would be linked to the London Inter-Bank Offered Rate (LIBOR) for the currency and period in question.

Where overnight money rates are available, such as in US dollars, foreign currency facilities may be geared to the overnight LIBOR. It will be appreciated that a daily change in overdraft rates geared to overnight money may be considered both inconvenient and administratively burdensome. Some banks will quote their own foreign currency base rate, which will be held fixed for, say, a week at a time and calculated on the basis of a composite rate for short-term funds. Exporters receiving sale proceeds in foreign currencies may very well use current accounts with overdraft facilities attached, expressed in these currencies to help maximise cash flow and minimise exchange exposure. This is achieved by borrowing on their foreign currency account at the time firm orders are received. The funds borrowed may then be sold for sterling, perhaps to reduce overdrafts or loan payments on sterling facilities. When the sale proceeds are eventually received they will be credited to the appropriate foreign currency account to expunge the borrowing. The exporter's exchange exposure in the transaction being covered at the time the sale contract was arranged with the spot sale of the currency for sterling.

Importers may also benefit from a similar arrangement regarding the settlement of foreign currency indebtedness, particularly after they have received foreign currencies from export sales at some earlier stage. In the author's opinion the use of foreign currency accounts in this manner for trade-related transactions can, in many circumstances, be more flexible and easier to control and manage than the use of fixed forward foreign exchange contracts and fixed-term borrowing. These facilities are available from both the indigenous clearing banks and from a large number of foreign and merchant banks in London.

2 Bank loan facilities

The principal difference between a bank loan and an overdraft is that the overdraft is based on a current account which the banker will expect to see fluctuate from credit to debit and back into credit, but not to go overdrawn and stay overdrawn. A loan, on the other hand, is invariably arranged on a separate loan account with an expressly designated purpose for the funds being drawn. Both banker and treasurer can monitor the repayment arrangements agreed for the facility quite simply. Most loans arranged in this fashion will have clearly identified repayment arrangements and this applies in particular to all foreign currency loans which are provided for a given period of time, at the expiry of which they must be repaid. This fixed term-lending can be priced on the basis of a fixed interest rate over the period of the loan, or on a floating-rate basis. The bank may agree to lend a given sum for, say, five years on a floating-rate basis based, say, on the six-month LIBOR rate. The rate will be adjusted every six months over the period of the loan in line with the current Inter-Bank money rates on the day of the interest determination.

11.04 FORFAITING

The development of forfaiting in the UK, as a popular method of non-recourse export finance, has been overshadowed by the very competitive ECGD short-term financial packages in the form of the 'Open Account Guarantee' and the 'Bills and Notes Guarantee'. Nevertheless, since the mid-seventies there has been a growth of forfaiting business and, so far as the UK is concerned, this is likely to continue.

One reason is the phasing out of the two ECGD short-term financial support facilities mentioned above, coupled with the continued corporate need for off balance sheet finance/outright payment.

Forfait finance provides exporters of goods or services sold on medium- to long-term credit with the ability to quote firm prices, including the financing cost, to an overseas buyer before sale contract negotiations are completed. The forfaiter will buy the buyer's obligations from the exporter at an agreed discount. In London there are many banks, but by no means all of them provide this service as do certain finance houses and discount companies. The buyer's obligations, which are purchased by the forfaiter without recourse to the exporter, can take the form of bills of exchange, promissory notes or, very rarely, the buyer's book debts. These obligations are usually drawn as a series of bills or notes often maturing at regular intervals, say, each six months over the total credit period being given to the buyer, say, seven years. If this was the case there would be 14 bills, the first maturing in six months and the last in seven years. As the bills are sold on a discount basis, the exporter would probably wish to arrange for the buyer to bear the cost of discounting. It is common practice, therefore, for the forfaiter to assist the exporter in calculating the amount of each bill so that when it is discounted it will equate to the interest cost the buyer has agreed to pay for the credit period granted. The forfaiter will be asked to quote an indication price and it is usual for the forfaiter to hold the price firm for, say, 48 hours to give the exporter time to negotiate with his buyer on a fixed funding cost basis. After concluding the sale contract the exporter can request a firm forfait price for the purchase of the entire series of bills, even though these may not be presented for several weeks, months or even, in certain circumstances, years later. This delayed presentation is particularly useful for exporters of capital goods who are then able to lock in firm funding costs without recourse, at the contract stage and well before shipment.

The forfaiter will almost certainly require that the bills of exchange are accepted by the buyer, or that the promissory notes made by the buyer are avalised or guaranteed by the buyer's bank. Other than this, the documentation underlying a forfait proposition is not excessive when compared with some medium-term financing and capital market propositions.

It has often been said that forfait finance tends to be expensive. There is no doubt that in the early to mid-seventies, when this type of facility was still a novelty, margins taken by forfaiters tended to be 'generous'. However, as forfait became more widespread with more financial institutions offering the service, the pricing terms became finer and generally geared to inter-bank rates. There still exists in competition the special export finance schemes, particularly the medium-term ECGD supplier credit Bank Guarantee facility.

11.05 INTERNATIONAL FACTORING FINANCE

Factoring contracts invariably provide a range of services in addition to finance. The nature of these services are discussed elsewhere in this publication. Finance may be provided under a factoring contract so that the exporter may draw cash against invoices presented to the factor. Payment of such monies may be made with or without recourse depending on the nature of the factoring agreement. As with forfait, factoring has sometimes been criticised for the relatively high costs involved so far as finance is concerned. This is not necessarily the case. Factoring charges are based on the amount of work involved and the nature of service provided and for this reason a proper comparison of like with like is difficult. So far as finance is concerned, however, factoring institutions which form part of a major bank grouping should be in a position to provide facilities to their own clients on terms which are no greater than the client could expect to enjoy from the bank in that group. Factors who are independent of such banking connections must rely on the money markets for their funding and it is conceivable that they may not be able to attract funds as cheaply as a major bank in these markets. If this be the case, the on-cost to the exporter, and in turn to the buyer, would be greater than equivalent finance through a major bank or factor associated with a major bank.

Export finance for goods which have been sold on open account terms or other short term deferred payment terms can be provided by banks on normal market or overdraft related rates under ECGD backed comprehensive guarantees as well as under a factoring agreement.

11.06 OFFICIAL ASSISTANCE FOR EXPORTS

The British Overseas Trade Board (BOTB) which advises the UK government on trade strategy also provides a range of direct export services. By regularly liaising with other governments it obtains and provides up to date commercial and industrial information in connection with overseas trade and arranges trade promotions, assists with associated publicity and provides finance. The BOTB sponsors the following two schemes:

> Export Marketing Research Scheme (EMRS); and
> Market Entry Guarantee Scheme (MEGS).

1 EMRS

Professional market researchers are employed by the BOTB to advise UK companies and trade associations on the best methods of conducting research into overseas markets. Subject to the proposition being acceptable to them, the BOTB will provide financial assistance to the extent of 50% of consultants' fees and expenses for individual companies and two-thirds of the fees and expenses of research consultants incurred by trade associations. Additionally, where a company employs its own staff in overseas research, the Board may reimburse up to half of travel and related costs incurred. Further financial support covering one-third of the following export marketing costs (excluding European community countries) may be available:

(a) establishment or re-organisation of a company's export department, including professional consultancy costs in connection therewith up to a maximum of £5,000;

(b) the cost of one member of staff for one year employed as a qualified overseas marketing research officer in a company's new export marketing research department; and

(c) the cost of specific published market research studies.

2 MEGS

This is designed for smaller- and medium-sized UK manufacturing firms to enable them to develop new overseas markets or to increase their market share, and at the same time spread the risks involved. In addition to UK manufacturing companies, the scheme also extends to certain sales organisations operating on behalf of one or more manufacturers under firm contract to those manufacturers. The scheme involves the funding of half of specific overhead costs associated with a new venture. No costs, as follows, will be eligible which are related to the production and distribution of the goods marketed and would include cost of market research and test marketing, continuing costs of existing facilities, costs incurred prior to the date of an application, entertainment costs, cost of activities which are subject to support from other sources of public funds, costs incurred when the venture is expected to make an annual profit, manufacturing costs, transport costs, capital investment costs, UK administration costs, costs of finance in respect of stocks, depreciation, interest charges, bank charges and commission payments directly related to the sales of the product in question.

The costs which are eligible are those incurred in the early years of a venture when it is expected to sustain an annual loss, and are:

(a) staff costs, including salaries, recruitment, relocation, overseas-based administration for sales and warehouse staff;

(b) training for selling and servicing of the venture products for overseas-based staff only;

(c) travel and expenses incurred by overseas-based staff and by home-based staff visiting the market, provided that there is a direct connection with the specified qualifying venture;

(d) the rental of overseas office accommodation including property and contents insurance, maintenance services, office equipment, local real estate taxes, office supplies and the purchase/running costs or rental of cars;

(e) sales promotion, including publicity, advertising, and the production of sales literature relevant to the specific venture;

(f) warehouse costs and showroom costs; and

(g) legal expenses incurred in establishing an overseas operation; external audit fees; costs and expenses incurred in registering patents, trademarks, licences and the checking and approval of getting the qualifying venture product to meet local standards.

The parameters of the scheme are as follows:

(a) ventures with planned eligible costs below £40,000 will not be considered. The minimum amount of any one venture is £20,000 and the maximum £125,000;

(b) coverage for half of eligible costs within the range £40,000 to £250,000; and

(c) where overhead costs exceed £250,000 the scheme may be applied but will have a maximum funding of £125,000. The funding will be made available at the commencement of a venture when it is expected that the proposition will run at an annual loss, provided that this period does not exceed five years.

Funds are normally made available after documentary evidence is produced, certified by an independent accountant and incurred during the year of the claim.

The cost of entering such a scheme is a flat rate charge of 3% of the funding required, plus a levy on sales receipts. The levy will be calculated on the assumption that the venture will be successful at 2½% over the weighted average of UK clearing banks' base rate. If the venture fails, the firm is exempt from any shortfall in repayment of the Department of Trade's funding which remains outstanding at the end of an agreed period. In other words, the Department of Trade is able to cover, with interest, funds provided so long as the venture is successful, but if it proves otherwise the exporter's position is not worsened by having to repay any of the benefits enjoyed under the scheme in earlier years.

Apart from market research and associated financial facilities indicated above, official support is given in respect of promotion, advice on individual export markets, publicity and credit insurance. In order to encourage overseas business, three overseas trade fair schemes are available. They are:

(a) all British exhibitions;
(b) the British Pavilion scheme; and
(c) the joint venture scheme.

In each case, the BOTB will provide space on the basis of a stand or display facility on preferential terms to those UK companies wishing to participate in promoting their products at overseas trade fairs. There are also financial facilities sometimes available for up to two representatives from each company participating in such promotions. Various forms of roadshow promotion or overseas seminars may also benefit from BOTB's support.

Economics, statistical and technical assistance and advice is available from various BOTB branches. Information covering tariffs and regulations, the economic climate, competition, business customs and basic data on travelling in various countries abroad, as well as specific market profiles, are available for most markets throughout the world. Daily up-to-date information is available from the Export Intelligence Service on overseas markets and export opportunities covering several thousands of different products and services. Overseas status reports on companies abroad may be obtained from the BOTB or, indeed, from the exporter's own bank.

The department of the British Standards Institution, called 'Technical Help to Exporters' (THE), will provide information and advice on technical matters to enable manufacturers to determine to what extent their products need to be changed to meet legal and/or marketing requirements for various overseas markets.

11.07 OTHER FINANCE FACILITIES

1 Confirming and export house facilities

A confirming house acts as agent, often purchasing agent, for an overseas buyer. It will receive commission paid by the buyer for its services, which include the provision of extended credit of up to 180 days' duration. There will be a contract of sale of goods between the buyer and the UK supplier with a confirming house entering an independent agreement with the seller, confirming the overseas buyer's order and thereby undertaking the risk of non-payment. Confirming houses provide finance on a non-recourse basis so that the supplier is able to obtain immediate payment after shipment of the goods without resort to his banking facilities.

Export houses include manufacturers export agents, export managers, a variety of merchants, buying or indent houses, finance houses and indeed confirming houses. Export houses other than confirming houses are normally merchants who buy as principal from manufacturers and then sell the goods abroad for their own account. Frequently finance is provided by the export houses paying the manufacturer after evidence of shipment and providing credit to the overseas buyers to whom they have onsold the goods.

2 Invoice discounting

Certain UK finance houses will offer a sales invoice discount facility. As a rule finance is the only service provided and, therefore, invoice discounting differs substantially from factoring facilities described elsewhere. Invoice discounting is almost always provided on a with recourse basis so that in the event of non-payment by the debtor, the finance company expects to recover from their client, the invoice issuer. There are usually wide margins taken between the invoice price and the amount advanced and the cost of such a facility tends to be higher than comparable bank lending.

3 Credit union finance

Various hire-purchase institutions can provide export/import finance by arranging an instalment credit contract in favour of a buyer/distributor/importer of goods. The initiative for these arrangements often stems from the exporter who may discuss his buyer's requirements with his local UK hire-purchase company. In turn, the hire-purchase company will contact its branch, or correspondent instalment credit institution in the buyer's country, to arrange the necessary contract in favour of the buyer. Finance may be provided either from the UK or locally in the buyer's country, depending on local credit and exchange control regulations.

11.08 COUNTERTRADE AND BARTER

Barter and other types of countertrade form a significant feature of world trade and are particularly convenient for developing countries short of cash or credit. Countertrade embraces some half-dozen techniques and is essentially a bilateral trade deal. The simplest form of countertrade is perhaps barter, involving a straight swap of goods for other goods, although probably this is the most difficult deal to accomplish in practice. Normally a combined use of goods and cash to pay for an export is involved with arrangements such as offset, buy back, counterpurchase, triangular compensation, full compensation, evidence accounts and switch trading. In the main, countertrade fits in well with the centralised economic planning of Comecon countries, which often places an emphasis on volume of out-put rather than price. Placing the responsibility for disposing of counterpurchased goods formally in the hands of Western exporters, countertrade helps to compensate for Eastern Europe's shortcomings in marketing. In third world countries shortages of foreign exchange to pay for imports, and a need to stimulate exports, have led to a global increase in countertrade.

Counterpurchase requires the exporter to accept part payment in kind for goods shipped. The percentage of the cash payment made can range from a small fraction of an overall contract value, to most of it, and the goods offered in exchange are generally unrelated to those provided by the exporter who may very well require the involvement of one or perhaps many other counterparties to dispose of his newly acquired goods. This form of countertrade is the most common arrangement and there are, of course, several varieties of counter-purchase structures, eg the 'junktim transaction' where goods are imported from one country against an undertaking from the exporter's country that future exports to the seller's country may be set off against the value of the goods being currently imported.

A buy back agreement generally involves the sale of capital goods in the form of plant and/or equipment, coupled with an arrangement to pay for them in terms of future out-put resulting from the goods purchased.

Offset arrangements often help to create employment and give the importing nation leverage to pay for the goods invested by the exporter in a developing country.

Triangular compensation may involve the movement of goods between three countries. If goods being offered in exchange for goods being imported are not saleable in the country from whence other goods are being imported, such goods would have to be sold in a third country. The proceeds in foreign exchange arising from the sale of the goods in the third country would, therefore, be available to pay for the goods being imported. Therefore, goods exported from country A to country B, are paid for as a result of sale proceeds from country C in respect of goods sold from country B to country C.

Some exporters who carry out regular countertrade transactions, may find it convenient to 'run a book' rather than to arrange for the counterpurchase of goods on an item by item basis. Evidence accounts are created to enable the exporter to record his own counterpurchased imports and endeavour to balance the book on, say, an annual basis.

Switch trading is normally associated with a form of triangular compensation involving a bi-lateral clearing agreement between the two countries and settlement in a hard currency through a third. It is often used for creating settlement of imbalances in long term bilateral agreements where one nation's trade surpluses with a partner country can be tapped by third parties so that, for example, UK exports to Bolivia may be financed from the sale of Hungarian goods to the UK or elsewhere.

11.09 CONTRACT AND OTHER GUARANTEES

Indirect financial support may be provided by a variety of guarantees issued by banks on behalf of their corporate clients and against a corporate counter indemnity.

Documents which do not conform to the terms of a letter of credit are nevertheless sometimes paid by the advising/confirming bank if the latter is satisfied that the discrepancies are specified in an indemnity, issued by the beneficiary's bank or sometimes the beneficiary himself. Without this the exporter would have to wait for his money until such time as the overseas buyer agrees to take up the documents (if he does) and pay for them despite the discrepancies between the credit and the documents presented thereunder. Bank guarantees are often given to a correspondent bank abroad in order to support local overdrafts or loan facilities provided for a customer, who will be possibly temporarily resident in that overseas country. Such facilities again would be supported by the individual or company's counter indemnity.

Documentary credits are sometimes used in place of a guarantee. This facility is often employed to avoid legal or fiscal complications which may arise in certain countries in connection with the issuing of a guarantee. A documentary credit might call for a statement made by a lending bank 'that payment of interest and/or repayment of principal is due and has not been received' on a loan. Should the lending bank, as beneficiary of such a credit, find itself in a position of being able to make such a statement then reimbursement of the amounts due can be effected under the documentary credit. Such arrangements are commonplace where a parent company's guarantee would normally be required, but owing to legal constraints, the guaranteeing of, say, an overseas subsidiary's indebtedness, is prohibited. The issuing of a documentary credit, however, which has the same effect so far as the lending bank is concerned, is not constrained in the same manner.

Tender guarantees are commonly required in connection with orders for capital goods and major contractual works. When a contractor places a bid for a particular project or order he is invariably required to have his bid supported by a bank's guarantee in order to discourage frivolous tenders and provide evidence that he is in earnest. The normal amount of a tender guarantee is 3% of the contract.

In due course on adjudication when the contract is awarded, the existing tender guarantee is usually converted into a performance guarantee. Performance guarantees are normally for an amount of between 5% and 10% of the contract amount. In the event that the contractor fails to fulfil his obligations under the contract now awarded to him, the money under the guarantee would be forfeit. The same would naturally apply, of course, with regard to the tender guarantee should he be awarded the contact and fail then to accept it after having tendered for it. These penalty monies are normally required in the form of unconditional guarantees. This means that the buyer in whose favour they are issued can exercise his option to call them at any time.

Conditional contractual guarantees are rare, although they are, of course, a good deal safer so far as the contractor is concerned.

Other contractual guarantees are sometimes required in respect, for example, of advance payments made to a contractor in order to get the work started. This enables the buyer to claim back funds in the event that he is dissatisfied with the contractor's progress. There are many occasions where companies or individuals are required to put up a deposit or margin in cash, or, as an alternative, arrange an appropriate bank guarantee instead. For example, a shipping company may make a claim for general average in which case the freight owners will not get their goods released to them until they put up an appropriate cash deposit or provide a bank's general average bond. Margin calls in some commodity and metal markets are also subject to a cash or guarantee requirement.

11.10 CREDIT INSURANCE AND BANK SUPPORT GUARANTEES

Credit insurance covers the risk of non-payment for goods rather than risk associated with the loss or damage to the goods themselves. In most OECD countries there exists a state credit insurer and a range of private credit insurance institutions. Export Credits Guarantee Department (ECGD) is a government department which assists UK exporters of both goods and services in two ways. First, they provide credit insurance cover for both del credere (buyer) risks and also for political and economic risks associated with non-transference of money from abroad. Second, they provide a variety of guarantees and specifically designed schemes against which banks may make available finance to support UK exports.

The private credit insurance market does not normally underwrite risks of a political/economic/transfer nature, but tends to restrict its cover to those risks associated with the buyers default.

A range of credit insurance policies are available from ECGD to meet the specialised needs of UK exporters of goods and services. The majority of export-ers' needs, however, are met by the short-term comprehensive guarantee, which is based on a whole turnover concept, and appropriate for exporters of consumer goods sold on cash on documents or credit terms of up to six months. For manufacturers of capital goods, specific guarantees are available for each contract.

The risks covered under the comprehensive short-term guarantee are as follows:

(a) insolvency of the buyer;
(b) the buyer's failure to pay within six months of due date for goods which he has accepted;
(c) the buyer's failure to take up goods which have been despatched to him (where not caused or excused by the policyholder's actions, and where ECGD decides that the institution or continuation of legal proceedings against the buyer would serve no useful purpose);
(d) a general moratorium on external debt decreed by the government of the buyer's country or of a third country through which payment is to be made;
(e) any other action by the government of the buyer's country which prevents performance of the contract in whole or in part;
(f) political events, economic difficulties, legislative or administrative measures arising outside the UK which prevent or delay the transfer of payments or deposits made in respect of the contract;
(g) legal discharge of a debt (not being legal discharge under the proper law of the contract) in a foreign currency, which results in a shortfall at the date of transfer;
(h) war and certain other events preventing performance of the contract pro-vided that the event is not one normally insured with commercial insurers; and
(i) cancellation or non-renewal of a UK export licence or the prohibition or restriction on export of goods from the UK by law (this risk is covered only where the pre-credit risk section of the guarantee applies).

For exporters who provide deferred terms of less than two years to their overseas buyers, ECGD can provide unconditional guarantees to lending banks who can make available finance through the open account scheme and bills or notes scheme at fine rates, namely 5/8% over base rate. Under the open account scheme, finance of up to 90% of the invoice amount is available and 100% under the bills and notes scheme. Credit insurance cover must be taken out prior to these schemes being used.

For financing medium term export credit, ECGD will issue specific bank guarantees. Advances of up to 100% of the contract amount may be made by the lending banks under this scheme for credit periods of normally two years and five years. Longer-term finance may be provided by buyer credit facilities where 80–85% of the contract value may be financed. As buyer credit arrangements involve major projects for contracts of £¼m or more, and these generally take some time to negotiate, both ECGD and the banks likely to be involved should be notified at an early stage of the intention to use such a facility. There are normally four legally enforceable agreements to be concluded co-terminously:

(a) a supply contract between the British supplier and the overseas buyer, for the supply of plant and equipment and possibly for construction of the project;

(b) a loan agreement between the financing bank and an overseas borrower to provide finance for the bulk of the payments under the supply contract or contracts;

(c) a guarantee given by ECGD to the financing bank to cover the risk of non-payment of principal or interest; and

(d) a premium agreement between the British supplier and ECGD.

11.1 EXAMPLES OF TRADE FINANCE INSTRUMENTS

Fig 11.1 A trade bill of exchange

```
                                   London 26 September 1986

Exchange for £200,000.00

At 30 days sight pay this sole bill of exchange
                to our order
the sum of two hundred thousands pounds sterling
value received which place to our account.


To    Bergems Import A/S
      Fisktorv 3
      Oslo
      Norway


                                   For & on behalf of
                                   UK Exports plc


                                   Authorised signatory
```

Fig 11.2 An ineligible bank bill of exchange

```
                                   London 25 September 1986

Exchange for US $ 150,00

At 60 days sight pay this sole bill of exchange
To the order of ourselves

The sum of United States dollars one hundred and fifty thousand only.
Value received.


To    The Royal Northern Bank plc
      100 Lombard Street
      London


                                   For & on behalf of
                                   UK Exports plc


                                   Authorised signatory
```

Fig 11.3 An eligible accepted bank bill of exchange

Drawn under credit No 48342 covering shipment of vehicles and spares from UK to Kuwait.

Exchange for £300,000.00   London 15 September 1986

At 90 days date pay this sole bill of exchange
                to our order

The sum of three hundred thousand pounds sterling
Value received.

To   UK Eligible Bank plc
      210 Lombard Street
      London

                                    For & on behalf of
                                    UK Exports plc

                                    Authorised signatory

Fig 11.4 A promissory note

MADRID 24TH DECEMBER 1985   US $ 123,457.78

On 24 DECEMBER 1985   for value received we promise to pay against this promissory note

to the order of KERRY EXPORTS LIMITED   the sum of

ONE HUNDRED AND TWENTY THREE THOUSAND FOUR HUNDRED AND FIFTY SEVEN AND 78/100 DOLLARS

effective payment to be made in   UNITED STATES DOLLARS   without deduction for

and free of any taxes, impost, levies or duties present or future of any nature

This promissory note is payable at BANCO DEL LLAMEDOS, MADRID

GINA ESPEDRILLES

AVENIDA COSTA DEL SOL

MADRID

ESPANA

CHAPTER 12

The role of financial futures

D. A. Ross and S. Taiyeb
Touche Ross

12.01 INTRODUCTION

Futures contracts are available not only for physical commodities like cocoa and silver but also for financial variables, such as interest rates and foreign exchange rates. In this chapter we will examine financial futures, where the contract is to buy or sell a financial instrument at a future date and where both the quantity and the price is fixed in advance. Although most of this material is relevant to financial futures generally, specific details will be considered with reference to contracts traded on the London International Financial Futures Exchange (LIFFE).

12.02 HISTORY OF THE FINANCIAL FUTURES MARKET

Financial futures have emerged out of economic necessity. Their dramatic growth can be related to the increased volatility of interest and exchange rates seen during the latter half of the 1970s and the early 1980s.

Figures 12.1 and 12.2 below show how volatile Eurodollar three-month interest rates and the $/£ exchange rate have become during the late 70s and early 80s. It is in response to the increased risks arising from such volatility that the financial futures markets have developed. This is because they allow corporations and other bodies to hedge their interest rate, exchange rate and stock market risks. They also allow traders to speculate in volatile instruments.

The first financial futures contracts in foreign currencies were traded on the International Monetary Market (IMM), a division of the Chicago Mercantile Exchanges, in 1972. These were followed in 1974 by a gold futures contract. In 1975 attention turned to interest rate futures with the introduction of the Government National Mortgage Association (GNMA) contract on the Chicago Board of Trade (CBOT). In 1976, this was followed by a three-month Treasury Bill contract on the IMM and by the CBOT's Treasury Bond contract in the following year. These three contracts proved particularly successful, and were joined by further futures contracts in US Treasury Notes, allowing trading to take place in a wide range of financial instruments with various maturities.

The remarkable growth of the Chicago exchanges led to the proposal in 1979 that a similar exchange should be created in London. Following a discussion document from a working party representing bankers, stockbrokers, commodity dealers, discount houses and money brokers, the Bank of England gave its

Fig 12.1 Three-month Eurodollar interest rates

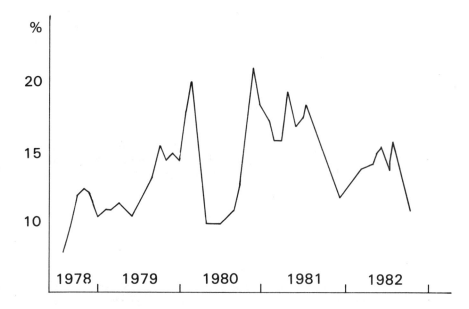

Fig 12.2 Dollar/sterling exchange rates

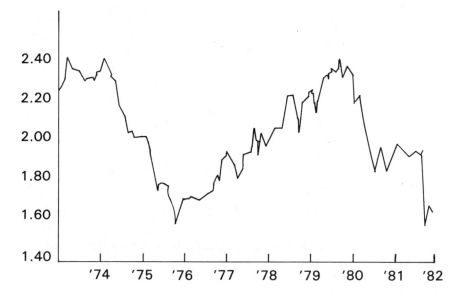

approval in early 1981 to the setting up of LIFFE (the London International Financial Futures Exchange). In September 1982 LIFFE commenced trading with three interest rate contracts and four foreign exchange rate contracts. The success of LIFFE is shown in Figure 12.3 below by the growth in the volume of trades. Figure 12.4 below shows the deepening of the underlying liquidity of the market as indicated by the increase in net open positions.

12.03 MARKET OPERATIONS

1 Nature of a futures contract

A financial futures contract is an agreement between a seller and a buyer to make and take delivery at a stated future date of a specified interest rate or currency commitment. Futures are similar to forward contracts in financial instruments. However, futures contracts differ from forward contracts in at least four respects:

(a) unlike the forward exchange markets, in which business is conducted by telephone and telex, financial futures contracts are traded exclusively by open outcry in designated 'pits' on the floor of the exchanges within specified trading hours. Even though orders are communicated to the floor by telephone and telex there are strict rules prohibiting 'kerb' trading;

(b) while it is possible, in the forward market, to deal for any reasonable amount and any reasonable future date, financial futures are standard contracts. They are for specific amounts to be delivered on a limited number of predetermined dates. This ensures that there can be no misunderstanding of what is being traded;

(c) all futures contracts are registered with a clearing house which then becomes the counterparty to each side of the transaction. In the case of LIFFE, it guarantees the performance of each transaction to the clearing member involved. An individual trader therefore has no need to concern himself with the credit standing of other traders. Once the guarantee is in place, the trader's risk is transferred to his clearing member and the clearing house; and

(d) only a tiny percentage (less than 2%) of financial futures contracts actually runs through to delivery. This is because market participants close out their positions once their objective has been met. A buyer closes out his position by making an offsetting sale of the same contract, whereas a seller makes an offsetting purchase. It is the ease of opening and closing positions that makes financial futures such a useful and flexible tool for managing risk.

2 Pricing of financial futures contracts

Here we will examine some categories of financial futures instruments traded on LIFFE: the short-term interest rate contracts; the long-term gilt interest rate contracts; and the foreign exchange contracts.

(a) Short-term interest rates

The short-term interest rate contracts are the three-month sterling and three-month Eurodollar interest rate contracts, which are both quoted on an index basis. That is, the price of a futures contract in the two instruments is always quoted as 100 minus the implied interest rate. This preserves the normal inverse relationship between prices and interest rates. The higher the implied interest

Fig 12.3 Average daily volume

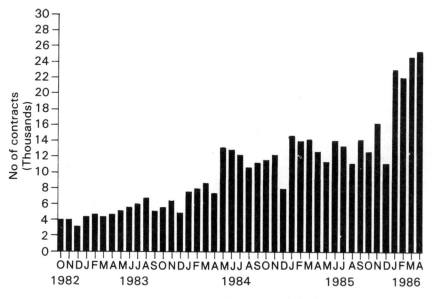

Fig 12.4 Total open interest

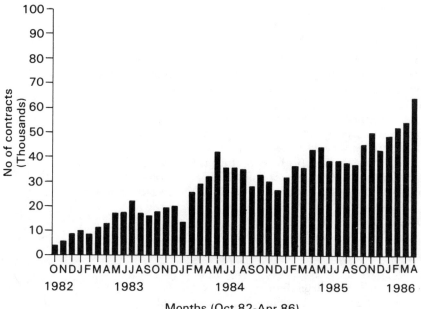

rate, the lower is the futures price. For example, one can lock in a 10% per annum rate of interest on a bank time deposit at some time in the future by purchasing a three-month contract at a price of 90.00 (100–10). If the price moves down to 89.50, the implied rate has risen to 10.50% (100–89.50).

Most of the exchanges define the minimum price movement of such contracts as one basis point. This may be called 'a tick', or one hundredth of 1% per annum of interest. LIFFE, as well as other exchanges, has also calculated for each tick its specific money value. The tick value is calculated as the tick size multiplied by the face value of the contract. The face value is $1 million for Eurodollar futures and £250,000 for sterling futures. The tick value is then calculated for one quarter of a year, as these are three-month instruments. For example:

Three-month Eurodollar interest rate Tick size = 0.01% of interest for three months
Value of tick = $25 (0.0001 × 3/12 × $1,000,000).

Three-month sterling interest rate Tick size = 0.01% of interest for three months
Value of tick = £6.25 (0.0001 × 3/12 × £250,000)

> Example:
>
> A trader buys 10 three-month sterling contracts at a price of 90.00. Five days later the position is closed by selling at 90.25.
>
> Profit = 10 contracts × 25 ticks profit ie (90.25–90) × £6.25 per tick
>
> Total profit = £1,562.50

(b) Long-term interest rates

Longer term futures contracts, such as the gilt contract on LIFFE, are quoted not on an index basis but on the same basis as gilts in the cash market, ie per £100 nominal value. The gilt contract on LIFFE is priced as a percentage of face value of a notional standard 12% coupon yield and 20-year maturity bond. For instance, suppose the market price of the LIFFE December gilt future was 99–16 on the 15 August. That is, the market is willing to pay £99 16/32 for £100 nominal of a 12% 20-year gilt for delivery in December.

The tick size for the LIFFE gilt contract is specified as £1/32 per £100 nominal. Once again the value of the tick is obtained by multiplying the tick size by the face value of the futures contracts. For the gilt future the face value is £50,000.

20-year gilt contract Tick size = 1/32 of 1 per cent
Value of tick = £15.625 (1/32 × 0.01 × £50,000).

> Example:
>
> A trader buys 10 gilt futures contracts at a price of 99–00. A month later the position is closed by selling at a price of 98–22.
>
> Loss = 10 contracts × 10 ticks loss ie (98–22 minus 99–00) × £15.625 per tick
>
> Total loss = £1,562.50.

(c) Foreign exchange contracts

Foreign exchange contracts are priced in terms of the underlying exchange rate. For dollar/sterling, the pricing system is similar to that in the ordinary foreign exchange forward market. The other LIFFE currency contracts, in yen, Deutschemarks, and Swiss francs, are quoted in terms of the number of dollars per unit of foreign currency, ie the reciprocal of the quotation used in the foreign exchange markets. Because of the very different values of the different currency units in terms of dollars, tick sizes differ between the different contracts. The tick value, however, is the same for all contracts of LIFFE except for sterling, as shown in table 12.1 below:

Table 12.1 Contracts against dollar

	Sterling	Deutschemarks	Yen	Swiss francs
Face value	£ 25,000	DM 125,000	Yen 12,500,000	SF 125,000
Tick size —				
0.01 cents per	£ 1	1 DM	100 yen	1 SF
Value of tick	$ 2.50	$ 12.50	$ 12.50	$ 12.50

A trader buys ten sterling-dollar contracts at a price of $1.4500. Ten days later the position is closed by selling at a price of $1.5000.

Example

Profit = ten contracts × 500 ticks ie ($1.5000 – $1.4500) × $2.50 per tick

Total profit = $12,500

(d) Summary

In all cases, the profit or loss on a financial futures market transaction is determined by multiplying the number of contracts by the number of ticks that the price has changed and by the tick value. In the futures market, the standard size of tick values makes it easy for market participants to calculate the cash change that results from a change in the futures price.

3 Price limits

Almost all futures contracts traded on an exchange are subject to daily price limits. These restrict the range of price movement which can take place in a day. Limits on price changes vary from one exchange to another. On virtually all US exchanges, when the daily price limit is reached in either direction, trading ceases for that trading day. On LIFFE, however, depending on the time of day, dealing may be suspended for only one hour. No price limit applies during the last hour of trading each day.

The aim of price limits is to ensure an orderly market and to limit uncontrolled speculation.

4 Commissions and transaction costs

On all the major exchanges trading financial futures, commissions are not fixed. The actual level of commission is therefore negotiated between individual clients and the broker or the member. It is, however, likely to be higher for non-members trading with a member of the exchange than it is between members.

There are, however, some general features of commissions on financial futures. Firstly, a commission will generally be quoted for a round turn; that is it covers both the opening and the closing of a position. It is normally payable when either the position is closed or delivery takes place. Second, levels of commissions are not influenced by the price of the underlying contracts. Third, reduced commissions are normally payable for day trades (when a position is opened and closed out on the same day), spread and straddle trades (see pp 193–194).

12.04 THE CLEARING HOUSE

1 The role of a clearing house

The mechanics of clearing-house operations on futures exchanges vary from market to market around the world. Every clearing house, however, performs certain crucial functions for an exchange. It carries out the function of matching and processing all trades. It registers and confirms all trades transacted on the market each day. It provides an up-to-date record, both centrally and for each clearing member, of the current position. Furthermore, once a contract is registered the clearing house becomes a party to every trade transacted. This is because it puts itself in the position of guaranteeing to clearing members the performance of every transaction entered into on the floor of the exchange. In effect, it substitutes itself for each counterparty and becomes the seller to every buyer and the buyer to every seller.

The clearing house also plays a crucial role in the delivery system. At delivery an outstanding long position has to be matched with a short position. It is the role of the clearing house to match these short and long positions according to specified rules.

For LIFFE, the clearing function is performed by the International Commodities Clearing House (ICCH), which is owned by the leading UK banks. It has experience of clearing futures transactions both in the UK and overseas. Only clearing members of the exchange are entitled to clear their transactions directly with ICCH.

A clearing member may be either an individual clearing member or a general clearing member. General clearing members have the right to clear other members' transactions as well as their own. Non-clearing members have to clear all their transactions through a general clearing member. In order to become a clearing member, certain conditions set by the exchange and the clearing house have to be satisfied, including a minimum net worth requirement.

Figure 12.5 below illustrates the roles of clearing and non-clearing members at LIFFE. Each member may either enter into transactions on his own account or, if he is a 'public order member', also on behalf of customers. By this arrangement participation on the exchange is extended to non-members.

Fig 12.5 Role of clearing and non-clearing members

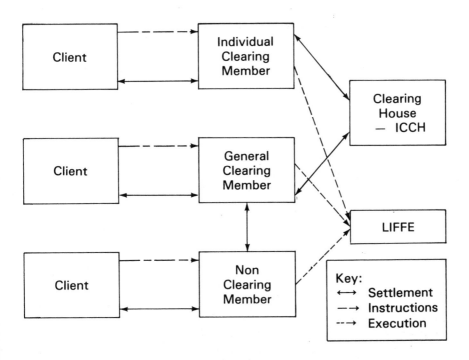

2 Margin requirements

In forward markets it is unusual for any money to change hands between the buyer and seller before the contract reaches maturity. In futures markets, however, the practice is very different. It is governed by a system of margins, the details of which are determined by the clearing house. The margin system has two components, initial margin and variation margin.

Let us deal with initial margin first. This margin provides protection to the clearing house in the event of a default. In such a case the clearing house could be forced to close out a member's positions at the current market prices. It might therefore sustain a loss, arising from changes in price during the current day's trading.

Thereafter, for as long as the contract remains open, it is 'marked to market' daily, that is each position is revalued daily based on the official settlement price for the previous day. Losses arising from this revaluation process must be paid to the clearing house also on a daily basis and profits, as and when they arise, can also be claimed daily. This daily flow of funds is termed 'variation margin'.

Example:

A client buys 10 Eurodollar contracts at a price of 90.00. On the second and third days for which the position remains open, the market first moves in his favour and then against him. The results can be summarised as follows:

	Settlement price	Initial margin	Variation margin	Net position
Day 1	90.00	$4,000	Nil	$ 4,000
Day 2	90.25	$4,000	$6,250cr	$10,250
Day 3	89.90	$4,000	$8,750dr	$ 1,500

On Day 1, as the settlement price is not different from the price at which the contracts are purchased, the only margin requirement is the initial margin of $400 per contract. On the following morning the purchaser has to lodge the $4,000 as initial margin. This sum will be placed with the clearing member.

On Day 2, the movement of 25 basis points in the client's favour gives rise to a profit of $6,250 (10 contracts × 25 ticks × $25 per tick), which is then credited to his equity account. The client, if he wishes, can withdraw this sum but in this instance this does not happen.

On Day 3, the market moves against the client's position by 35 basis points, giving a loss of $8,750. When this is debited, the residual balance is insufficient to satisfy the continuing initial margin requirement. A margin 'call' of $2,500 will have to be paid by the client on the morning of Day 4.

Although this system may appear a little cumbersome at first sight, in practice it provides safeguards for those using the market. It also has the advantage of paying profits as they accrue.

The initial margin varies for different instruments as shown in Table 12.2 below. These margins can also change from time to time.

Table 12.2 Initial Margin levels on LIFFE

	Margin requirements	
	Normal	Straddle
Three-month sterling interest rate	£1,000	£500
Three-month Eurodollar interest rate	$400	NIL
Long gilt future	£1,000	£250
Short gilt future	£1,000	£250
Currency futures	£1,000	$100
FT-SE Index future	£750	£250

Table 12.2 above also shows the margin requirements for a straddle position. A straddle position is defined as a simultaneous long and short position in different months of a single futures contract. Thus a typical straddle might be long June 1 three-month Eurodollar contract and short September 1 three-month Eurodollar contract. The initial margin on each pair of contracts is less than the initial margin on an outright position in a single contract. The reason for reduced margins is that the difference in price between the delivery months of a single contract is often less volatile than the absolute price for either month taken separately.

The rules on initial and variation margin payments apply only between the clearing members and the clearing house. Margin relationships, amounts and payments, between non-clearing members and a clearing member are technically negotiable, as are arrangements between clients and members of the exchange. Exchange rules, however, generally insist that such margins may not be less than the clearing member pays to the clearing house. Frequently a broker will insist on higher initial margin payments than are determined by the exchange and the clearing house.

12.05 USES OF FINANCIAL FUTURES

There are two main uses of financial futures, hedging and trading. Hedging reduces the risk of loss through adverse price movements in interest rates or currency rates. It is achieved by taking a position in futures contracts that is equal and opposite to an existing or anticipated position in the cash market. Everyone in the financial community is a potential user of financial futures to hedge their asset or liability positions. Hedging may be of benefit to banks, other financial institutions, pension funds, corporate treasurers and other city institutions.

Trading in financial futures is undertaken by those who are willing to assume price risk and hope to profit from the rises or falls they expect to occur in interest rates or exchange rates. Financial futures enable traders to take a view of the trend of rates, without actually having to buy or sell the underlying currency or financial instrument. Trading in financial futures is normally divided into three types:

(a) arbitrage, which is earning profits by taking advantage of temporary mispricing of cash instruments and futures contracts;
(b) spreading, which is taking a view on the evolution of the price differences between different futures prices;
(c) position trading, which is taking a view on absolute interest or exchange rate movements.

Both hedgers and traders are important to the financial futures markets. Traders provide liquidity to the market, allowing hedgers to buy or sell in volume without difficulty.

12.06 HEDGING WITH FINANCIAL FUTURES

The principles of hedging

The purpose of hedging is to neutralise a given cash market position against an adverse movement in interest or foreign exchange rates by transferring the risk from the hedger to someone else in the market. The hedger, therefore, is seeking to take a position in a related futures contract whose value will alter in an equal but opposite way to the instrument being hedged. By this action the hedger will 'lock-in' to current rates which are regarded as acceptable, but it should be remembered that, in so doing, he must be prepared to forego any 'windfall' gains if his perception of the likely movement of rates proves incorrect.

The principles of perfect hedging can best be illustrated by the following examples. The first example is of a typical long hedge. A long hedge in interest rates is used to obtain protection against exposure to interest rates falling or to protect the yield of a planned investment by purchasing futures contracts. The second example shows a typical short hedge. A short hedge is used to obtain protection against exposure to interest rates rising.

2 Example of a long hedge

A corporate treasurer may know in June that in three months time he will have £10m to invest for three months. Since he feels that interest rates may fall substantially during this period, he decides to 'lock in' to current yields. Futures contracts are therefore purchased to offset any movement of cash market prices before the purchase date. The effect of this hedge is shown in Table 12.3 below.

Table 12.3 Example of long hedge

Cash market	Date	Futures market
No transaction, interest rates on three-month time deposit of £10m is presently 10%. Gross interest income receivable = £250,000.	June 1	Buy 40 June three-month sterling interest rate contracts at 89.75 (interest rate 10.25%)
Invest £10m in a three-month time deposit at 7%. Gross income receivable = £175,000	Sep 1	Sell 40 June three-month sterling interest rate contracts at 92.75 (interest rate 7.25%).
Opportunity loss = £75,000		Profit on futures contracts = £75,000 (300 ticks × 40 contracts × £6.25)

This is a perfect long hedge, since the loss in income in the cash market of £75,000 is exactly offset by the gain in the futures market of £75,000.

3 Example of a short hedge

A firm has a £10m five-year loan at a 1% spread over the three-month sterling time deposit rate with three month rollovers. Since the treasurer believes that rates will rise by the next rollover date in two months' time, he decides to sell 40 futures contracts. The effect of this hedge is shown in Table 12.4 below.

Table 12.4 Example of a short hedge

Cash market	Date	Futures market
No transaction, current borrowing rate is 11% (10% + 1%) for £10m. Gross interest payable £275,000	March 1	Sell 40 June three-month sterling interest rate contracts at 89.50 (interest rate 10.50%).
Borrow £10m for three months at 13% (12% + 1%). Gross interest payable = £325,000	May 1	Buy 40 June three-month sterling interest rate contracts at 87.50 (interest rate 12.50%).
Increase in interest expense = £50,000		Profit on futures contracts = £50,000 (200 ticks × 40 contracts × £6.25)

This is another example of a perfect hedge. The firm's forecast of an interest rate increase was correct and it has to pay a further £50,000 in interest. This, however, has been compensated by a £50,000 profit in the futures market.

4 The basis risk

Hedging is not an exact science. Sometimes the hedger will face difficulties in calculating accurately the size of the exposure to be hedged. Furthermore it is only possible to deal in whole contracts. An exact balance between the two positions may be unobtainable. But the main reason why perfect hedges are not always achievable is 'basis' risk. The 'basis risk' is the difference between the cash and futures prices. This can vary considerably through time (see Figure 12.6 below.)

Fig 12.6 The relationship between yields in the cash and futures markets — the BASIS

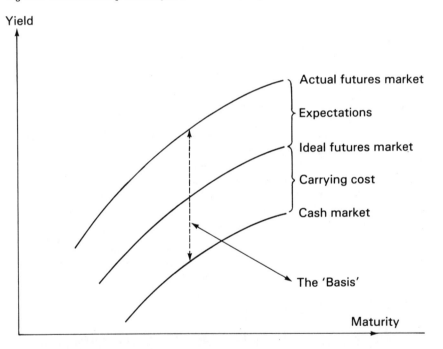

To illustrate the effect of a basis change, consider the short hedge example. On March 1 the basis was 50 points (futures price of 10.50% minus cash price of 10.0%). If the futures price on 1 May was 87.75 (interest rate of 12.25%) and the interest rate on the cash market was 12%, the basis would be reduced to 25 points (12.25% minus 12.00%), an implicit basis change of 25 points. The impact on the future gain would be to reduce the profit from 200 ticks to 175 ticks per contract. Profit on the futures contracts would be 40 × 175 × £6.25 or £43,750 instead of £50,000. This change in basis means that the futures gain covers only 87.5% of the cash market loss — an efficient but not a perfect hedge. If the basis had moved in the other direction, the firm would have made a 'windfall' profit.

5 Hedging in practice

(a) Analysing the exposure

Hedging involves a series of decisions which must be carefully evaluated in order to reduce risk effectively. For any hedger, the first step is to determine the size of his exposure. This must involve more than just considering the individual exposures which have to be hedged, since a company's finances may already contain natural hedges. If this is not done, what may appear to be a good hedging decision may in fact create a risky open position. Furthermore, in determining the net exposed balances the company must also take into account any additional future cash flows that may alter the exposure.

Having determined the net exposure for a given future period, the company then has to consider whether the risk is worth hedging. In order to do this, it must construct a probability distribution of expected future rates. The expected future interest rates along with the probability of rates, moving in an adverse direction, can then be determined. This information on rates can be combined with the net exposed balances to obtain the 'cash equivalent' of that risk.

The 'cash risk' figure can then be compared with the expected cost of hedging in order to determine whether the risk should be hedged. There are of course no hard-and-fast rules on when an exposure should be hedged. Any hedging decision should be related to the size of the firm, capital employed and the maximum percentage of shareholders' funds which management is prepared to allow to be exposed.

(b) Methods of hedging

If the firm concludes that the level of exposure is too high, it can hedge its exposure in a number of ways. First, it can alter maturity mismatches in the balance sheet and thereby increase the amount of natural hedge. It is, however, unlikely that any firm will be able to run a fully matched book at all times.

The second hedging alternative is to lock in borrowing and/or lending rates through the forward forward market. The yield curve of the cash market implies short-term interest rates at points in the future. Suppose that the current Eurodollar six-month interest rate is 8% and the three-month interest rate is 7.9%; then the three-month interest rate commencing in three months' time is determined as follows:

$$\left(\left[\left(\frac{\left[1 + \left(\frac{.08]}{2}\right)\right]}{\left[1 + \left(\frac{.079]}{4]}\right)\right]}\right) - 1\right] \times \left(\frac{360}{90}\right) = 0.794 \text{ or } 7.94 \text{ per cent}$$

The forward forward market is usually more advantageous to banks, because they can obtain the finest interest rates. For a non-banking corporation the futures market may be more advantageous.

The selection of a suitable hedging medium using financial futures is usually not as straightforward as it first appears, because the number of financial futures contracts presently available to hedge interest rate positions is still relatively small.

On LIFFE, the interest rate contracts are limited to two three-month instruments, and a 20-year long gilt instrument (15 to 25-year maturity). It is, however, possible to hedge one financial instrument with a futures contract on a different underlying instrument through a process known as 'cross-hedging'. But this exposes the hedger to another type of risk, since there is no guarantee that the interest rate on the two underlying instruments will move in line with each other. One way of overcoming this problem is to choose whichever futures contract has in the past proved most closely correlated with the instrument being hedged. It should always be remembered that the correlation can change through time and past correlations may not be good predictors of the future.

(c) Determining the hedge ratio

Once a suitable futures contract, which is highly correlated with the cash position and is suitably liquid, has been chosen, the next step is to determine the number of contracts required to produce a reliable hedge. In determining the number of contracts required, three factors should be considered. First, the face value of the contracts: for example, other things being equal one would need to purchase four sterling time deposit futures contracts each with a £250,000 face value to hedge £1 million of sterling CDs.

Second, since in constructing a hedge one is attempting to achieve 'money equivalency' between the two instruments, the hedge has to be weighted to allow for cash market maturities other than three months. For example, a movement of 0.01% in rates results in a cash movement of $25 for the three-month Eurodollar contract, but it would cause a change in value of $50 in a $1m six-month deposit.

Third, since the performance of a cross hedge will not be as satisfactory as a pure hedge, its performance can be improved by 'weighting' the hedge so that any difference in price movements between the futures contract and the instrument being hedged can be compensated. The number of contracts required to hedge a position in the cash market can therefore be weighted by the correlation co-efficient between the cash instrument and the futures price. If the correlation co-efficient between CDs and sterling three-month deposits is 1.15, this shows that on average a 1% move in sterling three-month deposit futures has been matched by a 1.15% move in sterling CDs. In order not to under-hedge it would be necessary to adjust the number of contracts bought by this co-efficient.

For example, a bank might wish to hedge an issue of £10m 90-day CDs in six months' time by selling LIFFE three-month sterling deposit futures contracts for a delivery month close to the date of the proposed issue. To find the right number of contracts to sell, it would not only divide the amount to be hedged (£10m) by the contract size (£250,000), but would also multiply the result (40) by the regression co-efficient (1.15) to adjust the hedge for the higher degree of risk associated with sterling CDs as compared with sterling three-month deposits. Therefore, instead of selling 40 contracts the bank would sell 46 contracts. If it was issuing 180 days CDs, the number of contracts would also need to be adjusted for money equivalency.

The above only applies to hedging with short-term futures contracts priced on an index basis. For a long-term futures contract like the 20-year 12% gilt a different approach is required. The problem of money equivalency does not apply here since these contracts are priced on the same basis as the cash market. However, the price of a particular instrument being hedged can move at a different rate, in response to an interest rate change, than the price of a standardised futures contracts being used to hedge it. Therefore the cash position should not always be hedged with an equal-valued futures position.

Instead, the conversion factor (this relates the settlement price of the standard long-term contract to *invoice* price for actual contracts at delivery) should be used to determine how many futures contracts to use in hedging. The number would be determined as follows:

$$\frac{\text{Face value of cash position}}{\text{Face value of futures contract}} \times \text{ conversion factor}$$

The gilt conversion factors are regularly published by LIFFE.

(d) Monitoring the hedge

Hedging can rarely be done exactly. Therefore, in order to achieve the best results, careful monitoring and periodic evaluation are required. Suitable systems will enable the hedger to keep a constant watch on both his cash and futures positions so that any adjustments which become necessary can be made.

6 Summary

In this section we have illustrated how hedging can be used to reduce absolute price risk. The success of the hedge will, however, depend on the degree of correlation between cash and futures, along with the accuracy of the basis forecast. Accurate basis forecasting will depend upon the hedger's knowledge of the seasonal and cyclical patterns of the different cash-futures relationships and the outlook in both the cash and futures markets.

Hedging cannot guarantee profits by correcting for poor management, unprofitable price levels, or a non-competitive price structure. It can, however, be effective in reducing risk. It allows a firm to budget for a certain return with a high degree of certainty whatever else happens to interest or exchange rates.

12.07 TRADING IN FINANCIAL FUTURES

Having discussed the techniques and strategies which can be adopted for hedging with financial futures we will now turn our attention to the other main use of futures contracts — trading. Traders are those investors who operate in the financial futures market in the hope that they can forecast movements in absolute or relative interest or foreign exchange rates better than the rest of the market. Traders generally, therefore, take on the interest or foreign exchange rate risk which hedgers are trying to off-load.

Traders are operating in volatile, high-risk instruments. The high leverage offered by financial futures markets means that big changes are possible in a trader's financial positions over very short periods of time. For example, if a trader wanted to set up a long position of $1m in Eurodollar time deposit rates, he could buy one futures contract on LIFFE and would be required to deposit only $1,000 as initial margin. If the future price were to rise by 50 basis points, he will show a profit of $1,250 (50 × $25 — the value of a point) or over 100% return on his original investment. However, if the rates had gone the other way, he would stand to lose over 100% of his original investment.

In this section we will discuss the various strategies that a trader may adopt along with how traders differ in their timing of futures market transactions.

1 Open position trading

Open position trading is taken on by those traders who take an overall view of interest rates moving in a certain direction. If a trader believes that interest rates are going to rise, which in turn implies that the futures prices will fall, he will sell the future now and buy it back after the futures prices have fallen, thus making a profit. Similarly, if he believes that interest rates are going to fall and as a result that futures prices will rise, he will establish a long position.

The following example shows the effect on a trader's position selling one three-month sterling interest rate contract at a price of 90.00 in the belief that interest rates will rise.

Example:

Day	Action	Futures price	Initial margin (£)	Variation margin (£)	Cumulative profit/loss (£)
1	Sell 1 contract	90.00	– 1000	—	—
2	Hold	90.25	—	– 156.25	– 156.25
3	Hold	89.95	—	+ 187.50	+ 31.25
4	Buy 1 contract	89.75	+ 1000	+ 125.00	+ 156.25

On Day 1 the trader had to deposit £1,000 as initial margin. At first, interest rates fell, thus pushing up futures prices, and the trader had to put up £156.25 variation margin. Thereafter futures prices fell and by Day 4 he was showing a 25 basis point profit, at which time he closed out his position by buying back a contract for the same period. He made a profit of £156.25 (25 × £6.25 per tick), which was paid to him along with the return of his initial margin of £1,000.

A trader may take an open position just before important economic statistics like money supply figures are announced. If the trader expects money supply figures to be higher than market expectations, he may open a short position in the hope that, if his assumptions are correct, interest rates will rise, prices will fall, and he will thus make a profit. This, however, can be very risky especially when government economic announcements are imminent. If the figures are contrary to the trader's expectations, he may suffer losses. One way of containing such losses is to use stop loss orders. These are discussed later in this section.

2 Spread trading

Spread trading, which is a less risky trading strategy, is often used by traders. This involves taking a view of the relationship between two different futures prices. A spread is defined as the purchase of one and the simultaneous sale of a different, but related, futures instrument.

The following example shows how the size of a spread can change on a three-month sterling contract.

Example:

Day 1   December futures price 90.00
March futures price 89.00
Spread = 90.00 – 89.00 = 100 basis points or ticks.

Day 2   December futures price 89.00
March futures price 87.75
Spread = 89.00 – 87.75 = 125 basis points or ticks.

Suppose in the above example a trader bought the December contract and sold the March contract. This is termed buying the spread. The profit effect would be as follows:

Day 1	Buy one December contract at 90.00	Sell one March contract at 89.00
Day 2	Sell one December contract at 89.00	buy one March contract at 87.75
Gain/Loss	Loss 100 ticks	Gain 125 ticks.

Net gain = 25 ticks × £6.25 = £156.25

If the trader had sold the December and bought the March futures contracts, he would have sold the spread and consequently lost money on that trade.

(a) Intra-contract spreading

Intra-contract spreading, known on LIFFE as straddle trading, involves the simultaneous purchase and sale of the same futures contract on the same exchange but for different maturities. The spread trader is interested only in the relationship between the two futures prices and not in the overall movement of interest rates.

(b) Inter-contract spreading

Inter-contract spreading is more complex, because it involves the simultaneous purchase and sale of futures contracts written on different underlying financial instruments on either the same or different futures exchanges. For example, an inter-contract spread on LIFFE might involve buying the December three-month sterling interest rate contract and selling the March three-month Euro-dollar interest rate contract. An inter-contract spread on different exchanges might involve buying a June three-month Eurodollar interest rate contract on LIFFE and selling a June domestic CD contract of the same maturity on the IMM in Chicago.

One of the complexities involved in inter-contract spreading is taking account of exchange rate movements. Let us consider the first spread mentioned above: a three-month sterling/Eurodollar contract spread on LIFFE. Even if a trader's prediction on the spread was right, his profit would be open to exchange rate movements since his profit/loss on the Eurodollar side would be denominated in dollars, while the profit/loss on the other side would be in sterling. The second spread mentioned does not, however, involve any currency risk.

3 Time scale of trading

Two types of trading have been discussed so far, open position and spread trading. Trading, however, can also be classified by the timescale of its operations. Normally three such scales are recognised.

Scalping	Scalpers hope to profit over very short periods of time by constantly trying to exploit the market. They will therefore trade the market constantly. They are a major source of liquidity in the futures markets.
Day trading	Day traders are involved in all aspects of trading but will not allow their position to remain open overnight. In this way they avoid the danger of large swings in prices between one day's close and next day's opening, but at the same time they cannot fully benefit from spread trading, because anomalies between futures prices may take days or weeks to take effect.
Longer-term trading	Longer-term traders are traders who hold open positions for as long as it is required to obtain sufficient profits or until their maximum acceptable loss limit has been reached.

12.08 CONCLUSION

In recent years, financial futures contracts have proved to be highly successful, with trading expanding rapidly. The growth in this market is the direct result of its ability to transfer risks from those who are unable or unwilling to bear them (hedgers) to those who are willing to do so in the hope of making a profit (traders). The futures market, therefore, allows the treasurer or the trader to exercise his view on the future level of interest rates and exchange rates. If the treasurer feels exposed to an unacceptable level of risk, he can protect his position in the cash market by taking an opposite action in the futures market. Conversely, if a dealer has a view on rates, he can act in the futures market, and if his views are proved to be correct, he will profit by his actions.

The benefits provided by financial futures can be summarised as follows:

(a) they are a flexible and inexpensive protection against the risks associated with changes in interest rates, exchange rates and stock prices;
(b) price quotations are competitive and transaction costs low;
(c) if necessary hedgers and traders may close out their positions quickly; and
(d) one can buy and sell contracts without ever owning the underlying security.

CHAPTER 13

The role of currency options

D. A. Ross and S. Taiyeb
Touche Ross

13.01 INTRODUCTION

Options are not new. A crude form of option trading in olive presses existed before 400 BC. In Amsterdam, in the early seventeenth century, a market existed in options on tulip bulbs. London, in the early eighteenth century, saw the development of options on securities. It was only in the post-Second World War bull market, however, that any real growth in stock options was seen. This culminated in the establishment of the Chicago Board Options Exchange in 1973 to trade US stock options.

Currency options are an adaptation of established stock options. The recent growth in currency options can be attributed to two factors: increased exchange rate volatility and the growth of international trade. Prior to 1971, exchange rates were not as variable as they are now. At the Bretton Woods conference in 1944, the industrial nations agreed to have their central banks buy and sell dollars to keep exchange rate movements within fairly narrow bands. With the failure of this system in 1971, most major currencies began to float with market forces. As a result, exchange rates have become much more volatile. For example, the average monthly range of fluctuation of the Deutschemark against the US dollar widened from 0.44 cents over the 1959 to 1971 period to 5.66 cents over the 1971 to 1982 period, a more than 12-fold increase.

At the same time as exchange rates were becoming more volatile, trade in goods and services between countries began to grow dramatically. This combination of volatile exchange rates and growing trade meant that more and more treasurers were looking for ways to hedge their foreign currency risk. It was to meet this need that exchanges and banks began to offer currency options.

13.02 THE NATURE OF CURRENCY OPTIONS

An option is a contract that gives its holder the right, but not the obligation, to buy or sell an asset on a future date at a specified price. Listed below are the definitions of the terms which are most commonly used in the options market.

Buyer A buyer of an option buys the right but not the obligation to buy or sell a currency. He pays a premium.

196

Seller A seller of an option grants the right to a counterparty to buy or sell foreign currency. He receives the premium.

Call option An option where the buyer has the right to buy the foreign currency.

Put option An option where the buyer has the right to sell the foreign currency.

Maturity This is the specified expiry date for the option contract. An option which can be exercised only on the expiry date is known as a 'European' option, while an option which can be exercised at any time up to the maturity date is known as an 'American' option.

Strike price This is the agreed exchange rate at which the option holder can buy or sell the foreign currency.

Since call or put options may be bought or sold, four basic trading strategies are possible. These strategies, along with the maximum profit or loss for each strategy, are shown in Table 13.1.

Table 13.1   Four basic trading strategies

		Maximum	
Strategy		*Profit*	*Loss*
(a)	Buy a call, ie obtain the right to buy a foreign currency	Unlimited	Premium paid
(b)	Sell a call, ie undertake to sell the foreign currency at the option buyer's request	Premium received	Unlimited
(c)	Buy a put, ie obtain the right to sell a foreign currency	Strike price	Premium paid
(d)	Sell a put, ie undertake to buy the foreign currency at the buyer's request	Premium received	Strike price

Each of the above positions has a different risk/reward profile. Why anyone should choose any particular strategy is explained in section 13.06 below.

13.03 OPTIONS, FORWARDS AND FUTURES

Currency options can be used just like an insurance policy against movements in exchange rates. In this respect they are an alternative to using the futures market or buying forward cover in the foreign exchange markets. There is, however, one crucial difference between these instruments. Whereas the option holder has the right but not the obligation to exercise his contract, forward or futures contracts are firm commitments to buy or sell an asset at a fixed price at a future date. Once forward or futures contracts are made, they must be fulfilled whether prices have moved favourably or not.

An option, therefore, provides protection against downside risk in the same way as a forward contract, but unlike a forward contract it retains the upside potential. This is because there is no obligation to exercise the option. This is the main advantage of options and is illustrated in Figures 13.1, 13.2 and 13.3 below.

Fig 13.1 The forward market

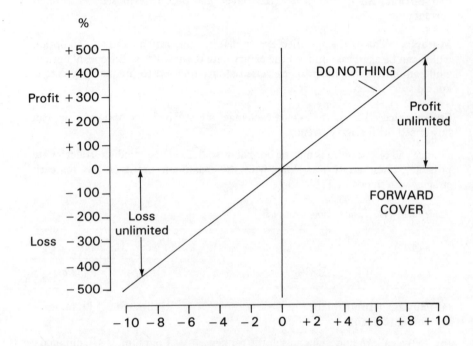

Per cent change in exchange rate at maturity

Figure 13.1 above shows the profit/loss associated with a forward cover contract compared with doing nothing. At maturity the hedger is protected from any adverse changes to the currency but he cannot benefit from any favourable movement in the exchange rate.

Figures 13.2 and 13.3 below show that by buying an option the hedger has the right to buy or to sell a currency at a specific price at a certain date. The loss to the hedger compared with the forward market is limited to the premium paid but the profit opportunity is unlimited.

The other main advantages of options are as follows:

(a)   the option buyer knows at the outset what the 'worst case' will be. Once the premium is paid, no further cash is payable. When the main objective is simply to limit downside risk, this is a powerful advantage. In many commercial applications, the option premium can be built into the pricing process, thus fixing minimum profit margins;

(b)   since there is no obligation to exercise an option, options are ideal for hedging contingent cash flows which may or may not materialise, such as tenders;

(c)   options provide a very flexible means of currency cover, offering a range of strike prices, whereas forward and futures markets only deal at the forward price existing now;

Fig 13.2 Buying a call option

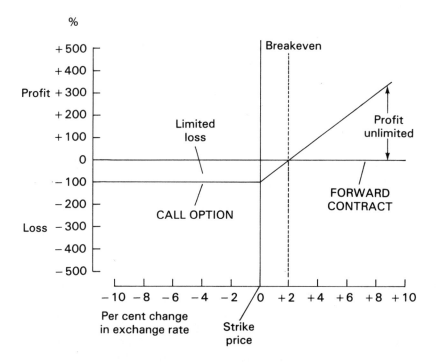

Fig 13.3 Buying a put option

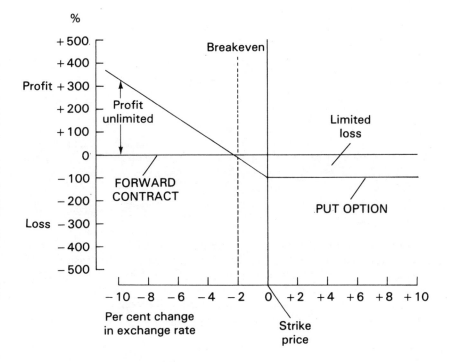

(d) options provide another possibility in the range of tools available to treasurers and traders. They can be used alone to achieve types of cover not otherwise available, and they can be used in conjunction with the forward and futures markets to achieve more complex hedges; and

(e) futures require daily margins to cover credit risk, while forwards require a credit line from a bank. An option buyer needs neither.

13.04 EXCHANGE TRADED AND OVER-THE-COUNTER (OTC) OPTIONS

Despite the advantages that currency options have over forward and futures contracts, no major market existed for these options until the European Option Exchange (Amsterdam), the Montreal Exchange and the Philadelphia Stock Exchange began trading in currency options in late 1982. Once currency options were established on these exchanges the banks began to offer similar services, thus creating an OTC market. Exchanges and banks, however, have different kinds of option contracts and trading procedures. These are discussed below.

1 Exchange traded options

Options on the exchange are dealt on the floor of the exchange in designated 'pits'. The method of matching buyers and sellers is by open outcry. Most of the options are American style with standard trading units and expiry dates. Contract standardisation helps to reduce the number of dimensions over which buyers and sellers must agree. Some flexibility is lost as a result, but standardisation is necessary for trading in a central place like an exchange. It would be an administrative nightmare to match customers with wide-ranging requirements of quantity and maturity.

All organised exchanges are affiliated with a clearing house, which is not only responsible for clearing trades on the exchange but actually places itself between buyers and sellers. In effect each party has a contract with the clearing house, which guarantees all contracts. To protect itself from losses, the clearing house requires that a security deposit, known as margin, be lodged by the party writing the option. The exchanges have, therefore, with the aid of the clearing corporation guarantee, created an instrument which people can trade without worrying about each others' creditworthiness.

Options on LIFFE and currency options on the London Stock Exchange are cleared and guaranteed by the International Commodities and Clearing House (ICCH). Options on the Philadelphia Stock Exchange are cleared and guaranteed by the Options Clearing Corporation (OCC). In Montreal and Amsterdam this function is provided by the International Option Clearing House (IOCH).

2 OTC options

OTC options are provided by a large number of international banks. Banks, however, do not provide trading floors for the exchange of orders. Instead, they quote prices directly to customers, usually by telephone. Since the customer who buys an option from a bank usually has a long-standing relationship with that bank, the customer has little concern that the bank will default on the option.

Options offered by banks, which can be either American or European style, are usually individually written. Banks tailor the contracts to the specific currency, quantity and maturity needs of each customer.

Banks sometimes reduce the risks they incur from selling OTC options by buying back a similar option on an exchange. When banks completely offset their option sales in this way, they are acting middlemen between customers and the ultimate sellers of the contracts.

3 Exchange traded v OTC

We have seen that the characteristics of the two option markets are substantially different. Summarised below is a list of advantages and disadvantages for each market:

(a) whereas OTC options are available in a large number of currencies, exchange traded options are only available in a limited number of currencies, albeit the main trading ones;

(b) OTC options are available in cross-currencies, i e between currencies other than the US dollar;

(c) OTC options are readily available for any exercise date up to one year and are also available beyond that period. Exchange traded options are normally only available for three-, six- and nine-month periods;

(d) OTC option prices are determined by the banks, whereas exchange traded option prices are determined by the market. As a result, in the exchanges the option price is basically the same regardless of the financial strength of the buyer. An individual can obtain the same price as the large corporate buyer;

(e) OTC options are often better suited for very large transactions, which may be difficult to place on certain exchanges;

(f) OTC option deals are not dependent on waiting for the market to open; and

(g) exchange traded options, because of their uniformity, are freely marketable, as opposed to OTC options, which are less easily saleable.

In summary, OTC options provide the better fit associated with a tailor-made article, but are not as marketable as an exchange traded option.

13.05 PRICING OF CURRENCY OPTIONS

The variables determining the price of a currency option can best be examined by breaking them into two major components:

(a) the intrinsic value of an option; and

(b) the time value of an option.

1 Intrinsic value

Intrinsic value is the amount an option is worth if it is exercised or converted into the underlying currency. It is, therefore, a function of the strike price of an option and the prevailing spot price of the currency.

A call option — the right to buy the foreign currency at the strike price for a limited period of time — has an intrinsic value only if the spot price is higher than the strike price. If a sterling call option were bought, say at strike price of $1.40 per £1, and if the present spot price was $1.50 per £1, the option would have an intrinsic value of 10 cents per £1. If it were exercised, the buyer would buy sterling at $1.40 and could sell it in the spot market at $1.50 and make a profit of 10 cents per £1. The net profit would, however, be reduced by the premium paid for the option.

A put option — the right to sell the foreign currency at the strike price — is worthless if the spot price is higher than the strike price. For a put option to have an intrinsic value the spot price has to be lower than the strike price. If, for example, a sterling put option were bought at $1.40 and, the spot price was $1.50, the buyer of the option would not exercise his option since he could get dollars at $1.50 per £1 in the spot market. If, however, the spot price was $1.35, the option would have an intrinsic value of 5 cents per £1. By exercising the option the buyer· could get $1.40 per £1 rather than $1.35 in the spot market.

When an option has an intrinsic value it is said to be 'in-the-money'. Options which are 'at-the-money' have a strike price equal to the spot price. 'Out-of-the-money' options (strike price less than spot price for call options and strike price greater than spot price for put options) have no intrinsic value.

2 Time value

Time value is the value of the option that reflects the possibility that the price of the underlying currency may change during the life of the option.

Fig 13.4 Call option intrinsic value

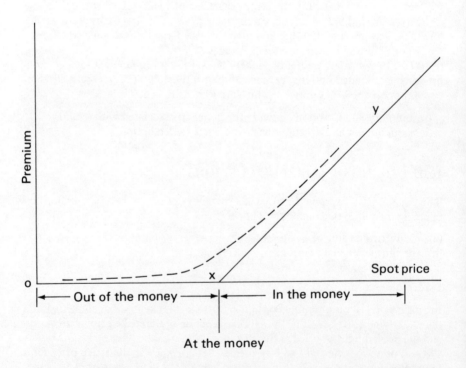

The time value is the difference between the option premium and its intrinsic value. Time value, which cannot be negative, is represented for a call option in Fig 13.4 above by the vertical distance between the intrinsic value boundary, OXY, and the broken line showing the premium at each spot price. The exercise price is X. At spot prices below X there is no intrinsic value, and hence the intrinsic value boundary line coincides with the horizontal axis. Above X intrinsic value increases almost cent for cent with the spot price of sterling, so the intrinsic boundary line slopes upwards at nearly 45 degrees from point X. This intrinsic value boundary sets limits to the value of the premium, which cannot fall below the boundary.

Figure 13.5 illustrates, in a similar fashion, the case of a put option. Again the exercise price is X.

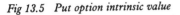
Fig 13.5 Put option intrinsic value

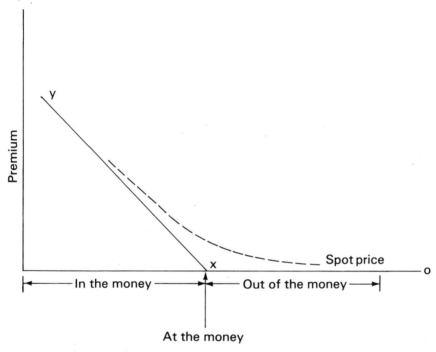

Time value is often misinterpreted as being solely a function of the time until the option expires. It is important to recognise that the time value includes the effects of other variables which can influence an option's price before it expires. The most significant of these variables are:

(a) time to maturity;
(b) interest rate;
(c) spot rate movements; and
(d) volatility.

In the discussion which follows we will consider each of these factors individually, each time assuming for simplicity that all the other factors remain constant.

Time to maturity

The longer the life of an option, the greater the time value. Let us consider two options which are identical except for their maturity dates. The holder of the option with the longer maturity date has all the benefits of the holder of the option with the shorter maturity date, but he can exercise his rights for a longer time. Therefore the price of the option with the longer maturity is usually higher.

(b) Interest rates

The time value of an option will change if the interest rate differential between the two currencies changes and other variables remain constant. An increase in domestic rates tends to push call prices up (and put prices down). A rise in foreign rates tends to push call prices down (and put prices up). In order to understand why, for example, the price of a call option should rise as domestic interest rates. rise, assuming the spot rates remain static, let us examine the cost of holding the underlying currency as an alternative to holding the call option. An increase in domestic interest rates will raise the 'cost of carry' of the underlying currency. The cost of carrying the underlying currency is the difference between the domestic and the foreign interest rates. The investor, instead of holding the call option, can borrow at the domestic interest rate to buy the foreign currency and then earn the foreign interest rate while holding it. Any increase in the domestic interest rate will lead to an increase in the cost of carry, thereby making the call option more attractive to the investor. This will lead to higher call option prices. Similarly any decrease in the domestic interest rate will push down call option prices.

The effects of interest rates on a put option price are the opposite of those on calls and are illustrated in Figure 13.6 below.

Fig 13.6 Interest rates effect on option prices

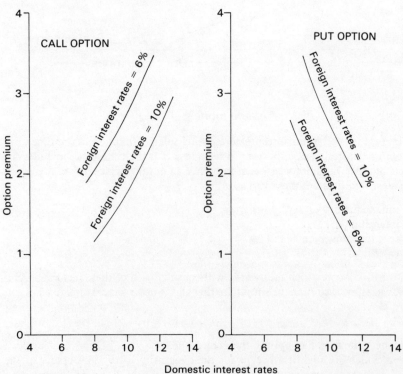

(c) Spot rate movements

The extent of the effect on an option price of a change in the spot price depends on the position of the spot price relative to the strike price. For deep out-of-the-money options the cost effect of a change in the spot price on the option price is relatively small. For deep in-the-money options the effect is almost 100% of the spot price movement. This relationship between the change in spot price and the change in option price is referred to as the hedge ratio or the 'delta' of the option. It represents the change in the option price for a one unit change in the spot price. The ratio changes continuously and only has integrity as a method of hedging options written (short positions) for marginal changes in prices. The reason the ratio can be used as a hedging method is that it shows the amount of the underlying currency an investor needs to hold to match the risk of a short call option position. This is shown in Fig 13.7 below.

Fig 13.7 Effect of spot rate movements on option price

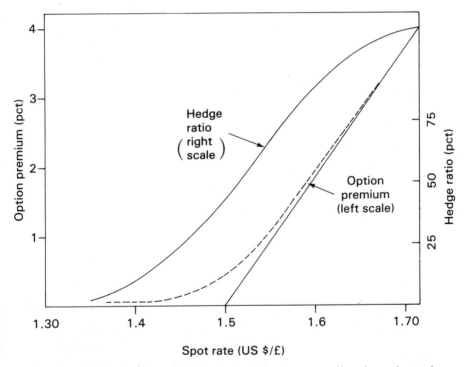

Spot rate (US $/£)

Let us consider the effect of spot price movements on a call option price under the following scenarios:

Scenario 1: Spot price $1.50, option strike price $1.60. The option is far out-of-the-money and as a result the delta is about 15%. Thus a 1 cent increase in the spot price will increase the option price by 0.15 cents.

Scenario 2: Spot price $1.50, option strike price $1.50. The option is at-the-money and the delta is therefore 50%. A 1 cent increase in the spot price will therefore increase the option price by 0.5 cents. This scenario is illustrated in Figure 13.7 above.

Scenario 3: Spot price $1.50, option strike price $1.40. The option is therefore deep-in-the-money with a hedge ratio of about 90%. Every 1 cent increase in the spot rate will push the option price up by 0.9 cents.

The largest portion of the price of a deep-in-the-money option is its intrinsic value. When the spot price increases the intrinsic value rises by the same amount; this dominates the increase in the option price and results in high hedge ratios. The behaviour of put option prices is similar.

It is important to stress that a given hedge ratio is applicable only at a specified spot and strike price. Furthermore, it is valid only for small price changes. At each new price the hedge ratio must be recalculated, and for a riskless net position to be maintained the underlying instrument position (spot or forward) must be adjusted.

(d) Volatility

Volatility is the annualised statistical measure of the degree of day-to-day fluctuations of the underlying exchange rate. It is one of the most significant variables influencing the time value of an option. Evaluations of volatility determine the likelihood that an option will become valuable and therefore exercised.

An option purchased on a stable currency (low volatility) will cost less than an option purchased on a currency whose rate changes frequently (high volatility). An option writer will demand to be paid more for an option with high volatility because of the increased probability of early exercise. Any increase in volatility will increase an option's time value, while a decrease in volatility will reduce an option's time value.

(e) Summary

In summary, during its life, an option will be worth the sum of its time value and its intrinsic value. At expiry, an option will be worth only its intrinsic value. The time value is therefore a wasting asset, since it declines to zero at expiry. The effect of a change in each variable, holding other variables constant, on the price of a call and a put option is summarised below:

Increase in variable	Effect on call option price	Effect on put option price
Time to expiry	Increase	Increase
Domestic interest rate	Increase	Decrease
Foreign interest rate	Decrease	Increase
Spot price	Increase	Decrease
Volatility	Increase	Increase

3 Currency option pricing models

In any discussion of option pricing it is important to distinguish between the option premium and the theoretical or 'fair' value of an option. So far we have referred to the option premium, which is the price an option buyer and seller agree to when they enter into a contract. It is therefore determined by demand and supply.

The fair value of an option, however, is derived from a mathematical model and depends on the accuracy of the data as well as the integrity of the model. It is the price at which buyers and sellers should expect to break even. It is, therefore, an estimate of what an option should sell for but not necessarily what it will sell for.

For most option traders and investors, fair value is the starting point in deciding whether the market price of an option is over- or underpriced. In trying to calculate the fair price of an option, standard option pricing formulae, developed in recent years, are used. The seminal work on theoretical option values was done in 1973 by Fischer Black and Myron Scholes. Their model, which is often known as the 'Black-Scholes' model, was originally developed for European style non-dividend paying stock options. They demonstrated that, under certain assumptions, it is possible to set up a perfectly hedged or riskless position, consisting of a long position in an underlying stock and a short position in options on that stock or vice versa, such that any profit resulting from the stock holding would be exactly offset by the loss on the option position and vice versa. The option premium at this equilibrium position is the fair value of the option.

The Black-Scholes model has been the foundation for most other option valuation models that have subsequently been developed. The model was first adjusted for stock options with dividends. Then Mark Garman and Steven Kohlhagen adapted the Black-Scholes model for options on foreign currencies. This model included the effect of interest rate differentials. Since the Black-Scholes model applies to European style options, it is not accurate for pricing American style options. Cox and Rubenstein therefore introduced the Binomial model, which is an approximation of the Black-Scholes model that allows for American style options.

The fair value of a currency option is a function of:

— Put or call
— Strike price
— Spot rate
— Domestic interest rates
— Foreign interest rates
— Time to expiry
— Expected volatility

Six of these seven variables are observable. The only variable which cannot be observed is the expected volatility of the underlying currency price. Even though it is easy to calculate the historic volatility of the underlying currency, it will not necessarily be a good predictor of the future. Expected volatility, therefore, is a matter of judgment.

One way of determining expected volatility is to look to the option market prices of exchange traded options. Using the market price of such an option we can determine, by iterative solution, the value of volatility that will cause the option model to yield a fair value equal to the observed market price. This is called the implied volatility, because it is the expected volatility implied by the market option price. Even though this is only a subjective measure, being governed by market factors such as sentiment, it is a useful guide.

For example, let us assume that the annualised volatility of the sterling/US dollar exchange rate was 15% over the past three months. If the implied volatility is 25%, we may consider the option to be over-priced. However, if we expect the volatility to be 40% over the next three months, the option is underpriced. In any case, implied volatility is a measure by which to judge option prices.

13.06 PRACTICAL USES OF CURRENCY OPTIONS

Having described what options are and how they are priced, we will now look at a few practical uses of currency options that are appropriate for corporate financial management.

1 Buying a call option

The first technique considered here is buying a call option in home or base currency to hedge a foreign currency receivable. The buyer of the option will have the benefit of hedging the risk, while leaving open the opportunity for overall profit improvement in the event of a rise in the foreign currency.

To illustrate the way this technique works, let us assume that a German exporter has a $5m receivable due in three months' time. The present spot exchange rate is DM 2.02 and the three-month forward rate is DM 2.005. The exporter is concerned about a decline in the US dollar but at the same time wants to benefit from any Deutschemark weakness. He therefore decides to buy a three-month Deutschemark call option at a strike price of DM 2.005 at a cost of 2.5% on a principal value of $5m for a total premium of $125,000 (.025 × $5m) or DM 252,500.

The effect of this strategy can best be illustrated by considering the results at expiry at various DM spot rates — DM 1.80, DM 2.005 and DM 2.20.

DM 1.80   If the spot rate at expiry is DM 1.80, the investor will exercise his call option and buy DM and sell US dollars at 2.005. The gross saving from having used the option in this case will be DM 0.205 per dollar (2.005–1.80) or a total of DM 1,025,000. The net savings after including the cost of the option will be DM 772,500. If he had hedged his receivable in the forward market (at DM 2.005), his savings would have been DM 1,025,000 since there is no cost involved in the forward market.

DM 2.005   If the spot rate at expiry is the same as the strike rate, the investor will not incur any exchange losses and the option will expire worthless. He will, however, incur the cost of the option premium of DM 252,500. This is the maximum an option buyer can lose and so represents a known risk at the time of the option purchase.

DM 2.20   Finally, if the spot rate at expiry is DM 2.20, the option buyer will not exercise his option. He will therefore lose the option premium of DM 252,500. However, because the investor will now be able to sell his US dollars and buy DMs at DM 2.20, he will benefit against the forward rate by DM 0.195 (DM 2.20 — DM2.005). The gross currency profit will be DM 975,000. The net profit including the cost of the option will be DM 722,500. Thus in this case, even though the cost of the option is lost, he profits from a beneficial move in the currency. This would not have been possible through a forward cover contract.

Figure 13.8 below illustrates the profit/loss at the various spot rates at expiry compared with the forward market.

2 Buying a put option

The second technique is the use of options to protect a currency declining against the dollar. In this case, the investor would buy a put on the currency. This would give him the benefit of a hedge against a fall in the currency while allowing him

Fig 13.8 *Profit/loss profile of buying DM call option*

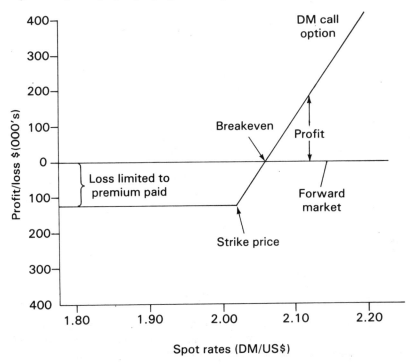

the opportunity of profiting from a rise in the currency. The fundamentals of put buying are almost identical to those of call buying, since the put option is a mirror image of the call option.

Again to illustrate the features of using an option compared with a forward or futures contract, let us assume a US exporter has a £10m sterling receivable in six months' time. The current exchange rate is $1.50 and the exporter buys a £10m sterling put option for expiry in six months at a strike price of $1.47 (the same as the six-month forward rate) for a premium of 4%. As in the last example, let us consider the effect of this strategy at various sterling spot prices at expiry:

$1.80 If the spot rate at expiry is $1.30, the company will exercise the option and get $1.47 for every pound sterling. The profit, however, will be less than would have been made by selling the sterling forward in the forward market. This is because the company has paid 4% to buy the right to sell sterling at $1.47. In the forward market there would have been no cost, since the forward rate was also $1.47.

$1.50 If the exchange rate is $1.50, the company will not exercise its option. It will instead sell sterling in the open market at $1.60. If it had used the forward or futures market, the company would have been locked into $1.47. It would not have profited from the rise in sterling.

3 Writing covered call options

Having evaluated the various option buying techniques, let us now consider option writing. The objective in this case is to generate extra income on a long currency position by writing a 'covered call option'. This strategy will afford the writer the benefit of extra income, although he assumes an opportunity risk.

Example:

An investor is long £1m in a bank deposit account. He purchased the sterling at a rate of $1.48. The current spot rate is also $1.48.

In order to generate extra income on his bank deposit, the investor sells a pound sterling six months' call option at a strike price of $1.50 for a premium of 4%. If at expiry the exchange rate is below $1.50, the option holder who has the right to buy dollars will not exercise his right and the option writer will keep the 4% premium. This represents additional income over the bank deposit rate.

If the pound is above $1.50, the investor will again keep the premium, but in this case the option will be exercised against him. The investor will have to sell £1m at a rate of $1.50. If the exchange rate is above $1.50 plus the 4% premium received, that is above a rate of $1.56, the investor will have missed an opportunity for capital gains because of having written the option.

4 Currency options for corporate exposure management — a case study

The following case study illustrates the use of currency options by a multinational corporation. It shows how this corporation successfully used options together with the traditional foreign exchange forward market to hedge its exposures.

Organisation

This US-owned multinational corporation has manufacturing companies in the UK, Germany and Spain. Its parent treats the European operations as a profit centre. It has set up a Head Office organisation in the UK to co-ordinate the European activities. The European treasurer is responsible for managing over £700m of cash, and has a diverse portfolio of foreign currency exposures including £4b of currency purchases a year.

Management of exposure

During the late 1970s the group was earning over £1b a year and there was little pressure to manage foreign currency exposures. Profits or losses from exchange rate fluctuations could easily be absorbed by the group. In the early 1980s, however, profitability declined owing to the sharp downturn of the world economy and increased competitive pressure in the industry. A 10% strengthening of the Deutschemark in 1981 would have reduced the group's profits by over 60%. An exposure management team was therefore set up to manage the risk.

Types of exposure

Of the various types of exposure, the main one arises from operating transactions. These dwarf the balance sheet translation exposure risk. Operating exposure is the risk to future cash flow of changes in exchange rates. The group knows the short-term net operating exposure accurately, because it has systems which analyse the costs and revenue by currency of each type of product which is produced in Europe. The net operating exposure that results from the pattern of trade between countries where goods are produced and countries where they are sold is short Deutschemarks and pesetas and long other European currencies, particularly sterling. In the longer term it is unlikely that the net operating position will change dramatically, since the manufacturing bases cannot be changed in response to currency movements. Net worth exposure is managed by the US parent.

Objective

The main objective of the exposure management team is to reduce the group's foreign currency risks, provided that the cost of doing so is not excessive. In deciding whether to cover the risk the team compares the forward rates with budget rates and the corporation's latest forecast of exchange rates. The general guideline, however, in determining the proportion of individual exposure to hedge is as follows:

Criteria	Exposure Hedged %
Forward rates worse than budget rates by over 1%	Uncovered
Forward rates worse than budget rates by less than 1%	Up to 25%
Forward rates equal to or better than budget	Up to 50%
Forward rates better than budget rate by over 2%	Up to 75%

Hedging techniques

The main technique used for hedging currency exposures is the forward market in preference to currency options. The reasons are:

(a) Size Individual exposures run into hundreds of millions of dollars and it is not possible to hedge many of these in the options market.

(b) Availability Currency options, both exchange traded and OTC, are available only for the major currencies. Sometimes only OTC options are available for certain cross-currencies. Since the operating exposure of the European operations is mainly on a cross-currency basis, it is not possible for the corporation to hedge all its exposures in the options market.

(c) Cost Senior management is usually reluctant to pay the up front premiums for options.

Despite these limitations, over the last couple of years options have assumed a more significant role in the group's hedging programme.

Exchange traded v OTC

The group mainly uses the OTC market, because most of its exposures are in the cross-currencies. Furthermore, the OTC market has the capacity for very large transactions along with flexibility on strike prices, settlement dates and the possibility of European style options. However, if exchange traded options are a viable alternative for any particular transaction, they will be used since their liquidity in specific strike prices and dates makes them a great deal easier to sell.

Examples

The following are a few examples which illustrate how the group has actually used options to cover currency risks.

(a) Buy DM call/sterling put options The group has a substantial short Deutschemark long sterling position. The group hedged part of this exposure by buying Deutschemarks and selling sterling in the forward markets. This strategy worked well in the early part of the year when sterling declined. In the second quarter, however, in view of the possibility of sterling becoming stronger, it was decided to increase the cover not in the forward market but by buying DM call options. This limited the downside risk, but left the company able to take advantage of any upside gain. From senior management's point of view this strategy was satisfactory, because the effective exchange rate (strike price plus the premium) was better than that assumed in the annual budget, but it still allowed them to take advantage of further currency gains. In the event the options were not exercised, because sterling strengthened and the foreign currency transactions were executed spot.

(b) Sell DM put/sterling call options Along with the purchase of DM call options for short-term maturity through the second and third quarters, the group continued to purchase Deutschemarks in the forward market, because sterling was expected to weaken in the period. By the year end over 50% of the group's sterling exposure for the next year was hedged and no further forward transactions could be undertaken, because the forward rates were worse than those assumed in the financial plan. Furthermore, since it was considered that the short-term sterling strength was over, the corporation was unwilling to pay high premiums for DM calls. It was therefore decided to use some of the remaining short Deutschemark position by writing DM put options at strike prices which were better than those assumed in the budget. Thus, if the option is not exercised, the corporation earns the option premium; if it is exercised, the corporation purchases its Deutschemarks at a rate it is willing to accept in any event.

(c) Purchase DM calls/US $ put and simultaneously sell FF calls/US $ put Towards the end of 1985, the corporation, along with most other people, was forecasting a French franc devaluation after the elections in France in March 1986. Since the European operations have a significant long French franc operating exposure, it decided to cover 75% of this exposure (for the first nine months of 1986) by selling French francs forward against Deutschemarks. Consideration was also given to buying DM calls/FF put options, but since the cost of the option was high it was decided not to pursue this strategy.

Instead the group evaluated the possibility of buying at-the-money DM calls/ US $ put options and simultaneously selling at-the-money FF calls/US $ put options. Obviously this strategy did not fully cover the risk, but, it was considerably cheaper than either the forward market or the purchase of DM call/FF put options. The successful outcome of the strategy was dependent not only on a French franc devaluation but also on further depreciation of the US $. The group would, of course, be at risk if the French franc appreciated, but this risk was considered of low probability.

Since the general outlook for the dollar was bearish at the time, part of the DM/FF exposure was hedged using this strategy. As things turned, out not only did the dollar depreciate further but the FF did indeed devalue as expected. The corporation therefore exercised the DM calls/US $ puts which it had purchased and also kept the premium income on the DM calls/FF puts that it had sold.

It must be stressed that this was not a risk-free hedging strategy. The group only considered using it because the bulk of its exposure was already hedged on a 'risk-free' basis.

Other corporate finance issues

CHAPTER 14

Taxation aspects of corporate finance

N. R. Noble and G. J. Nuttall
Field Fisher & Martineau

14.01 INTRODUCTION

This chapter considers the main tax rules which apply to capital raising. It considers firstly the rules applicable to different forms of loan capital (14.02–07) and methods whereby a UK company can raise loan finance and pay interest, or its equivalent, gross, whilst still obtaining a tax deduction (14.08). For comparison it describes the rules applicable to share capital and those applying to interest rate and currency swaps (14.09–11). Finally, other factors influencing the form of finance are mentioned, such as tax deductions for investors/lenders, the accrued income scheme, the bond washing provisions and stamp duty (14.12). Space does not permit a discussion of VAT considerations. Some statutory provisions have been paraphrased for ease of reference.

14.02 STANDARD LOAN STOCKS INCLUDING DEBENTURES

1 Definition

There is no tax definition of loan stock for the purposes of a UK resident company obtaining a tax deduction for interest paid or as regards the deduction of tax from that interest. For present purposes it is treated as meaning a loan which is reasonably long term.

2 Tax deduction

A loan stock will not normally be an advance from a bank within the Taxes Act 1970, s 251(3) and so a UK resident company will only obtain a tax deduction for interest paid if it complies with the conditions of the Taxes Act 1970, s 248:

(a) the interest must be yearly interest (ie interest on a loan expected to last more than one year);
(b) the interest must not represent a distribution;
(c) the interest payment must be borne by the company;
(d) the liability incurred to make the interest payment must be incurred for a valuable and sufficient consideration;
(e) the company must either:

    (i)   exist wholly or mainly for the purposes of carrying on a trade; or

    (ii) the interest payment must be laid out wholly and exclusively for the purposes of a trade; or

    (iii) the company must be an investment company; or

    (iv) the interest must have been capable of being eligible for relief under the Finance Act 1972, s 75 if the company had been an individual; and

(f) if the interest payment is made to a non-resident, then one of the following additional requirements needs to be satisfied:

    (i)   the company must deduct basic rate tax under the Taxes Act 1970, s 54 or a reduced or nil rate of tax under a double tax treaty; or

    (ii) the company does not deduct basic rate tax under s 54 by reason of the provisions applying to Eurobonds in the Finance Act, 1984, s 35, or

    (iii) the payment is a payment of interest within the Taxes Act 1970, s 249. Section 249 applies in particular where interest is in fact paid outside the UK and the loan is either incurred for the purpose of non-UK activities of the trade or the interest is payable in a currency other than sterling, or

    (iv) the interest is payable out of income brought into charge to tax under Schedule D, Case IV or V.

3 Deduction of UK tax

On the assumption that the loan lasts for more than one year and that the loan is not an advance from a bank, a UK resident company borrowing in the UK must deduct basic rate tax at 27% from interest payments on the loan stock under the Taxes Act 1970, s 54. In the case of the payment of interest to a non-resident, this can be a requirement if the company is to obtain a tax deduction. In these cases, however, a non-resident lender will frequently be entitled to a reduced or nil rate of UK withholding tax under a double tax treaty. The rate of UK withholding tax can, for instance, be reduced to nil in the case of the USA and the Netherlands and to 10% in the case of Japan. Even though withholding tax is not deducted or is only deducted at a rate of 10% by virtue of a double tax treaty, the terms of the Taxes Act 1970, s 248 that basic rate tax under s 54 of that Act must be deducted are treated as satisfied.

14.03 EUROBONDS (FINANCE ACT 1984, s 35)

1 Definition

A Eurobond for the purposes of the Finance Act 1984, s 35 is a security which is:

(a) issued by a company;

(b) is quoted on a recognised stock exchange (as defined);

(c) is in bearer form; and

(d) which carries a right to interest.

2 Tax deduction

A UK resident company obtains a tax deduction for interest paid on a Eurobond under the Taxes Act 1970, s 248 in exactly the same manner as for a standard loan stock. In the case of the payment of interest on the Eurobond gross, a tax deduction is only obtained if the conditions in 3 below are observed.

3 Deduction of UK tax

The company can pay interest on a Eurobond gross without the deduction of UK basic rate tax if the following conditions are satisfied:

(a) the person by or through whom the interest is paid must not be in the UK; or
(b) the person by or through whom the interest is paid is in the UK but:
    (i) either it is proved that the beneficial owner of the Eurobond and the interest is not resident in the UK; or
    (ii) the Eurobond is held in a recognised clearing system (ie Euroclear or Cedel). In a case where the Eurobond is held in a recognised clearing system, the person by or through whom the interest is paid must on demand from the Inland Revenue deliver an account of any payment of interest or if no demand is received that person must file a written statement within 12 months specifying its name and address and describing the payment.

The reference to the person by or through whom interest is paid is to the principal paying agent, or a sub-paying agent, but not to the company itself. If the above conditions are not satisfied, then the company must deduct basic rate tax under the Taxes Act 1970, s 54 or a reduced or nil rate of tax under a double tax treaty as in the case of standard loan stock.

14.04 DEEP DISCOUNT SECURITIES (FINANCE ACT 1984, s 36 AND SCH 9)

1 Definition

A deep discount security is a redeemable security which has been issued by a company at a deep discount, other than broadly a share in the company or a security where the amount payable on redemption is determined by reference to the movement in the retail prices index or a similar general index of prices published by a government agent or government of a territory outside the UK. A deep discount means a discount which exceeds 15% of the amount payable on redemption of the security or more than $\frac{1}{2}$% for each complete year between the date of issue and redemption. A deep discount security within the Finance Act 1984 can only be issued by a company and therefore care needs to be taken where the issuer is a government.

2 Tax deduction

The company will obtain a tax deduction for the income element of the accrued discount in each income period. An income period is each period for which a payment of interest falls to be made or, if no interest is payable, the year ending immediately before each anniversary of the date of issue. The conditions for obtaining a tax deduction are set out in Sch 9, para 3:

(a) the cost of paying the discount on redemption must be borne by the company;
(b) the income element must not otherwise be tax deductible;
(c) the company must:
    (i) exist wholly or mainly for the purpose of carrying on a trade; or
    (ii) the deep discount security must have been issued wholly and exclusively to raise money for the purposes of a trade; or
    (iii) the company must be an investment company; and

(d) the discount on redemption must not be a distribution within the Taxes Act 1970, s 233(2)(d).

There is a delay of the deduction until redemption for the income element on the deep discount security if the company and the lender are associated or group companies or, where the company is a close company, if the investor is a participator, an associate of a participator or a company controlled by a participator in the close company.

3 Deduction of UK tax

The discount on a deep discount security can be seen as either a discount or rolled-up interest. In so far as it is interest, the Taxes Act 1970, s 54 is specifically excluded from applying to the discount on sale or redemption of a deep discount security where the discount represents income of the seller or the holder chargeable to tax under Sch D, Case III or IV (Sch 9, para 1(9)). Such a discount can therefore be paid gross. In so far as it is a discount s 54 cannot apply to it because s 54 only applies to interest. There is, of course, no question of the application of s 54 to the proceeds of sale of deep discount securities on their sale before redemption.

14.05 STERLING COMMERCIAL PAPER

1 Definition

There is no statutory definition of sterling commercial paper. Sterling commercial paper, however, normally constitutes promissory notes with maturity periods of less than 12 months which either bear a discount or pay interest or do both. The tax rules applying to sterling commercial paper are set out in the Bank of England Press Release dated 29 April 1986, para 6 and in the interim guidelines published by the British Bankers Association.

2 Tax deduction

If the amount of the discount of sterling commercial paper exceeds ½% per complete year pro rata for a period of less than one year, the sterling commercial paper can be a deep discount security and a deduction will be obtained under the conditions set out in 14.04.2. Sterling commercial paper is considered by the Inland Revenue to be a security for the purposes of the deep discount security legislation, although in other circumstances (e g in relation to qualifying corporate bonds) such short-term paper may not be considered as a security. If it is a deep discount security the issuing company should state the income element on any certificate (Finance Act 1984, Sch 9, para 1(8)). However, in practice, the absence of this information will not invalidate the right to deductibility if the other conditions are met. If the sterling commercial paper pays interest, then the provisions of the Taxes Act 1970, s 248 may not apply to give a tax deduction because the interest is not yearly interest, nor will it necessarily be paid to a bank, stockbroker or discount house. Therefore the issuing company may only obtain a tax deduction if the interest is paid wholly and exclusively for the purposes of the company's trade. An investment company will not obtain a tax deduction. (The provisions relating to bills of exchange discussed in 14.06 below will not be applicable because a promissory note will not be a bill of exchange.) A company will similarly obtain a tax deduction for any discount whether or not it is deep, if the discount is given wholly and exclusively for the purposes of the company's trade. It will not obtain a tax deduction if it is an investment company.

3 Deduction of UK tax

If the discount on sterling commercial paper is a deep discount security then the company does not need to deduct basic rate tax from the discount under the same conditions as in 14.04, 3 above. There is no requirement that the company deducts tax at the basic or a double tax treaty rate from interest payable on sterling commercial paper because the loans made in a sterling commercial paper programme will normally be expected to last for less than one year. The interest payable will therefore be short interest and the conditions of the Taxes Act 1970, s 54 will not be applicable. Section 54 will not apply to any discount which is not a deep discount because the discount will be either rolled up interest which is short interest or it will be a discount to which s 54 does not apply.

14.06 BILLS OF EXCHANGE (FINANCE ACT 1984, s 42)

1 Definition

There is no definition of a bill of exchange for the purposes of s 42, so the term bears its ordinary commercial meaning.

2 Tax deduction

The company obtains a tax deduction for the discount on the bill of exchange as a charge on income under the Taxes Act 1970, s 248 provided that the following conditions are observed:

(a) the bill of exchange must be drawn by the company and be accepted by a bank and be discounted by that or any other bank or discount house;
(b) the discount suffered by the company must not otherwise be deductible from the company's profits;
(c) the discount must be ultimately suffered by the company; and
(d) the company must exist wholly or mainly for the purposes of carrying on a trade, or the bill must be drawn to obtain funds wholly and exclusively expended for the purposes of a trade carried on by the company, or the company must be an investment company.

An investment company will need to rely on s 42 in order to obtain a tax deduction for a discount on a bill of exchange. A trading company which is paying the discount wholly and exclusively for the purposes of its trade should normally obtain a deduction for the discount as a trading expense and should not need to rely on s 42.

3 Deduction of UK tax

There will be no need to deduct basic rate tax from the amount of the discount, either because the discount will be rolled up interest, which is short interest, or it will be a discount to which s 54 does not apply.

14.07 BANK OVERDRAFT

1 Definition

There is no definition of a bank overdraft in the tax legislation for the purposes of this section. It is, however, assumed that the bank or a branch is carrying on a bona fide banking business in the UK and that the interest is payable in the UK.

2 Tax deduction

Interest payable on the bank overdraft may or may not be short interest depending upon whether the overdraft is expected to last more than 12 months. The company will obtain a deduction as a trading expense for interest payable on a bank overdraft, whether the overdraft is expected to last more or less than 12 months, provided that the interest is incurred wholly and exclusively for the purposes of the company's trade. If the interest is not paid wholly and exclusively for the purposes of the company's trade, then the company can still obtain a tax deduction for the interest paid if the conditions of the Taxes Act 1970, s 248 are satisfied, and this will again be the case whether the overdraft is expected to last more or less than 12 months.

3 Deduction of UK Tax

If the interest payable on the overdraft is short interest, there is no need to deduct UK basic rate tax because s 54 only applies to annual interest. If the interest is in fact annual interest, then there will still be no need for the company to deduct basic rate tax because s 54(2) provides that this need not be done when interest is payable in the UK on an advance from a bank carrying on a bona fide banking business in the UK.

14.08 METHODS OF PAYING INTEREST GROSS AND OBTAINING A TAX DEDUCTION

1 Introduction

There are three methods in particular whereby a UK resident company can arrange its loan capital so that *interest* on that capital can be paid gross, whilst still enabling the company to obtain a tax deduction. If any of these methods are not available, the company can have recourse to discounted securities.

2 Short interest

It is possible for a company to pay interest gross and still receive a tax deduction if the company ensures that the loan on which interest is payable is for less than one year and that the interest is paid wholly and exclusively for the purposes of the company's trade so that it obtains a tax deduction as a trading expense. The danger of this method is that the company will for instance obtain a bank borrowing originally intended to be for less than 12 months but which in fact is then rolled over so that the loan extends beyond the 12-month period. It may be easier to satisfy the requirements of this method by the company issuing sterling commercial paper which has to be repaid within the 12-month period and then, if necessary, making a new issue of sterling commercial paper to a new investor.

3 Eurobonds

Perhaps the most convenient method whereby a company can raise long-term finance, permitting it to pay interest gross and to obtain a tax deduction, is to issue Eurobonds qualifying within the Finance Act 1984, s 35 and Sch 9. This method involves the company issuing a qualifying Eurobond and then appointing a non-UK principal paying agent and non-UK sub-paying agent. In this way it is not necessary to deliver any returns to the Inland Revenue under s 35, nor is it necessary to check the residence position of investors or for the Eurobonds to be held in a recognised clearing system. The interest payable by the company still needs to qualify under s 248 so that the company can obtain a tax deduction.

4 Dutch finance vehicle

The conditions for a company to issue a qualifying Eurobond may not be desirable in all cases (eg it may not be practical for the Eurobond to be quoted on a recognised stock exchange). In these circumstances, it may be best for the UK company to set up a Dutch resident subsidiary. The Dutch resident subsidiary will issue the Eurobond which need not be quoted. The Dutch subsidiary can pay interest on the Eurobond gross since the Netherlands has no system of withholding tax on interest. The Dutch subsidiary will make a loan of the funds to the UK company taking a 0.25% term if the loans are Hfl 1 billion or less, a 0.1875% term if the loans are between Hfl 1 and 3 billion and a 0.125% term if the loans exceed Hfl 3 billion. The UK company will pay interest gross to the Dutch finance vehicle under the UK/Netherlands double tax treaty which provides for a nil rate of UK withholding tax. The UK company can at the same time obtain a tax deduction for interest provided that all the conditions of the Taxes Act 1970, s 248 are complied with. In particular the condition that interest is paid to a non-resident having made the necessary deduction under the Taxes Act 1970, s 54 will be satisfied because a nil rate of withholding tax under a double tax treaty is treated as satisfying this condition.

5 Discounts

In cases where it is not practical for the UK company itself to issue Eurobonds or to use a Dutch finance vehicle, the UK company can issue a deep discount security, sterling commercial paper at a discount or bills of exchange at a discount in which case there is no requirement to deduct UK withholding tax. A tax deduction can be obtained at the same time for the discount provided that the appropriate conditions are satisfied.

14.09 ORDINARY SHARE CAPITAL

1 Definition

The main definition of ordinary share capital for tax purposes is contained in the Taxes Act 1970, s 526. It is defined as all issued share capital of a company other than share capital which entitles the holder to a dividend at a fixed rate and which has no other right to share in the profits of the company.

2 Tax deduction

A UK resident company paying dividends on ordinary share capital obtains no tax deduction for those dividends. This should be contrasted with a company paying interest on loan capital where a tax deduction is normally obtained. The company does, however, obtain the equivalent of a tax deduction in the system of advance corporation tax ('ACT'). The difference between the ACT system and the tax deduction for loan interest is one of the factors which needs to be taken into consideration when determining whether a company should raise capital by means of loan capital or share capital. The system of ACT works as follows. A company paying a dividend has to pay ACT equal to 27/73 of that dividend. The ACT paid on a dividend can then be set against the company's corporation tax liability. Therefore, in straightforward circumstances, a company which has profits in excess of £500,000 and which therefore pays corporation tax at a rate of 35%, would be in the following position. Taking each £100 of its profits, the company would have to pay corporation tax of £35, meaning that it could pay a dividend of £65 in respect of each £100 of those profits. If the company declared a dividend of £65, it would have to pay ACT of £24.04 (ie £65 × 27/73). An individual shareholder would be deemed to receive a gross dividend of £89.04 (ie £65 + ACT of £24.04). He would be liable to income tax in full on that dividend although the ACT would count as basic rate tax already deducted.

Therefore the individual would only be liable to pay higher rates of income tax. An exempt shareholder can reclaim the ACT paid on a dividend. A non-exempt corporate shareholder receives a dividend of £65 and is then liable to no further tax on it (Taxes Act 1970, s 239). A number of factors need to be considered both by the company raising finance by way of share capital and by the investor providing the finance. As regards the company, it will note that the income yield of share capital is generally lower than the income yield on loan capital. At the same time, whereas the company will need to generate £100 of pre-tax profits in order to pay interest of £100 (assuming that a tax deduction is obtained), the company will need to generate £100 of pre-tax profits in order to pay a dividend of £65. As regards the corporate investor, it needs to recall that it will be liable to corporation tax at 35% on any interest received, whereas any dividend received will not bear any further tax. Both the issuing company and the investor will need to take into account a possible increase in the rate of corporation tax which makes the differences between interest and dividends more marked.

3 Deduction of UK tax

The deduction of UK tax in the case of dividends is the ACT payment. ACT at 27/73 always has to be paid on dividends unless the issuing company is not resident in the UK (Finance Act 1972, s 84(1)), or the issuing company can pay gross under a group income or consortium income election, or the investor is entitled to an ACT refund under a double tax treaty and the issuing company operates an arrangement giving credit at source (eg the G Arrangement). An overseas investor may well prefer to provide finance by way of loan capital because it can in most circumstances ensure that it receives interest gross. In contrast dividends can never be received without at least some payment of ACT (or withholding tax).

14.10 PREFERENCE SHARE CAPITAL

1 Definition

The relevant definition is that for a preference dividend contained in the Taxes Act 1970, s 526, where a preference dividend is defined as a dividend payable on preferred shares at a fixed rate. Where a dividend is payable on preferred shares partly at a fixed rate and partly at a variable rate, the preferred dividend is that part of the dividend payable at a fixed rate. Preference shares put an investor providing capital to a company in the form of shares in a position which approximates more closely to that in loan capital arrangements in that the investor is assured of a fixed rate of return on his capital but only if there are distributable profits.

2 Tax deduction and deduction of UK tax

ACT is payable on a preference dividend in the same way as on an ordinary dividend except that the fixed rate dividend is such amount as, after the payment of ACT, equals the guaranteed dividend. This is because the 'net' dividend (excluding ACT/tax credit) is fixed, so that the actual payment does not vary with changes in the rate of ACT, although the 'gross' amount does vary. Preference shares can be used as a tax advantageous method of providing capital to a company. This is done in the following manner. The relevant subsidiary of a borrowing group which has substantial tax losses issues preference shares to the lender with the appropriate agreed fixed rate of dividend. The subsidiary is not concerned about obtaining a tax deduction for any dividend because the borrowing group has substantial tax losses to cover its profits, and a deduction for interest would merely increase those losses. The subsidiary of the borrower therefore pays the dividend on the preference shares to the lender without any payment of ACT under a consortium income election. The lender then receives a preference dividend and is not liable to corporation tax on it by virtue of the Taxes Act 1970, s 239. In this way the lender can increase his after-tax rate of return on his provision of capital, and the borrowing group can negotiate a lower cost of finance on its raising of capital because the lender is effectively utilising his tax losses.

14.11 INTEREST RATE AND CURRENCY SWAPS

1 Purposes and example of interest rates swap

The following is an example of a floating to fixed interest rate swap. One of the purposes of such an interest rate swap is to reduce the costs of finance. This is achieved by the following. It may be that the rate of interest payable by a strong credit company in the capital markets is lower than that payable in the bank credit market. It can therefore be advantageous for a strong credit company wishing to borrow on a floating basis to issue fixed rate bonds on a capital market and then to swap into a floating rate loan because it can obtain a floating rate borrowing at a comparatively lower rate of interest. In the following example the strong credit company issues a US $110m 11% Eurobond maturing in 1989 and effectively converts this into a floating rate obligation at a cost of ¼% under LIBOR as shown in Fig 14.1 below.

Fig 14.1 Interest rate swap

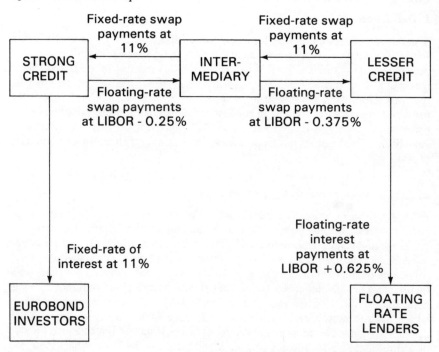

In the circumstances shown in Fig 14.1 above, the strong-credit company effectively borrows on a floating-rate basis at ¼% under LIBOR when the rate of interest if it had actually borrowed on the bank market may have been ¼% over LIBOR. There would be a corresponding benefit to the lesser credit company.

2 Purpose and example of currency swap

The purpose of a currency swap may again be related to the cost of finance. A particular US company may be A rated by Standard and Poors and therefore be able to borrow on an A-rating basis on the US markets whereas it may be able to borrow on a AAA-rating basis on the Swiss market. If the US company wishes to borrow in US dollars, it can be to the advantage of the US company to borrow on the Swiss market in Swiss francs and then to swap this loan into US dollars as in the example shown in Fig 14.2 below.

3 Tax deduction/swap payments

In the case of the two examples of interest rate and currency swaps, the counter-parties are making swap payments to each other in respect of interest (swap pay-ments) through the intermediary. Both the relevant counterparties and the intermediary want to be certain that they will obtain a tax deduction for such payments. It is necessary to take into account the following points:

(a) the swap payments are clearly not interest because the payments are not in respect of a loan between the parties. Each counterparty still remains liable under its separate loan arrangements and pays interest under those arrangements;

Fig 14.2 Currency swap

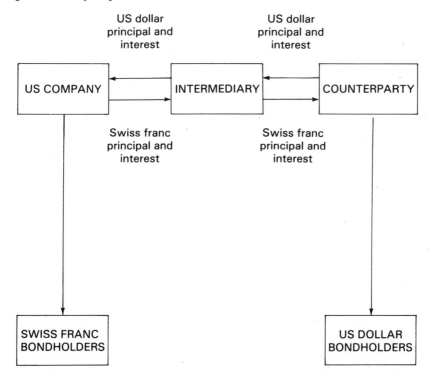

(b) one of the effects of the swap payments not being interest is that the Taxes Act 1970, s 130(f) can potentially apply to prevent a Sch D, Case I deduction where the swap forms part of a capital transaction as regards the person making the swap payment. If the swap payment had been interest, it would have been specifically excluded from the application of the Taxes Act 1970, s 130(f) by virtue of the wording of that subsection. The swap payment can only potentially relate to a capital transaction in the context of a currency swap. No capital changes hands in the case of an interest rate swap. As a matter of practice a swap payment under a currency swap is treated as interest where paid to a recognised bank (a bank) with the overall effect that in these circumstances s 130(f) does not have effect;

(c) the Taxes Act 1970, ss 251(2)(b) and 251(3) are treated as applying to a swap payment under a currency but not an interest rate swap where the swap payment is made to a bank. Therefore a Sch D, Case I deduction will be obtained in priority to a deduction under the Taxes Act 1970, s 248 for a swap payment made to a bank under a currency swap whether or not lasting for more than one year, because s 251(3) will apply;

(d) a person making a swap payment may be able to obtain a tax deduction under Sch D, Case I, but in particular the swap payment must be made wholly and exclusively for the purpose of its trade (Taxes Act 1970, s 130(a)). As already explained, s 130(f) can prevent a Sch D, Case I deduction where the payment is made to someone other than a bank under a currency swap. A Sch D, Case I deduction can be obtained for a swap payment in respect of an interest rate swap relating to a capital transaction because s 130(f) does not apply. A Sch D, Case I deduction can only be obtained for a swap payment in respect of a currency swap relating to a capital transaction if it is made to a bank, because s 130(f) is treated as not applying and s 251(2)(b) and s 251(3) are treated as applying;

(e) swap payments can be treated as annual payments even in such circumstances where they are not because, for instance, they are not pure income profit of the recipient (eg the recipient is a bank or a swap dealer). However, a swap payment cannot be treated as an annual payment where the person making the payment can obtain a Sch D, Case I deduction; and

(f) where the swap payment is not an admissible Sch D, Case I deduction, a person making a swap payment can obtain a tax deduction under the Taxes Act 1970, s 248 because the swap payment is treated as an annual payment and all the conditions in s 248 must be complied with. The effect of the swap payment being treated as an annual payment is that UK basic rate tax must be deducted from it under the Taxes Act 1970, s 53 unless a reduced or nil rate is deducted from it under a double tax treaty or it is paid gross to a bank.

4 Deduction of UK tax/swap payments

It follows from all the comments in 3 that:

(a) a swap payment can be paid gross if it is a Sch D, Case I expense for the person paying it (eg a bank or a swap dealer). It follows that, where a swap payment is made other than to a bank in the context of a currency swap which forms part of a capital transaction as regards the payer (eg it relates to a long-term borrowing), the swap payment cannot be made gross on this basis because there is no Sch D, Case I deduction by virtue of the Taxes Act 1970, s 130(f);

(b) a swap payment can be paid gross where it is Sch D, Case I income of the recipient but the payer will only obtain a tax deduction in this case under Sch D, Case I unless the recipient is a bank. It will not be able to obtain a deduction under the Taxes Act 1970, s 248 except in the case of a gross payment to a bank, because the payment will not have been treated as an annual payment under s 53;

(c) a swap payment may be paid gross to a bank or by a bank in the same terms as in the Taxes Act 1970, s 54(2) (ie where agreement is entered into in the ordinary course of business) and in particular in the case of a payment to a bank this will not prevent a tax deduction under s 248. As regards a bank, payments and receipts under swap agreements entered into by a bank will normally be on revenue account and within Sch D, Case I. An exception is where the swap payments are not made wholly and exclusively for the bank's trade or where they are made for capital purposes to a person other than a bank. In this instance, the bank should perhaps treat the swap payment as an annual payment and deduct tax at a basic or a double tax treaty rate, otherwise it will obtain no tax deduction;

(d) in circumstances other than (a) (b) and (c) basic rate tax must be deducted unless a double tax treaty applies if the payer is to obtain a tax deduction. If the payer is not concerned about obtaining a tax deduction it can pay gross; and

(e) even if the swap payment can be paid gross under (a), (b) or (c), in cases where no Sch D, Case I deduction can be obtained, it can be treated as an annual payment and have basic rate tax deducted from it under the Taxes Act 1970, s 53. The payer will then obtain a tax deduction under the Taxes Act 1970, s 248 except where s 251(3) applies (ie a swap payment under a currency swap lasting more than one year made to a bank), provided that all the conditions of s 248 are observed. The rate of tax deducted can be reduced or removed if the recipient can obtain protection under a double tax treaty either on the grounds of an article similar to Art 6 of the UK/US Double Tax Treaty (ie that the swap payments are business profits of the recipient and the recipient has no permanent establishment in the UK) or on the grounds of an article similar to Art 22 of the UK/US Double Tax Treaty which frees from UK tax income not specifically covered elsewhere in the treaty. It should be noted that swap payments may only be business profits of a recipient if it carries on a financial trade. There is no need to deduct tax even if the swap payment is treated as an annual payment where it is made to a bank.

5 Conclusions/swap payments

(a) A counterparty can pay gross to a bank and obtain a tax deduction either under Sch D, Case I or under the Taxes Act 1970, s 248. Gross payments to non-banks may deny the payer a tax deduction if it cannot obtain a Sch D, Case I deduction because the swap payment will not have been treated as an annual payment under s 53.

(b) A counterparty can pay gross to a person other than a bank and obtain a tax deduction if it can obtain a Sch D, Case I deduction or if the recipient of the swap payment has appropriate protection under a double tax treaty.

6 Swap arrangement fees

A swap agreement will normally provide for the payment of an arrangement fee (swap fee) to the person who has arranged the swap. In so far as the swap fee is paid to the intermediary and is loaded into the swap payment over the life of the swap, the swap fee has the same treatment as the swap payment. If the swap fee is paid to a person other than the intermediary or separately from the swap payment, then a tax deduction can only be obtained under Sch D, Case I. The swap fee cannot be treated as an annual payment and so no deduction can be obtained under the Taxes Act 1970, s 248. The swap fee will not be an incidental cost of obtaining finance and so no deduction will be obtained under the FA 1980, s 38. If a counterparty cannot obtain a deduction for the swap fee where this is being paid to a person other than the intermediary it may be better for the swap fee to be charged to the intermediary in the form of an introductory fee in respect of which the intermediary would normally receive a Sch D, Case I deduction. A swap fee not forming part of a swap payment can always be paid gross because it is not treated as an annual payment.

7 Swap option payments

There may be included in an interest rate swap a provision whereby there is a cap or floor or both (collar) imposed on the amount of the swap payment. Taking the interest rate swap in Fig 14.1, there may be a provision whereby the intermediary agrees to a cap imposing a ceiling on the swap payments to be made by the strong credit in return for a fee from the strong credit with the result that, if LIBOR passed the cap, the strong credit would continue to make swap payments at the capped rate and the intermediary would finance the difference out of its own resources in making swap payments to the lesser credit. Alternatively there may be a provision whereby the intermediary agrees to a floor on the swap payments to be made by it to the lesser credit in return for a fee from the lesser credit with the result that, if LIBOR went below the floor, the strong credit would make swap payments below the floor and the intermediary would finance the difference out of its own resources in making swap payments to the lesser credit. In so far as the fee for the ceiling or floor (swoption fee) is loaded into a swap payment over the life of the swap, the swoption fee can have the same tax treatment as the swap payment. In so far as the swoption fee is paid in the form of a premium, a Sch D, Case I deduction can be obtained provided that the fee is paid wholly and exclusively for the purposes of the relevant counterparty's trade. The swoption fee will not relate to capital so that s 130(f) will not prevent a Sch D, Case I deduction. If the swoption fee is not paid wholly and exclusively for the purposes of the counterparty's trade, no tax deduction can be obtained under s 248 because the fee will not be an annual payment. The fee will not be an incidental cost of obtaining finance and so no deduction will be obtained under the FA 1980, s 38.

14.12 OTHER FACTORS INFLUENCING THE FORM OF FINANCE

1 Tax deductions on capital

The various taxing provisions providing reliefs particularly as regards the subscriptions for share capital may often have a crucial effect on the investor/lender in determining whether he provides finance in the form of loan capital or share capital.

(a) Business Expansion Scheme (Finance Act 1983, s 26, Sch 5)

This can give individuals an income deduction for the subscription price for ordinary shares in a qualifying unquoted company. The deduction is obtained principally in the year of assessment in which the shares are issued. Business Expansion Scheme relief is not obtained if finance is raised in the form of preference shares or loan capital.

(b) Finance Act 1980, s 37

Section 37 provides that an individual investor who has subscribed for shares in a qualifying unquoted trading company may obtain an income deduction for any capital loss on a disposal of those shares, provided that the conditions of s 37 are satisfied.

(c) Finance Act 1981, s 36

Section 36 provides a relief equivalent to that in the Finance Act 1980, s 37 where the subscription is made by an unassociated investment company.

(d) Debt on a security

In contrast to shares where an investor/lender can obtain a revenue deduction for the provision of capital even in a case where the capital is not lost (ie under the Business Expansion Scheme), an investor/lender can only ever obtain a capital loss on the 'loss' of loan capital. A capital loss is only available if the loan capital is either a debt on a security or falls within the provisions of the Capital Gains Tax Act 1979, s 136. The effect of a loan being a debt on a security, however, is that any capital gain made on the disposal of the loan will also be subject to tax on capital gains. 'Debt on a security' is not defined. An authoritative guide on the meaning of that phrase is contained in *W T Ramsay Ltd v IRC* [1981] STC 174. The principal conditions are that the security:

(a) must be marketable;
(b) must carry a market rate of interest and in particular it must be possible to make a gain on the disposal of the security as well as a loss; and
(c) must be an investment.

The above will not apply to a debt on a security which is a qualifying corporate bond (as defined later).

(e) Loans to traders (Capital Gains Tax Act 1979, s 136)

If a loan is not a debt on a security, the investor/lender will then only obtain a capital loss on it when it becomes irrecoverable if it falls within the provisions of s 136. The conditions which have to be satisfied in order for s 136 to apply are as follows:

(a) the loan must not be a debt on a security;
(b) the loan must be used by the borrowing company wholly and exclusively for the purposes of its trade, not being a trade of money lending;
(c) the borrowing company must be resident in the UK;
(d) the loan must become irrecoverable;
(e) the investor/lender must not have assigned its right to recover the loan;
(f) the investor must make a claim to the Inspector of Taxes; and
(g) the investor and borrower must not have been group companies when the loan was made or subsequently.

A possible advantage of a loan falling within s 136 is that, whereas the investor/lender can obtain a capital loss on the loan becoming irrecoverable, the investor/lender will not be liable to tax on capital gains on the disposal of such a loan. However, loss relief already obtained can be clawed back under s 136(5) on a subsequent recovery.

(f) Qualifying corporate bonds (Capital Gains Tax Act 1979, s 67, Finance Act 1984, s 64)

The definition of a qualifying corporate bond is contained in s 64. In order to be a qualifying corporate bond, the bond must be a security which satisfies the following conditions:

(a) the bond must from the time of issue have been quoted on a recognised stock exchange in the UK, or have been dealt in on the Unlisted Securities Market, or the bond must have been issued by a body, shares stocks or securities of which were at the time of issue quoted on a recognised UK stock exchange or were dealt in on the Unlisted Securities Market;
(b) the bond must at all times represent a normal commercial loan as defined by the Finance Act 1973, Sch 12, para 1(5);
(c) the bond must be denominated in sterling with no provision for a conversion or redemption in any other currency; and
(d) the bond must have been issued after 13 March 1984, or must have been acquired by a person after that date other than by way of an excluded disposal (as defined).

No chargeable gain or allowable loss arises on the disposal of a qualifying corporate bond. Qualifying corporate bonds may therefore be attractive to investors/lenders if they consider that a capital gain is likely, because the gain will be tax free.

2 Accrued income scheme (Finance Act 1985, ss 73–77 and Schs 22 and 23)

Before the introduction of the accrued income scheme, many investors/lenders were effectively converting income into capital by selling bonds cum div. The element of the sale price attributable to the accrued interest was treated as capital in the same way as the rest of the sale price and the purchaser was taxable on the entire amount of interest if received by it. The above, of course, meant that the seller would only pay the lower rate of tax then applicable to capital gains on the accrued interest, or would pay no tax at all if it was non-UK resident without a branch or agency in the UK. The accrued income scheme was therefore introduced to prevent this. A seller is deemed to receive income equal to the amount of interest accrued up to the date of sale. It is necessary to be clear as to the exact securities to which the accrued income scheme applies. The scheme applies to all securities other than:

(a) shares in a company;
(b) securities the interest on which is a distribution within the Taxes Act 1970, s 233(2)(d)(iv) (ie loans to associated non-resident companies);
(c) national savings certificates;
(d) war savings certificates;
(e) certificates of deposit within the Finance Act 1968, s 55; and
(f) any redeemable security where the amount payable on redemption exceeds the issue price and there is no other return on the security.

The application of the accrued income scheme to securities can make certain forms of capital more or less attractive. Therefore the accrued income scheme does not apply to shares in a company and in particular to preference shares. The scheme also does not apply to certificates of deposit, and for these purposes sterling commercial paper has the same treatment as a certificate of deposit. Where the accrued income scheme does not apply to securities, it is still necessary to consider in particular the Taxes Act 1970, ss 469–475 ('the bond washing provisions').

3 Bond washing provisions

The bond washing provisions are contained in the Taxes Act 1970, ss 469–475. Section 469 takes effect where an owner agrees to sell or transfer securities (which includes shares) and by the same or a collateral agreement agrees to buy back or re-acquire the securities or acquires an option which is subsequently exercised to buy back the securities. In these circumstances, if the owner does not receive the interest on the securities, he is deemed to do so and is taxable on that interest. There are two important exceptions to s 469. It does not apply if:

(a) the securities are subject to the accrued income scheme; or
(b) the securities are Eurobonds or foreign government stock and the owner carries on a trade which consists wholly or partly in dealing in securities and the person who agrees to buy the securities carries on such a trade.

Section 469 also applies where a trader in securities agrees to acquire securities and by the same or a collateral agreement agrees to sell back the securities or acquires an option which is subsequently exercised to sell back the securities. In these circumstances the transaction is ignored for the purposes of computing the trader's trading profits, but only if he receives interest on the securities. This part of s 469 does not apply as regards securities which are subject to the accrued income scheme nor to securities which are Eurobonds or foreign government stock if the original vendor is a dealer in securities. A Eurobond for the purposes of s 469 is a security which:

(a) is neither preference stock nor preference share capital;
(b) is issued in bearer form;
(c) carries a right to interest at a fixed rate or at a rate bearing a fixed relationship to a standard published base rate;
(d) does not carry a right to any other form of benefit whether in the form of participation in profits or otherwise (although this condition is treated as not breached if the Eurobond is convertible or contains rights to subscribe for further securities); and
(e) the interest on which is payable without any deduction in respect of income tax or any similar tax imposed by a territory outside the UK.

Foreign government stock means stock which is issued by a non-UK government and which is denominated in a non-sterling currency.

Taxes Act 1970, s 470

Section 470 applies where the owner of any security sells or transfers the right to receive interest in respect of the securities without selling or transferring the securities themselves. In these circumstances the interest is deemed to be the interest of the owner and of no other person.

Taxes Act 1970, ss 471–474

These sections apply where person A purchases securities and then subsequently sells them, with the result that the interest on the securities is receivable by person A. Section 471 then has the effect that, if person A is a dealer in securities the purchase price for the acquisition of the securities is treated as being reduced by a portion of the interest received. That portion is the interest accrued on the securities for the period when they were not held by person A (ie the proportion which the period from the date the securities last went ex div to the date of the purchase bears to the period from the date when the securities last went ex div to the date on which they went ex div after the date of purchase). Section 471 does not apply in the following circumstances:

(a) if the period between person A's date of purchase and his taking steps to sell the securities exceeds six months;
(b) if the period in sub-para (a) exceeds one month and the Inland Revenue are satisfied that the purchase and sale are at market value and that the sale is not made in connection with an arrangement made before or at the time of purchase;
(c) if the securities are subject to the accrued income scheme;
(d) if person A makes the subsequent sale in the ordinary course of its business as market maker in the kind of securities concerned. A market maker for these purposes is a person who holds himself out at all normal times in compliance with The Stock Exchange Rules as being willing to buy and sell securities of that kind at a price specified by it and is recognised as doing so by the Council of The Stock Exchange;
(e) if the securities are overseas securities bought by person A on a stock exchange outside the UK in the ordinary course of his trade as dealer in securities, and the interest is brought into account in computing person A's

profits for UK tax purposes and (if relevant) person A elects not to take any credit under the Taxes Act 1970, s 497 or s 498 (double tax relief). Overseas securities are securities of a government or of any body of persons resident outside the UK; and

(f) if the securities are Eurobonds bought by person A in the ordinary course of his trade as a dealer in Eurobonds. A Eurobond has the same meaning as for s 469.

Sections 469, 471 and 472 are only relevant if the securities are not subject to the accrued income scheme. They are therefore particularly relevant to shares. They do not necessarily apply to sterling commercial paper which, although it is not within the accrued income scheme, is arguably not a security (although treated as such for the purposes of the deep discount security legislation).

4 Stamp duty and capital duty

(a) Loan capital (Finance Act 1986, s 79)

There is no stamp duty (or stamp duty reserve tax) the issue of any bearer loan capital or on the transfer of any loan capital except in relation to loan capital which:

(a) at the time of the transfer of the loan capital carries a right to conversion into shares or other securities or carries a right to the acquisition of shares or other securities. This means that convertible bonds or bonds with warrants will be stampable;

(b) at the time of transfer or before carries or has carried a right to interest which exceeds a reasonable commercial return on the nominal amount of the capital;

(c) at the time of transfer or before carries or has carried a right to interest which falls or has fallen to be determined by reference to the results of a business or the value of property; or

(d) at the time of transfer or before carries or has carried a right to repayment of an amount which exceeds the nominal amount of the capital and which is not reasonably comparable with what is generally repayable under the terms of issue of loan capital listed in the Official List of The Stock Exchange.

Loan capital which carries a right to interest, or to an amount payable on redemption by reference to an index showing changes in the general level of prices payable in the UK over a period substantially corresponding to the period between issue and repayment, does not fall within paras (b)–(d) above.

(b) Share capital

In contrast there is stamp duty at ½% on the transfer of registered shares. There is stamp duty at 1½% on the issue of UK bearer shares but there is no stamp duty on the transfer of such shares by way of delivery. There will be no stamp duty but these can be stamp duty reserve tax on a contract for the sale of registered shares which is followed by no transfer unless the shares are in a clearing system. There is no stamp duty reserve tax on the transfer of bearer shares by delivery. There is stamp duty or stamp duty reserve tax at 1½% in connection with the issue of depository receipts or the transfer or issue of shares with a clearing system.

5 Capital duty

No capital duty is payable on the issue of loan capital whereas capital duty at 1% is payable on the subscription price for share capital.

The effect of the above is that an investor/lender may, if everything else is equal, prefer to purchase loan capital because there will be no stamp duty cost on the acquisition. An issuing company may also prefer to issue loan capital because there is no capital duty cost on issue.

CHAPTER 15

Corporate reorganisations

T. J. Davies
Field Fisher & Martineau

15.01 INTRODUCTION

The mid-1980s witnessed a flush of takeovers and so-called 'mega' takeovers (eg Guinness/Distillers, Hanson/Imperial, and Burton/Debenhams), a substantial increase in the popularity of management buy-outs (eg Leyland Bus, and Mecca Leisure), substantial corporate rationalisation, and rapidly changing financial markets and interest rates. All of these factors have contributed, and will continue to contribute, to the impetus for corporate reorganisation.

1 The nature of a reorganisation

Corporate reorganisation may take many forms and may be effected pursuant to the powers of a company under its memorandum and articles of association or, where such powers do not suffice, pursuant to statutory provision. The term 'reorganisation' is not defined in the Companies Act 1985 but it may be taken to include the following situations:

(a) a reconstruction, that is an arrangement whereby the undertaking or part of the undertaking (but not merely assets) of a company are transferred to another company, the shareholders in which are substantially the same as those of the first company. This is known as the 'substantial identity test';

(b) an amalgamation or share for share merger, that is the bringing together of the businesses of two companies by an exchange of shares. This may be done by a new company acquiring all the shares of two existing companies so that the new company becomes the holding company of the two existing companies. This was the means by which Habitat Mothercare and British Home Stores merged their respective businesses, both companies becoming subsidiaries of a new holding company called Storehouse. Alternatively, the shareholders in one company (Company A) may exchange their shares for shares in another company (Company B) with the result that Company B becomes the holding company of Company A. The key element in a true amalgamation is that the consideration for the acquisition of shares in one company is satisfied principally in shares of the acquiring company and not in cash;

(c) a demerger, that is where the trading activities carried on by a single company are divided so as to be carried on by two or more companies not

236

belonging to the same group or the trading activities of a single group are divided so as to be carried on by two or more independent groups;

(d) a distribution in specie, that is a distribution by a company to its shareholders of specific assets such as shares in a subsidiary. This is also a form of demerger;

(e) a reduction of share capital;

(f) a purchase by a company of its own shares;

(g) a reverse takeover;

(h) the reconstruction of the assets and/or liabilities of a company; and

(i) a management buy-out.

2 Statutory provisions

A shareholder in a company normally cannot be compelled to sell or dispose of his shares, nor can his rights as a member be modified without his consent. Similarly, a creditor of a company cannot be compelled to give up his security or to accept the creation of prior charges. In addition, for the protection of both creditors and shareholders, there is a general prohibition on companies reducing their share capital. Unqualified, these principles would severely restrict the scope for corporate reorganisation. Accordingly the Insolvency Act 1986 and the Companies Act 1985 contain the following mitigating provisions:

Insolvency Act

(a) s 110 empowers the liquidator of a company, with the sanction of a special resolution of the company in general meeting and, in the case of a creditors' voluntary winding up, with the sanction of the court, to transfer the whole or part of the business or assets of a company to another company in exchange for shares or other interests in or benefits from the transferee company;

(b) s 1 provides a simple procedure whereby a company can conclude a legally effective voluntary arrangement with its creditors;

(c) s 8 provides that the court may make an administration order directing that the affairs, business and property of a company be managed by an administrator appointed by the court;

Companies Act

(a) s 425 empowers the members or creditors or any class of members or creditors to agree to a compromise or arrangement with the company which, subject to the sanction of the court, will be binding on all the members or creditors or class thereof as the case may be;

(b) s 135 empowers a company to repay capital to its members subject to the reduction being approved by special resolution of the company in general meeting and being confirmed by the court; and

(c) s 162 empowers a company to purchase its own shares subject to complying with the detailed provisions in Chapter VII of the Act.

These statutory provisions are considered in greater detail in subsequent sections of this chapter.

3 The rationale of reorganisation

The share capital structure and asset/liability structure of a company should be under constant review to ensure optimum utilisation of shareholders' funds. In that regard the following questions will be particularly relevant:

(a) would expansion of the company's operations be facilitated by a major change in ownership of the company? eg where shareholder factions cannot agree on corporate policy;

(b) does the company have reserves which are surplus to the requirements of its existing and projected business operations? If so, the company should be considering returning a proportion of the excess capital to shareholders by way of reduction of share capital or by purchasing its own shares?;

(c) does the company have any under-utilised fixed assets or any operations not making a satisfactory contribution to group profits which could be sold and the resources more efficiently employed?; and

(d) could the company's liabilities be restructured either to enable increased borrowings, with a view to expansion, or to reduce gearing?

15.02 INSOLVENCY ACT 1986, s 110

1 Procedure

Where a company is proposed to be, or is, in the course of being voluntarily wound up, the Insolvency Act, s 110 empowers the liquidator, with the sanction of a special resolution of the company and, if the company is the subject of a creditors' voluntary winding up, with the sanction of the court or of the committee of inspection (if any) appointed by the creditors, to transfer the whole or part of the company's business or property to another company in exchange for shares or other interests in or benefits from the transferee company. Provided that the articles of association of the transferor company contain power to make distributions in specie, those shares, interests or benefits are then distributed to the members of the transferor company in accordance with their rights in a winding up. The transferee company will normally agree to meet the liabilities of the transferor company. Alternatively, the transferor company will retain sufficient assets to meet its liabilities. In any event, if within one year of the special resolution sanctioning the arrangement, an order is made for winding up the transferor company, the special resolution will not be valid unless sanctioned by the court. Thus for 12 months a s 110 arrangement may be upset.

2 Rights of dissenting members

A sale or arrangement in pursuance of s 110 is binding on the members of the transferor company. However, if a member does not vote in favour of the special resolution and expresses his dissent in writing to the liquidator within seven days of the passing of the resolution, he may require the liquidator either to abstain from carrying the resolution into effect or (at the liquidator's option) to purchase his interest at a price to be determined by agreement or arbitration. That price is likely to be the equivalent of what he would have received on an ordinary winding up. If the liquidator elects to purchase a dissenting member's interest, the purchase money must be paid before the company is dissolved and must be raised by the liquidator in such manner as may be determined by special resolution of the company. Members who give no notice of dissent still cannot be compelled to accept shares in the transferee company, and in such event the shares to which they are entitled will normally be sold by the liquidator for their benefit.

3 Section 110 in operation

Section 110 provides a relatively simple means of reorganisation and is particularly useful where there is not likely to be any significant dissent amongst shareholders. The following are typical situations where the section might be employed:

(a) Two groups of shareholders wish to continue separately a trade carried on by Company A. Two new companies, Company B and Company C, each issue shares to Company A in exchange for part of its business and assets. Those shares are distributed to Company A's two groups of shareholders so that one group holds shares in Company B and the other holds shares in Company C. Company A's trade is thus effectively partitioned. Company A is then dissolved.

(b) The shareholders of Company A and Company B wish to amalgamate the businesses of their respective companies. A new company, Company C, issues shares in exchange for all the shares in Company A and Company B. Company A and Company B are then dissolved and their assets distributed in specie to Company C.

(c) Company A is in financial difficulty but its business would remain viable within a larger group, and the shareholders wish to retain an interest in the business. Company A sells its business and assets to Company B in exchange for shares in Company B. Those shares are distributed to the shareholders of Company A.

15.03 COMPANIES ACT 1985, s 425

1 Ambit

The Companies Act 1985, s 425 provides that if a majority in number representing three-fourths in value of the creditors or any class of the creditors or the members or any class of the members, present in person or by proxy, agree to a 'compromise or arrangement' with a company and that compromise or arrangement is sanctioned by the court, it will be binding on all the creditors or class of creditors or on the members or class of members as the case may be.

Although 'arrangement' is expressly stated to include a reorganisation of the share capital or the consolidation or division of shares of different classes, neither 'compromise' nor 'arrangement' are defined in the Companies Act. However, it is clear that the ambit of s 425 is much wider than that of the Insolvency Act, s 110 which is restricted to a company which is to be wound up and gives rights to dissenting minority shareholders. Section 425 has no such limitations and can thus be used for any of the schemes outlined in section 15.02, 3 above, but without the need for the scheme to incorporate a company dissolution. Section 425 can also be used to alter special rights attached to shares or to alter the terms of a company's debenture stock or to convert non-redeemable shares into redeemable preference shares. A creditor could not normally be bound by an agreement between a company and its other creditors, but s 425 can be used to effect a scheme obliging secured creditors to accept the creation of a prior charge upon the company's assets. It can even be used to effect a scheme requiring creditors to give up their security in return for fully paid shares of the company.

2 Explanatory statement

Section 426 requires that a statement explaining the effect of any compromise or arrangement must accompany every notice summoning a meeting pursuant to s 425. This explanatory statement must, in particular, state any material interest of the directors of the company (whether as directors, members, creditors or otherwise) and the effect on those interests of the proposed compromise or arrangement insofar as it differs from the effect on the like interests of other persons. If the meeting is convened by advertisement, that advertisement must include an explanatory statement or notification of the place at which and the manner in which creditors or members entitled to attend the meeting may obtain copies of the explanatory statement. If rights of debenture holders are affected, the explanatory statement must deal with the interests of any trustees of any deeds securing the debentures.

3 The role of the court

A meeting for the purpose of considering a scheme proposed under s 425 can only be convened by order of the court and, if the scheme is approved by such a meeting, it is only binding if it is subsequently sanctioned by the court. In exercising its discretion the court must satisfy itself that:

(a) the class to which the scheme purports to relate is accurately identified. For persons to constitute a true class, they must be able to consult together as to their common interests. Preferential creditors, secured creditors and unsecured creditors have divergent interests and must be regarded as separate classes and there may be further classes within those classes, for example where secured creditors have different security. Similarly, where some shares are fully paid and others are partly paid the respective shareholders must be regarded as separate classes. In *Re Hellenic & General Trust Limited* it was held that the majority shareholder in that company, which was also a wholly-owned subsidiary of the proposed purchaser of the shares of the company, constituted a separate class from the other shareholders because it had a community of interest with the purchaser;

(b) the meeting or meetings were duly convened and held;

(c) the resolutions were passed both by a majority in number of those members of the class present and voting and by the holders of three-fourths in value of the aggregate holding of such persons, e g if 50 members of a class attend a meeting of whom one member holds 10,000 shares and the remainder hold 100 shares each, those 49 shareholders cannot validly approve a scheme against the wishes of the single shareholder holding 10,000 shares because they do not hold the necessary three-fourths in value. Conversely, the holder of the 10,000 shares cannot validly approve the scheme against the 4,900 votes of the remaining shareholders because there would not be a majority in number;

(d) those who attended the meeting were fairly representative of the class, e g if there are 5,000 shareholders and 100,000 issued shares and just 15 members, together holding only 200 shares, are present, and vote, and the statutory majorities are achieved, the court would be unlikely to be satisfied that the class was fairly represented at the meeting; and

(e) the scheme is fair and equitable. If a scheme is approved by a large majority vote and the court considers that it is fair, it is unlikely to exercise its discretion on the grounds of the commercial merits of the scheme.

Under s 427 the court has wide powers to facilitate a scheme including the power to order the transfer of the whole or any part of the undertaking or liabilities of a company to another company. The court also has power to impose conditions on its approval. Accordingly, a scheme should include provision for the company to agree to any modification which the court may require.

4 Effect of court sanction

Once the court has sanctioned a scheme, it is binding on all the creditors or members who are parties to it and on the company. If the company is in the process of being wound up, the scheme is also binding on the liquidator and contributories. The scheme will not, however, be effective until an office copy of the order sanctioning it has been filed with the Registrar of Companies.

15.04 VOLUNTARY ARRANGEMENTS

Insolvency Act 1986, s 1 provides that the directors or the administrator or liquidator of a company may make a proposal to its shareholders and to its creditors for a composition in satisfaction of its debts or a scheme of arrangement of its affairs. This 'voluntary arrangement' procedure provides a means by which a company may come to terms with its creditors with the minimum of formality. It is particularly suitable for small companies experiencing financial difficulties which, given time, are capable of being overcome. The person making the proposal nominates a qualified insolvency practitioner to act as 'nominee' and provides him with details of the proposed arrangement and of the assets and liabilities of the company. The nominee must report to the court within 28 days whether he considers that the proposal should be put to meetings of the shareholders and creditors. If he feels that it should be and the court agrees, he will call these meetings to consider the proposal. If a liquidator or administrator proposes an arrangement under which he will act as nominee, the meetings of the shareholders and creditors may be called without any report being made to the court. If the arrangement is approved at the shareholders' and creditors' meetings, it will be binding on the company and on all those who had notice of, and were entitled to vote, at the meetings. However, the arrangement cannot restrict the rights of secured or preferential creditors without their agreement. Furthermore, if the arrangement unfairly prejudices the interests of a creditor or shareholder he may, within 28 days of the result of the meeting being reported to the court, apply to the court for the approval of the arrangement to be revoked, suspended or modified.

Once a voluntary arrangement has been approved the nominee will become the supervisor of the arrangement unless the shareholders' and creditors' meetings appoint another insolvency practitioner to act in his place.

15.05 ADMINISTRATION ORDERS

1 Grounds for an order

The Insolvency Act 1986, s 8 provides that the court may make an administration order directing that, during the period for which the order is in force, the affairs, business and property of the company shall be managed by an administrator appointed by the court. The procedure is designed to assist in the preservation of the profitable parts of the business of a company which might otherwise be put into liquidation. The court may make an administration order if it is satisfied that the company is or is likely to become unable to pay its debts and that the making of the order would be likely to achieve one of the following purposes:

(a) the survival of the company, and the whole or any part of its undertaking, as a going concern;
(b) the approval of a voluntary arrangement under the Insolvency Act, Part 1;
(c) the sanctioning of a scheme of arrangement under Companies Act 1985, s 425; or
(d) a more advantageous realisation of the company's assets than would be effected on a winding up.

An application for an administration order may be made by one or more of the company, the directors or creditors but may not be made in respect of a company which is already in liquidation.

2 Effect of a petition

Once a petition is presented no resolution may be passed or order made to wind up the company and leave of the court is required before any steps may be taken to enforce any security over the company's property or to repossess goods subject to any hire purchase agreement. The court's permission is also required to commence or continue any other actions or proceedings against the company or its property.

3 Conduct of the administration

On appointment the administrator takes into his custody or control all the property to which the company is or appears to be entitled. The administrator has the power to do all such things as may be necessary for the management of the affairs, business and property of the company and his powers override those conferred on the company or its officers, the exercise of which (insofar as they could interfere with the administrator's powers) is subject to his consent. The administrator also has powers to dismiss and appoint directors and to call meetings of the members or creditors.

Within three months of the making of the administration order (or such longer time as the court may allow) the administrator must send a statement of his proposals for achieving the purpose specified in the administration order to all of the company's creditors and to the Registrar of Companies, and he must convene a creditor's meeting on at least 14 days' notice and lay a copy of the statement of his proposals before that meeting. He must also send a copy of the statement to all the members of the company or publish a notice informing them where they may apply for a free copy. The administrator must report to the Registrar of Companies and to the court whether his proposals are approved. If they are not approved the court may make such order as it thinks fit, including the discharge of the administration order. The administration of a company will come to an end only when the court discharges the order on the application of the administrator or of a creditor or member of the company.

15.06 REDUCTION OF CAPITAL

1 Purpose of capital reduction

A company may wish to repay capital because:

(a) it is in excess of its needs; or
(b) it has been lost or is unrepresented by available assets and reality needs to be reintroduced to its balance sheet; or
(c) fresh capital can be obtained more cheaply elsewhere.

In addition, the court has power under the Companies Act 1985, s 461 to order a company to purchase the shares of any member if he has been unfairly prejudiced by the conduct of the company's affairs. Such an order may provide for the reduction of the company's capital.

2 Procedure

The Companies Act 1985, s 135 provides that a company may reduce its share capital provided that:

(a) its articles of association contain the power;
(b) the reduction is approved by special resolution of the company in general meeting; and
(c) the reduction is confirmed by the court.

This procedure need not be followed where a company redeems redeemable shares in accordance with its articles provided that the Companies Act 1985, s 160 (regarding financing such redemption) is complied with, nor where a company forfeits shares for non-payment of calls pursuant to its articles.

A capital reduction may be effected in any way but in particular by:

(a) extinguishing or reducing the liability in respect of share capital not paid up, e g by reducing £1 shares partly paid up as to 50p each to fully paid up 50p shares; or
(b) returning paid up capital, e g by reducing £1 fully paid shares to 50p shares and paying back 50p per share; or
(c) returning paid up capital on the basis that it may be called up again.

3 Rights of shareholders

Where a capital reduction is because of loss of capital and if there is only one class of shares, the same proportion of each share must be cancelled. If there is more than one class of share the reduction should be borne in the reverse order of priority to that which would apply on a return of capital in a winding up. Conversely, if a company is returning excess capital, the court will usually sanction the reduction where rights in respect of capital are observed even if preference shareholders are thereby prevented from sharing in the future prosperity of the company.

4 Confirmation by the court

When a company has passed a resolution to reduce its share capital, it must apply to the court for an order of confirmation before the reduction can be effective. If the proposed reduction involves either a diminution of liability in respect of unpaid share capital or the payment to a shareholder of any paid up share capital, any creditor of the company who would be entitled to prove against the company in a winding up is entitled to object to the reduction. The court will only confirm the reduction if it is satisfied that every creditor who is entitled to object to the reduction has either consented to it or his debt or claim has been discharged, determined or secured.

The court may dispense with the consent of particular creditors if satisfactory security is provided. In practice dispensation is usually sought on the basis that the company's realisable assets exceed the aggregate of its total liabilities, the amount of any proposed repayment, and its remaining paid up capital.

If a reduction of capital is confirmed by the court, it will approve a formal minute stating the new capital structure of the company. That minute together with a copy of the order must be filed with the Registrar of Companies. The reduction only takes effect from the date of the certificate issued by the Registrar. Once the certificate has been issued the reduction cannot be upset.

15.07 PURCHASE OF OWN SHARES

1 Funding and authority

The Companies Act 1981 ended the long-established principle that a company could not buy its own shares. The Companies Act 1985, s 162 now provides that any company may purchase its own shares provided that:

(a) the articles of association authorise the purchase; and
(b) the purchase is made out of distributable profits (within the meaning of s 263 of the Act) or out of the proceeds of a fresh issue of shares.

2 'On market' and 'Off market' purchases

Shares may be purchased either 'on market' through a recognised investment exchange, or 'off market', ie under a contract of purchase.

An on market purchase must be authorised in advance by an ordinary resolution of the company in general meeting which must specify the maximum number of shares that may be purchased, the maximum and minimum prices which may be paid for the shares and the date on which the authority is to expire, which may not be more than 18 months after the passing of the resolution.

An off market purchase may only be made in pursuance of a contract of purchase, the terms of which must be authorised in advance by a special resolution. If the company is a public company, the resolution must specify a date on which the authority is to expire, which must not be later than 18 months after the date on which the resolution is passed. In determining whether 75% of the votes cast at the Extraordinary General Meeting are in favour of the special resolution, the votes attached to the shares proposed to be purchased must be disregarded. Any member may demand a poll on the resolution, irrespective of any provision regarding the calling of polls in the articles of association. A copy of the sale/purchase agreement must be available for inspection by members at the registered office of the company not less than 15 days before the meeting, and at the meeting itself.

3 Effect of purchase

Once a company has purchased its own shares they will be treated as cancelled and the amount of the issued share capital diminished by their nominal amount. The authorised capital will remain the same. Stamp duty at the rate of ½% is payable on the amount of the consideration.

The company must deliver a return to the Registrar of Companies within 28 days of the purchase specifying the date of purchase and the number of shares purchased and (if applicable) a copy of the sale/purchase agreement must be kept at the registered office for ten years and that copy must be open to any member for inspection.

4 Substantial purchase by a listed company

A purchase by a listed company of 15% or more of its issued equity share capital within a period of 12 months must be made either by way of a tender offer or a partial offer to all shareholders proportionate to their respective shareholdings. A tender offer must be made on The Stock Exchange at a stated maximum price and notice of the offer must be given by means of an advertisement in two national newspapers at least seven days before the offer closes.

A tender offer or partial offer involves two separate circulars to shareholders as follows:

(a) First circular This explains the proposal and incorporates a notice of extraordinary general meeting for the purpose of:

(a) amending the articles of association (if necessary) to authorise the purchase by the company of its own shares; and

(b) authorising the proposal itself and specifically the parameters within which any purchases from directors or substantial shareholders or persons connected with them might be made. (This is in order to comply with the Companies Act 1985, s 320 and the requirements of The Stock Exchange).

The circular will constitute a Class 1 circular and if shares are to be purchased from persons having a Class 4 relationship with the company (ie normally a director or substantial shareholder), the circular will constitute a Class 4 circular, in both cases involving compliance with the applicable provisions of chapter 2, section 3 'Admission of Securities to Listing'.

(b) Second circular Assuming that the resolutions proposed at the extraordinary general meeting are passed, this circular contains the details of the tender offer or (as appropriate) the partial offer.

15.08 DEMERGERS

1 Meaning

The term 'demergers' is the creation of taxation rather than company law. The Finance Act 1980, s 117 and Sch 18 introduced certain exemptions from tax, stamp duty and capital duty where the trading activities carried on by a single company are divided so as to be carried on by two or more companies not belonging to the same group or the trading activities of a single group are divided so as to be carried on by two or more independent groups. In introducing these exemptions it was the Government's intention to remove some of the disincentives to the fragmentation of composite businesses. The then Chancellor of the Exchequer commented that 'there are cases where businesses are grouped together inefficiently under a single company umbrella' and 'could in practice be run more dynamically if they . . . were allowed to pursue their own separate ways under independent management', in other words if they were broken up. Certainly the introduction of the demerger provisions facilitated the use of the Companies Act 1985, s 425 and in particular made distributions in specie more attractive.

A demerger cannot be a reconstruction or amalgamation because a demerged division is not carried on by substantially the same persons as before the demerger; rather a demerger is the exact opposite of an amalgamation.

2 Taxation reliefs

The detailed tax legislation is beyond the scope of this chapter but the principal reliefs available, if the demerger conditions are satisfied, are as follows:

(a) Income tax

An individual shareholder to whom a distribution is made consisting, for example, of shares in a subsidiary of the transferee company, will not be treated as income of the individual shareholder subject to income tax.

(b) Corporation tax

Advance corporation tax will not be payable on a distribution by a company pursuant to a demerger and there are certain reliefs from corporation tax where a company leaves a group, provided it does so purely pursuant to the demerger.

(c) Stamp duty

No stamp duty is payable on any document executed solely for the purpose of effecting an exempt distribution pursuant to a demerger, eg any document transferring shares in a subsidiary to the shareholders of the distributing company and any document for transferring a trade or shares to a transferee company.

(d) Capital duty

No capital duty is payable on any document entered into for the purposes of effecting an exempt distribution pursuant to a demerger, eg the issue of shares by a transferee company to the shareholders of a distributing company. However, capital duty is still payable on the initial capitalisation of the transferee company.

15.09 REVERSE TAKEOVER

1 Nature

A reverse takeover is a takeover by one company (Company A) of another larger company (Company B). If the consideration for the acquisition is satisfied wholly in shares, this will result in the former shareholders of Company B becoming the majority shareholders in Company A. Where the consideration is in cash, then assuming that the acquiring company does not have very large cash reserves, it will need to raise cash, possibly by means of a rights issue or by a placing of its own new shares with institutional investors or, alternatively, by some form of debt financing. This latter form of finance may involve a consortium of banks or other institutions, as in the case of the much publicised but abortive bid by the Australian company, Elders IXL, for the much larger UK company, Allied-Lyons. It is beyond the scope of this section to explore the possible variations of such arrangements but clearly a reverse takeover financed by debt will substantially alter the balance sheet of the acquiring company. Banks and institutions backing the acquirer will need to be satisfied that having secured its target company, the acquirer will be able to service its existing and new debt commitments from profits generated within the new group. In this regard lenders will also need to be satisfied that whatever proposals are made for discharging the debt, they do not involve the acquired company in giving financial assistance for the purchase of its own shares in breach of the provisions of the Companies Act 1985, Chapter VI, because this may render their security unenforceable.

A reverse takeover by a listed company will constitute a super Class I transaction and will require the sanction of its shareholders in general meeting.

2 Back-door listings

A private company may use a reverse takeover to gain a public listing instead of applying for a listing itself. A 'back door' listing may be effected through a public company, which is smaller in terms of assets or profits (or both) than a private company, making a share for share exchange offer to the shareholders of the private company who will then become the majority shareholders in the public company. This will involve an application for a new listing for the new and much larger public company. Although this may appear an attractive means of obtaining a listing for a private company, in practice the expenses may be almost as large and the time scale just as long as in the case of a conventional listing.

15.10 RECONSTRUCTION OF ASSETS AND/OR LIABILITIES

1 Assets

A company reorganisation need not involve a reconstruction of its share capital. If a company has assets which are surplus to its requirements or subsidiaries which are extraneous to its future development plans, they may be sold off. Alternatively, a company may consider that one of its subsidiaries would do better if it was floated off. A 'listed spin off' affords the parent company the opportunity to realise part and retain part of its investment in the 'spin off' company without breaking it up.

If a company is taken over, rationalisation of its assets and/or activities may be expected to follow. However, care must be taken to ensure that such asset disposals do not entail an acquired company giving financial assistance for the purchase of its own shares in breach of the provisions of the Companies Act 1985, Chapter VI.

A change in corporate philosophy may precede the disposal of certain assets or companies in a group. This may occur when a particular product or geographical market experiences a down turn or where a company's management simply concludes that the resources tied up in a particular business could be more efficiently utilised in other parts of the group. Such rationalisation may be part of a survival plan for a company in difficulties, eg before it was taken over by BTR, Dunlop had already sold off its tyre-manufacturing interests as part of a recovery programme.

2 Liabilities

A company reorganisation can take the form of a reconstruction of its liabilities as well as a reorganisation of its assets. The composition of a company's liabilities and the gearing of its balance sheet can influence the market value of its shares and may therefore affect its capacity to raise new equity capital. Debt reduction or refinancing may take many forms (see ch 7 above) but will usually have one or more of the following aims as its objective:

(a)   reducing the proportion of debt to overall assets;

(b)   deferring the maturity of the company's borrowings;

(c)   reducing the cost of servicing loans or debentures by refinancing them from cheaper sources of finance;

(d)   releasing assets which are the subject of secured borrowings, e g traditional secured borrowings may be replaced by borrowing on a negative pledge unsecured basis whereunder the borrower covenants that its total external borrowings will not exceed, say, 10% of its total tangible assets and that its secured liabilities will not exceed, say, 20% of such assets; and

(e)   introducing greater flexibility as to debt maturity, e g by refinancing a debt by the issue of redeemable preference shares.

15.11 MANAGEMENT BUY-OUTS

1 Buy-out situations

In management buy-outs, that is the acquisition of businesses from their owners by those involved in their day-to-day management, have gained increasing popularity in recent years. This is principally due to the sale of peripheral businesses by companies rationalising their activities, increased availability of finance, and greater awareness amongst managers of buy-out possibilities. The most common management buy-out situations are as follows:

(a)   the restructuring or rationalisation of a group may result in it selling off particular parts of its business which do not constitute part of its main business, or which do not make a satisfactory contribution to group profits;

(b)   viable parts of a business in receivership or liquidation may be sold off as a going concern by the receiver or liquidator;

(c)   shareholders of a privately-owned company who are making plans for their retirement may sell to the existing management; and

(d)   the owners of a business may be doubtful about its future prospects while the management may be more optimistic.

2 The buy-out business

For many businesses which constitute potential buy-out situations there is likely to be little current profitability or positive cash flow. However, the management (as opposed to the owners) may believe that if they could control their own costs and determine their own marketing and product development policies they could improve the profitability of the business. Such a belief must be tested objectively; managers proposing to mount a buy-out must make a realistic assessment of their own individual strengths and weaknesses and of the market in which the buy-out business operates. They will also need to be sure that, if they are breaking away from a group, they will retain within the bought out business the necessary personnel for proper financial management, effective marketing and the development of new products.

3 The buy-out vehicle

The normal legal entity or vehicle for a buy-out will be a limited company. The management or buy-out team will usually become shareholders in the buy-out vehicle and that vehicle will then raise additional finance to make the acquisition. In order to avoid taking over any undisclosed liabilities within the company operating the buy-out business, or perhaps because the buy-out business represents only part of the activities of that company, the buy-out team may prefer to to buy the assets of the buy-out business rather than shares in the operating company.

4 Financing

The buy-out team will want a substantial equity or share participation in the buy-out vehicle because it is that which will give them a direct interest in improving operating efficiency and profit performance. However, they are unlikely to provide more than a small proportion of the cost of acquiring the buy-out business from their own resources. This means that the buy-out vehicle is likely to have a high ratio of loan capital to equity capital. While potential backers may be prepared to lend to a highly geared business, they will need to be satisfied that it will have a high positive cash flow to service interest charges on preferential and loan capital. For this reason buy-outs frequently, but not invariably, involve cash generative businesses with substantial assets which can provide collateral security.

The subject of management buy-outs is explored more fully in ch 4.

Index